U.S.S.R.

Alaska

Canada

The Aleutians

Volume 7, Number 3 / 1980 / Alaska Geographic®

Chief Editor: Lael Morgan

Contributing Editors

Lydia Black • G. Vernon Byrd • James A. Estes • Raymond Hudson • Robert D. Jones Jr.
William S. Laughlin • Frederick A. Messing • Alonzo H. Moser • A.P. Okladnikov
Elaine Rhode • Charles A. Simenstad • Henry Swanson

The Alaska Geographic Society

To teach many more to better know and use our natural resources

Editors: Robert A. Henning, Lael Morgan,
  Barbara Olds, Carol A. Phillips
Associate Editor: Penny Rennick
Designer: Dianne Hofbeck
Cartographer: Jon.Hersh
Photographs by Lael Morgan except as noted

Library of Congress Cataloging in Publication Data
Main entry under title:

The Aleutians.
   (Alaska geographic; v. 7, no. 3 ISSN 0361-1353)
   Includes index.
   1. Aleutian Islands—Description and travel.
2. Aleutian Islands—History.   3. Natural history—
Alaska—Aleutian Islands.   I. Morgan, Lael.
II. Series.
F901.A266 vol. 7, no. 3   [F951]   917.98s   [979.8'4]
ISBN 0-88240-145-9   80-17331

ALASKA GEOGRAPHIC®, ISSN 0361-1353, is published quarterly by The Alaska Geographic Society, Anchorage, Alaska 99509. Second-class postage paid in Edmonds, Washington 98020. Printed in U.S.A.
THE ALASKA GEOGRAPHIC SOCIETY is a nonprofit organization exploring new frontiers of knowledge across the lands of the polar rim, learning how other men and other countries live in their Norths, putting the geography book back in the classroom, exploring new methods of teaching and learning—sharing in the excitement of discovery in man's wonderful new world north of 51°16'.
MEMBERS OF THE SOCIETY RECEIVE *Alaska Geographic®*, a quality magazine in color which devotes each quarterly issue to monographic in-depth coverage of a northern geographic region or resource-oriented subject.
MEMBERSHIP DUES in The Alaska Geographic Society are $20 per year ($24 to non-U.S. addresses). (Eighty percent of each year's dues is for a one-year subscription to *Alaska Geographic®*.) Order from The Alaska Geographic Society, Box 4-EEE, Anchorage, Alaska 99509; (907) 274-0521.
MATERIAL SOUGHT: The editors of *Alaska Geographic®* seek a wide variety of informative material on the lands north of 51°16' on geographic subjects—anything to do with resources and their uses (with heavy emphasis on quality color photography)—from Alaska, Northern Canada, Siberia, Japan—all geographic areas that have a relationship to Alaska in a physical or economic sense. In early 1980 editors were seeking material on the following geographic regions and subjects: the Kobuk-Noatak area, the Seward Peninsula and glaciers of Alaska. We do not want material done in excessive scientific terminology. A query to the editors is suggested. Payments are made for all material upon publication.
CHANGE OF ADDRESS: The post office does not automatically forward *Alaska Geographic®* when you move. To insure continuous service, notify us six weeks before moving. Send us your new address and zip code (and moving date), your old address and zip code, and if possible send a mailing label from a copy of *Alaska Geographic®*. Send this information to *Alaska Geographic®* Mailing Offices, 130 Second Avenue South, Edmonds, Washington 98020.
MAILING LISTS: We have begun making our members' names and addresses available to carefully screened publications and companies whose products and activities might be of interest to you. If you would prefer not to receive such mailings, please so advise us, and include your mailing label (or your name and address if label is not available).

The cover
Green hills and blue inlets surround the communities of Unalaska and Dutch Harbor.
(Lorie Kirker)

Right
Mist moves in across the distant hills near Hot Springs Bay on Akutan Island.
(David W. Shapiro)

Far right
The wet Aleutian climate turns the summer tundra to deep green velvet on Umnak Island.
(Lorie Kirker)

Editor's note: The Pribilof Islands, Saint Paul and Saint George, were uninhabited when discovered in 1786 by G. L. Pribylov, but Russians soon colonized them, using Aleuts from the Chain to harvest valuable fur seals which migrated there annually to breed and give birth to their young. Descendants of the original Aleut sealers thrived and multiplied while Aleuts from other islands continued to settle there, attracted by work opportunities, kin or marriage, until today Saint Paul is the largest Aleut settlement in Alaska, and neighboring Saint George, though smaller and more isolated, is also a viable community.

Because the Pribilofs, like the mainland Aleut communities of Belkofski, King Cove and Nelson Lagoon, lie outside the physical boundaries of the Aleutian Chain, they are not included in this issue of *ALASKA GEOGRAPHIC®* or covered in detail on the pull-out map which accompanies it. However, they share the rich history of Aleut people and remain today very much a part of the modern Aleut nation.

The skies break into glory in this dramatic photograph of Unalaska Bay, taken from Morris Cove, Unalaska Island.
(Martin Butz)

Contents

This issue includes a large pull-out map of the Aleutian Islands.

The Aleutians . . . a name that has come to mean to me fog, rough, smoking islands of basalt, volcanic ash and green grass, rain, sleet, sometimes snow, terrible winds and seas, sometimes unbelievably blue skies and fluffy clouds and a stillness broken only by the sounds of the seabirds, the gentle wash of surf on black sand beaches—a faraway place suspended between the worlds of the East and West, visited rarely, even largely unknown by the people of Alaska to whom the Aleutians are attached like a jigsaw puzzle piece of an elephant's trunk.

It's over a thousand miles from end to end, and crosses the international dateline to become both the farthest west and the farthest east of American soil. It's sparsely inhabited and will unlikely support any truly large settlement in the foreseeable future.

A lonely place with rich history, the Aleutians will for me always have a strange fascination. Here there has been struggle, man against his environment, man against man, and there should be feelings of fear and dismay, but there is instead, strangely, a deep feeling of peace.

Our Roving Editor Lael Morgan has found that peace in this strange land and in covering the bush beat has come to love both the land and its people. Her research has been thorough, in dusty archives and in tossing Aleut dories. She knows the Chain. We felt her affection for the area made her deserving of the title Chief Editor of this issue of *ALASKA GEOGRAPHIC®* and her vast accumulation of Aleutians material dictated that nobody could do the job better. That information, carefully distilled over the past years of gathering and winnowing, plus Mrs. Morgan's sensitive camera lens, has resulted in a book that was due, and we think will be deserving of great plaudits.

Sincerely,

President
The Alaska Geographic Society

Above
An unnamed volcano in the Eider Point area west of Amaknak Island.
(Stephen Bingham)

Opposite
Otkriti Cove, shown on a calm, sparkling day, is near a sea lion rookery on the south side of Agattu Island.

Massacre Bay on Attu, site of the murder of 15 Aleut warriors by the Russians, was an important battle scene nearly 200 years later during World War II.
(Dennis Goodwin)

Preface

Sometimes, when I am away—when I am working in the city and bothered by things that Aleuts are bothered by like hard sidewalks and too many people and air that even out-of-doors seems claustrophobic—I remember the beginning of a book by the late Corey Ford titled *Where the Sea Breaks Its Back*, and I smile again.

Years ago, when I was very young, I crossed the North Pacific from Vancouver to Japan; and one day, as our ship rounded the top of the great circle, I noticed a string of strange, bare mountains rising out of the sea along the northern horizon. They resembled heaps of smoking slag; the sun, striking their sides, gave them a greenish cast like verdigris on copper. I asked a fellow passenger what they were. "Illusions," I thought he said, but now I realize he said they were Aleutians.

Often I, too, have thought the Aleutian Islands must be illusions, for they are strange and beautiful beyond reality. And although I wish to keep their secret, paradoxically I also yearn to share their magic.

These islands are, as yet, unspoiled, protected well by the bad name they earned from their earliest discovery by Outsiders. In a lifetime of travel and photography they remain my favorite place— unmatched for physical magnificence and a welcome retreat in their stunning remoteness—but their bad reputation is honestly come by and I'll detail it to discourage the faint of heart.

Number one notorious is the Aleutian weather—the worst in the world according to the U.S. Coast and Geodetic Survey's *Coast Pilot*, which is a usually conservative publication. Winds of 120 miles per hour are not uncommon in season and the season is all year long. The Aleutian wind collapses tents, collapses houses; people cannot walk against it. But what a spectacular thing to see and experience; the splendid seas it creates! Sailors are never bored here, and birds and man do some remarkable flying.

It rains a lot. An average of only eight sunny days a year,

It is no secret that Lael Morgan's heart is in the Aleutians—"my favorite place on earth," she calls these remote and misty islands. Here she enjoys the green tundra of Atka Island with young friend Mary Snigaroff, whose picture appeared on the cover of Morgan's 1979 volume of ALASKA GEOGRAPHIC®, Alaska's Native People.
(Judy Zaochney)

some experts have reported, although I think they mean uninterrupted morning to evening sunshine. A lot of Aleutian days are off and on: a little sun, a little rain, terrific rainbows. What more could a photographer want, assuming he's smart enough to shroud his camera in a plastic bag and have a little patience?

Finally, there is the isolation which has quite literally driven men mad, especially some stationed here during World War II. Of some 200 islands, only six have villages and these qualify as the most remote settlements in America. Adak is a Navy base; Attu has a small Coast Guard station, and there are a couple of ranches, but the rest of the Chain is deserted give or take an occasional shipwreck or U.S. Fish & Wildlife expedition. Television, telephones, even mail service and visits from traveling physicians, educators and salesmen are at a minimum, indeed.

But because this is a photo book, there are also some superbly positive truths about the Aleutians I cannot hide: breath-taking landscapes and seascapes; animal and bird colonies of wonderful uniqueness; remarkable fishing, hiking, climbing and diving.

Vastly rich is this watery realm.

And the people—perhaps you can tell from the faces that Aleutian living requires a different breed of men and women. Life is hard and human beings are so few in these islands that they tend to value each other more than most.

It amuses me now that when I first traveled to the islands I was afraid. I knew no one, had heard nothing but bad about the Chain and it was a low point in my personal life, too.

How surprised I was to find that this was the country where I belonged, that in the Aleutians my mind will forever rest peaceful, even when I'm distant seas away.

Lael Morgan

Acknowledgments

Special thanks to: Mrs. Lillie McGarvey of Anchorage and Unalaska; Dr. Juergen Kienle, Geophysical Institute, University of Alaska, Fairbanks; Robert R. Coats, David M. Hopkins, Tom Miller and Tau Rho Alpha, U.S. Geological Survey; Bruce Marsh, Johns Hopkins University; E.R. Engdahl, Cooperative Institute for Research in Environmental Sciences, University of Colorado/NOAA; Tom Spitler and the Pete Culbertsons of Adak; Capt. George Putney, *Aleutian Tern;* the U.S. Fish & Wildlife Service; Alaska Department of Fish & Game; U.S. Coast Guard; Dr. Clifford Amundsen and Edward Clebsch, University of Tennessee; Douglas W. Veltre, Anthropology Department, Anchorage Community College; Andrew Gronholdt, Sand Point; Iliodor Philemonof, Anchorage; Father Paul Merculief, Nikolski; Grant Hale and John Haile Cloe, Command Historians, Department of the Air Force; Ms. Renne Jaussaud, National Archives; William Draper, New York City; R.N. De Armond, Juneau; Mr. and Mrs. Henry Wheaton and Joe Kelly of Anchorage; Mr. and Mrs. John Seller, Glen Ellen, California; Flora and Phil Tutiakoff, Unalaska; Ruth Shaishnikoff, Sue Chase Hall, Abi Dickson, Vernon Robinson and Frank Poplawski of Unalaska; Don Hodley, Amaknak; Randy Caldwell and the Norm Isacsons of Squaw Harbor; the Terry Millers of Umnak and Kodiak; the Milt Holmes of Chernofski; Capt. Magne Nes, *Northern Aurora;* Richard Ellis, New York City; Renee Balhuta, University of Alaska Archives, Fairbanks; Gary C. Stein, Anthropology and Historic Preservation, Cooperative Park Studies, University of Alaska; Ernest D. Leet, Lt. Comdr. (Ret.); the U.S. Navy; Ounalashka Village Corporation; the Aleut Corporation; the Aleutian/Pribilof Islands Association, Inc.; and the village of Atka.

In 1962 these delightful little girls of Nikolski were photographed as they enjoyed cutting and eating putske, *wild cow parsnip, which tastes much like celery. From left, sisters Dora and Marsha Dushkin still reside in Nikolski; their cousin Ann Dushkin, at right, now Ann Kyle, lives with her family in Sand Point.*
(Christy Turner)

The water here at valley's end
at Summer's Bay
shallow as the palm of your hand
is filled with light.

This poetry and the excerpts that introduce each chapter are from "Summer's Bay" by Raymond Hudson, written in 1968 while he was in Vietnam, and dedicated to Anfesia Shapsnikoff, his beloved friend and mentor in Unalaska.

Hudson is shown in a photo on page 78. "Summer's Bay" appears in its entirety on page 223; it is a fitting tribute to Hudson's adopted home and the proud race of people featured in this issue of *ALASKA GEOGRAPHIC®*.

One of the many scenes of peaceful beauty in the Aleutians is Unalaska's Summer Bay (Hudson's Summer's Bay), called Imagninskoe *by Father Veniaminov.*
(Lorie Kirker)

. . . Islands
between sea and ocean
Aleutian Islands
split circle of vanished people . . .

1
Introduction

The Aleutian Chain is a bridge between two continents and the slender wedge between two seas, the longest archipelago of small islands in the world. In this day of advanced technology, much of its flora and fauna—its very physical makeup—remains an enigma. In fact, it has yet to be thoroughly explored. Mountains, waterfalls, canyons, lakes and petrified forests that elsewhere would be national landmarks, go unnamed, often unmapped here.

Although the Chain hosts the greatest arc of active volcanoes in the United States, it is one of the very few in the world that has not been catalogued by the International Association of Volcanologists. And much of the sea, with its vast Aleutian Trench and Bering Canyon, perhaps the largest in the world, remains to be thoroughly explored.

We know the islands' aboriginal people had a technically advanced and highly fascinating civilization, but their history has been all but obliterated, leaving us to sleuth over archaeological digs and mummy caves for tantalizing clues.

Nor have scientists yet unlocked the mysteries of earthquakes and tidal waves which have long bedeviled the area, nor pin-pointed the large caches of crude oil thought to exist beneath Aleutian seas.

Within the last two decades the Chain has been considered so remote that the Atomic Energy Commission successfully argued it was the best place in the United States to test atomic weapons, yet it is startling to realize that the Aleutians have twice been the center of world attention.

They were the route by which the Russians discovered Alaska in 1742 and were once the source of vast riches for them. Then, during World War II, strategists on both sides figured that if the Japanese could take the Aleutians it would give them a beachhead on the U. S. mainland and cut off our lend-lease traffic to Russia as well.

Aleutian soil was the first American ground actually occupied by the Japanese and the first recaptured, although these battles are scarcely remembered except by soldiers who fought them and families of the dead, and there is no memorial here of note other than markers honoring fallen Japanese troops.

But quietly the islands and their people are coming into their own. Without hoopla—until recently almost without press—Unalaska is about to become the busiest money-making port in the United States, and the future of Aleutian resources looks better yet.

As for the Aleuts themselves—brutalized and slaughtered by early Russian freebooters, displaced during World War II, and repeatedly dismissed by scientists and educators as "destined for extinction"—they have stubbornly survived, are now increasing in number, and recently regained control of vast acreages of their homeland.

The story of these islands has been too long neglected. Even the map of this area is traditionally relegated to an undersized inset on the larger map of Alaska.

This issue of *ALASKA GEOGRAPHIC®* is an attempt to set the record straight and to introduce you to one of the richest areas in Alaska, both in heritage and potential.

McDonald's Cove at Agattu is perhaps the first place where Russians spilled Aleut blood. In 1745 Nikolai Chuprof landed with a small party and Natives attempted to take their muskets. According to historian Hubert Howe Bancroft, "One bullet took effect in the hand of a native; the crimson fluid gushed forth over the white sand, and a long era of bloodshed, violence and rapine for the poor Aleuts was begun."

Left
Mount Ballyhoo (elevation 1,589 feet, on Amaknak Island) is said to have been named by author-adventurer Jack London, although historians haven't figured out when he actually traveled here. Perhaps it was on his return from the Klondike, for it was a common event for ships to put in at Unalaska for water and coal.

Below
When Aleuts get a full day of sun they usually make the most of it. Here Feddie and Anna Krukoff do their washing and patch their roof on a rare fine day at Nikolski.

Above
Henry Swanson of Unalaska went on the last legal sea otter hunt in the Aleutians as a boy of 15 in 1910 with his stepfather, who was a well-known whaling captain in the Arctic. They took 12 baidarkas and a 24-man crew on a larger ship. A trapper and trader, Swanson has spent a lifetime in the Aleutians and probably knows the region better than almost any man.

Right
Comstay Bay, one of Adak's many beautiful spots, offers no clue that the island houses Alaska's largest naval base.

That fury . . .
Shook the sea of these islands,
Sent creation's terrible passion . . .
Centuries of steam and rock . . .

2
The Beginnings

The Aleutian Chain forms the westward arm of the Alaska Peninsula which extends within 500 miles of the Kamchatka Peninsula of Asia; 54° 51′ north, 163° 22′ west in the extreme east (Unimak) and 52° 55′ north, 172° 42′ east to the west (Attu). In addition, this survey encompasses the Russian Komandorskies, 300 miles west of Attu, and the Shumagins, just to the southeast of Unimak, which, if not actual physical extensions of the Chain, are bound to it by virtue of close proximity and history.

The Aleutians are actually crests of an arc of submarine volcanoes approximately 1,400 miles long and 20 to 60 miles wide which rise to a maximum height of 9,372 feet above sea level and 32,472 feet from the ocean floor.

The semicircular Chain appears to date back 70 million years to the latest Miocene and Quaternary ages which marked greatly increased volcanic activity in the North Pacific. Island status was achieved some 400 million years ago although parts of the arc have sometimes been submerged due to glacial melt and tectonic effects.

To the geologist, the formation of island arcs is one of the most challenging features of the earth's surface and, although many theories have been brought forth, none is entirely satisfactory. Many today support the concept that the earth's crust is broken into six major and several smaller plates which spread and push against each other. According to this theory the Pacific plate sinks down deep under the American plate which underlies the Bering Sea, eventually causing molten lava to rise from the bowels of the earth and erupt from the volcanoes we know as the Aleutians.

In more mature arcs this activity sometimes forms a secondary front which may account for the newest of the Aleutian Isles: Amak, which came to the surface about 7,000 years ago, and Bogoslof, which emerged in the late 1700s.

The Pacific side of the Chain is bordered by the Aleutian Trench. This extraordinary trough is more than 2,000 miles long and 50 to 100 miles wide with a maximum depth of over 25,000 feet where the Pacific plate bends down beneath the American plate.

To the north of the Chain the Bering Sea is shallow in the east and deep in the west. The continental shelf edge intersects the Aleutian arc just east of Unimak.

The Bering Canyon is one of the world's largest known slope valleys, being approximately 249 miles long and reaching a maximum depth of 10,667 feet. It is suspected that submarine erosion was caused by runoff from the Kuskokwim River and nearby streams during a glacial period when sea level was lowered by runoff from advancing or retreating glaciers, a phenomenon known as eustacy. Canyon deposits were mainly laid down in the Neogene times and it is therefore assumed that the canyon came into being prior to the end of the Tertiary time.

The geological record of the Aleutians has great gaps due in part to the low Ph factor of the soil which prevents preservation of fossils and plant pollens; however, the sediments are dominated throughout by volcanic rock and sediments derived from them.

Minerals of commercial value are scarce both in variety and quantity. Gold, sulfur,

Akutan volcano belched fire and smoke throughout the fall of 1978, causing grief to numerous processing boats anchored in Akutan harbor, as fallout made it difficult to keep facilities clean. Island residents have long lived at the foot of this 4,275-foot volcano without disaster, although lava flows run to the sea on a distant side of the peak.

The Ancient Bridge

Excerpted from an article by *A. P. Okladnikov,* Institute of History, Philology and Philosophy of the USSR Academy of Sciences, Siberian Division, as it appeared in *The ALASKA JOURNAL®,* Autumn 1979

The geography of northeast Asia and northern North America points to the most probable route that Old World groups followed in their migration to the New World. The shortest distance between Asia and America is found in the Bering Strait, where Big and Little Diomede and Saint Lawrence Island served as stepping stones. Saint Lawrence Island is renowned for its ancient Eskimo sites excavated by Henry Collins. What better spot to look for traces of "the First Americans" than there?

It is now established that a land bridge existed during glacial times. Scientists have designated this area Bering Land, or Beringia. The concept of Beringia was first introduced in the 1920s by Pyotr Sushkin, a Soviet academician, who devoted his life to the study of Siberia's ornithofauna.

It is believed that a land mass, more than 1,000 miles wide, linked the Chukchi Peninsula with Alaska at two different times. The first time was approximately 65,000 to 35,000 years ago. The land bridge was submerged and later reestablished during the Later Wisconsin glacial period—about 28,000 to 25,000 years ago. The land bridge must have existed until about 11,000 to 10,000 years ago when it was completely submerged by the advancing sea. The Bering and Anadyr straits were flooded, Alaska was separated from Siberia, and Saint Lawrence Island, the Pribilofs and the Aleutians were cut off from continental America.

The existence of Beringia facilitated intensive migration of different species of plants and animals, including human beings, from continent to continent. Soviet scientist, A. Scher states that as far back as the early Quaternary period, Beringia was a major focus in the territorial spread of cold-resistant mammals that inhabited the subarctic areas—the moose, musk ox and bison, for example. Their descendants undoubtedly constitute the pride of America's fauna.

The migration of animals continues today. Some birds of the Chukchi Peninsula and the Anadyr Valley, such as the Canada goose and the wagtail, fly to California every year. Rivers in Siberia and Alaska share the same fish species—salmon, grayling, pike, common sucker, minnow and others. North America abounds with Siberian plants.

Due to recent discoveries, a theory has developed in the scientific community regarding Pacific routes to the New World, routes that lay either along the Asian continent by way of the Okhotsk coast

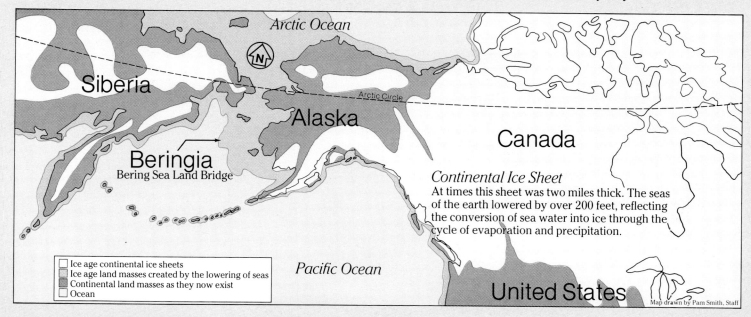

Beringia
Bering Sea Land Bridge

Continental Ice Sheet
At times this sheet was two miles thick. The seas of the earth lowered by over 200 feet, reflecting the conversion of sea water into ice through the cycle of evaporation and precipitation.

☐ Ice age continental ice sheets
☐ Ice age land masses created by the lowering of seas
☐ Continental land masses as they now exist
☐ Ocean

Arctic Ocean
Pacific Ocean
Siberia
Alaska
Canada
United States
Arctic Circle

Map drawn by Pam Smith, Staff

and Kamchatka, or the island group—Japan, the Kuriles and perhaps along the southern coast of the Bering Land Bridge to the Aleutians. Discoveries on Anangula, a small uninhabited island in the Aleutian Chain, have greatly contributed to the validity of this premise.

In 1973, at an international symposium in Khabarovsk on ancient Beringia, the idea to organize a joint expedition of American and Soviet archaeologists to the Aleutian Islands was developed. At this symposium were two eminent American scientists, David Hopkins and William Laughlin, who have made considerable contributions to research of "the First Americans" problem.

The expedition occurred during the summer of 1974. Working together at the site of the Blade Culture on Anangula, Laughlin and I found thousands of stone artifacts. An on-the-spot analysis, as well as at our mess-room on the island's high rocky shore, considerably expanded our knowledge and understanding of "the First Americans."

We uncovered a series of elements linking the oldest culture of the Aleutians with the cultures of northern and central Asia. There were at least eight such elements based on the shape and method of stone tool manufacture. The second substantial achievement of our joint expedition was tracing the subsequent cultural development of Anangula's inhabitants.

It was proven conclusively that the ancient Blade Culture was not an accidental episode in the history of the Aleutian Islands.

During the excavation of the village site, on the eastern coast of Anangula, I had the good fortune to make some unexpected and rare finds. First, I came upon a broad, regularly shaped prismatic blade, retouched on one side only—the same type as at the Blade Culture site. Fifteen minutes later, I found a bifacial andesite point, worked on both sides. Both artifacts were found in the same layer, indicating they had been made at about the same time. Thus, a link between the two cultures—the unifacial blade culture and the bifacially chipped artifact culture—was found. In other words, components were found that link the earlier Aleuts of Anangula with the later Aleuts, who have always manufactured bifacial blades.

It should be noted that Anangula's bifacial points are very similar to those found by Soviet archaeologist Nikolai Dikov on the Kamchatka Peninsula at a settlement on the shores of Lake Ushki. The hypothesis that Aleutian culture was influenced by groups on Kamchatka had been raised earlier—now, it is confirmed by facts. □

copper and coal have thus far generated the most interest.

It is debatable whether a glacial ice sheet covered the entire Chain during the Pleistocene ice age or whether icecaps were regional, leaving some islands unscathed, but glaciers still cover many volcanoes in this area.

It is well established that during early Wisconsin times the area was connected to Asia by a land bridge which ran from Siberia in the area of the Anadyr River to the Pribilofs and then south via Port Moller on the Peninsula to terminate at Umnak. Over this bridge Asian people and game migrated during a period of several thousand years, the Aleuts favoring southern limits, keeping in contact with the sea on which they had long depended. Many settled at Samalga Pass, southern terminus of this route which was astonishing for its diverse and prolific sea life, enriched by the upwelling Pacific waters as they met the Bering shelf. Even today this area boasts the largest concentration of marine mammals in the world and probably one of the strongest bird populations.

The oldest known settlement in the Aleut world, which dates back 8,000 years, is Anangula (Ananiuliak) Island at the northern end of Samalga Pass off Nikolski. As deglaciation proceeded from west to east, descendants of early migrants apparently spread out through the Chain and were, perhaps, joined by migrants from other areas to become a great maritime nation.

The fate of the Anangula people remains in question, however, for the site appears to have been occupied less than a century when a heavy cover of volcanic ash rained down from Okmok, probably killing local fauna and flora on which inhabitants depended. The 4,000-year gap between settlement here and evidence men again lived in the area appears to correspond to a period of volcanism.

Early estimates that Aleut population ulti-

Dr. William S. Laughlin and students work on excavation of ruins that date back nearly 4,000 years at the long studied and anthropologically important midden at Chaluka, Nikolski village on Umnak Island.
(Christy Turner)

mately reached 25,000 have been challenged by researchers today who point out Aleuts traditionally maintained two or more villages, moving from one to another according to the seasonal availability of game. It is more likely that population crested around 16,000, still a considerable density for the given land mass and instability of the area.

Volcanic eruptions and earthquakes, today a common threat, were probably even more disruptive when the Chain was in early states

of development, and the tidal waves and land-slides they spawned appear to have plagued settlers throughout the ages.

At least 26 of the Chain's 46 active volcanoes appear to have erupted since written history began in 1760; however, the remoteness of population centers and severity of the climate still discourage geologists from studying this lively area. (Please see page 208.)

Even when observers are present, most are untrained, and clouds resulting from condensation of water are sometimes confused for volcanic smoke. Then, too, names of the islands have sometimes been confused or wrongly located on the charts. Some volcanoes reported early as active appear to have been dormant for centuries and it is sometimes difficult to know which volcano is being talked about in early Russian literature.

In 1907 Thomas A. Jaggar, a pioneer volcanologist fresh from studying the catastrophic explosion of Mount Pelee in the West Indies (1902) and an eruption of Vesuvius (1906), undertook a four-month expedition to the eastern Aleutians. Severely hampered by rain, fog, and the fact that his transport was a sailboat, the trip raised more questions than answers, and Jaggar ultimately set up shop at Kilauea Volcano in Hawaii, which proved a more congenial climate for study.

He returned to the Chain several more times, however, and in 1927 attempted to establish an Aleutian Geophysical Observatory, but funding was not forthcoming. In 1929 he managed to put seismographs on Kodiak and at Dutch Harbor, but there was no funding for professional staffers.

Father Bernard R. Hubbard, a Catholic priest, whetted national interest in the subject in 1932 by making the first ascent of Shishaldin (via pack dogs) and visiting Bogoslof, both breathlessly chronicled by the *Saturday Evening Post.* But since Hubbard was more of an adventurer than a serious researcher, the main point he seems to have established was that Aleutain field trips are not for the faint of heart.

The enormous investment made in the Chain by the U. S. military during World War II revived interest in volcanic study with an eye to prediction, especially after an eruption near a military outpost on Chuginadak claimed one life (1944) and activity of Okmok on Umnak Island threatened a large base there (1948).

In the fall of 1945 the U. S. Geological Survey undertook its first serious volcanic study of the Chain, extending field work through 1948.

The most striking feature of Alaska volcanoes was found to be the presence of many calderas (craters of volcanoes that have collapsed), which are uncommon in other areas. And the basic structure of the Chain appeared to differ from the norm.

"Formerly, it was assumed that the Aleutians, like the Hawaiian Islands, are immense, rather simple volcanoes built up directly from

the ocean floor, with only their tops above water," wrote D. G. Robinson after studying the eastern Chain in 1948. "Now evidence is growing that most of the Aleutian volcanoes have been building above the present day sea level on a platform of older rocks evolved 60 to 70 million years ago so that the bulk of each present volcano is now above sea level and has been since its formation."

Unfortunately, since the late 1940s—with the exception of work done by Bruce Marsh in the study of the Aleutian arc and geothermal potential of the Chain — most of Alaska's volcanic work has been confined to the Alaska Peninsula which is an extension of the Aleutian "Ring of Fire."

However, secrets of these volcanoes may ultimately be unlocked through the work of seismologists, a study of growing interest because damage caused by earthquakes and the tidal waves which sometimes follow them are far more wide-sweeping than lava eruptions in a sparsely settled region.

Between 1904 and 1959 Japan was hit with eight earthquake shocks that registered 7.9 or more on the Richter scale, against nine for the Kuriles and two for the Aleutians. Between 1947 and 1959 Japan suffered 80 violent jolts, 11 of which registered 7 or above and one that was 8.5, while the Aleutians recorded 20 of a magnitude of 7 or higher and one of 8 (an increase probably due to better reporting).

A turning point came on April Fools' Day 1946, when the Aleutians suffered a rocker that caused Outsiders to realize the Chain played an important part in world events and monitoring was essential.

The magnitude of this earthquake, which occurred southwest of Unimak under the Aleutian arc was 7.4 but it sent tidal waves of more than 100 feet to the nearby shore, obliterating Scotch Cap lighthouse and killing five.

Seismic sea waves spread out from the Aleutians, much as waves do when a rock is cast in the water, sweeping the Pacific at over 500 miles per hour. Although scarcely noticeable at sea, this tsunami slammed into Hawaiian shores less than five hours later, killing 159, injuring 163, and causing an estimated $25 million damage.

Far from spent, the tidal wave raced on to Chile, buffeting those shores 18 hours after the initial quake, then rebounded to hit the other side of Hawaii. The inundation came without warning and is rated the worst natural disaster in Hawaiian history.

Two years later the U. S. Coast and Geodetic Survey established a seismic wave sea (tsunami) warning system for Hawaii. The system worked so well that when a major seismic disturbance of magnitude 8.1 seized the Chain in March of 1957 causing waves of even greater force than the 1946 disaster, the Hawaiian islands were evacuated without loss of life, although some $53 million in damages was recorded.

Atomic testing in the Aleutians renewed interest in earthquake studies there, and from 1970 to 1973 a sophisticated network of seismic devices monitored the Amchitka area. Finally, in 1974, a far-flung seismograph network was established, centered at the U. S. National Weather Service Adak Observatory.

Shortly after this system was installed, scientists recorded a large number of very shallow earthquakes near Great Sitkin just prior to a single eruption.

Currently seismic areas of the Chain are being carefully defined and this hopefully will result in dependable methods of prediction and a better knowledge of plate tectonics.

Understanding will not diminish the volatile nature of the Chain, however. It remains on the edge of two very active plates. As explained by Dr. Juergen Kienle of the Geophysical Institute, University of Alaska, "These are the seams of the world and it's never going to calm down. That's where things are happening."

This dramatic painting by Darrel Millsap conveys the mind-bending immensity of the Unimak tidal wave of April 1, 1946. Generated by a massive earthquake deep in the Aleutian Trench, this wave, over 100 feet high, demolished Scotch Cap Light, killing five coastguardsmen. The far-reaching effects of this disaster eventually claimed hundreds of lives in the Hawaiian Islands.
(*Oceans*/The Oceanic Society)

Approaching storm clouds envelop Pogromni Volcano, 6,568 feet high, at Cape Sarichef, Unimak Island.
(John E. Sarvis)

Bogoslof

Bogoslof, most recently formed of the Aleutians, gives us some idea of how the Chain may have come into being. Known as the "disappearing island," it first was reported by navigators in 1768 but seldom appeared in the same form or location twice.

Captain James Cook put it on his map as "Ship Rock, 60 miles west of Dutch Harbor in 1778 and on St. John's Day, 1796, a second peak (Castle Rock) emerged just southeast of the first. The thundering force of this eruption could be heard by residents of Dutch Harbor who named the island after the churchman Ioanna Bogoslova."

In 1806 a major convulsion was felt in the area, flame was reported coming from the sea and the isle apparently increased in size. When surveyed in 1826 Castle Rock was two miles long, 0.75 miles wide and 349 feet high.

During a third eruption, reported by a whaling ship in 1883, a huge tabular mass appeared about a mile northwest of Castle Rock which was officially named Grewingk but commonly known as Fire Island or New Bogoslof. Bombs, debris and the products of erosion later formed a bar joining the new isle with Ship Rock, but it subsequently washed out leaving a deep channel.

Another cone was reported active in 1886, and photographs taken by the crew of the U. S. Revenue Cutter Service *Albatross* when they went ashore in 1891 show the island was still smoking.

The officers of the USRCS *Perry* surveyed a newly risen dome in 1906 (400-foot Mount Metcalf) and named it after their ship. The following year, in July, the officers of the USRCS *McCullough* discovered a second new peak of 500 feet and named it after their vessel.

Volcanist Thomas Jaggar, who went ashore August 7 of that year, reported McCulloch Peak a typical lava dome which had blown away half of Perry on formation and was surrounded by a ring of steaming salt water. Nonetheless, wildlife had taken full advantage of the island.

"The rocky cliffs were covered with thousands of murres, their chicks and eggs; and the birds darkened the sky in flight," he wrote. "The stench from offal and rotten eggs was intense.

"The sea was full of fish, the beaches were full of sea lions, the hot lava and air were full of birds. Thus life and deadly volcanism lived together."

Justifiably, the scientist congratulated himself on good timing.

"On September 1 after we left, the crater exploded, throwing sand and dust a distance of 100 miles to the east. The middle heap was engulfed, leaving only a lagoon; and the remaining peaks were shrouded in a heavy mantle of debris. Such a history of building and bursting and spreading out as a shoal has gone on for more than 111 years. Bogoslof is the peak of a submarine Pelee several thousand feet above the sea bottom. It is always active, the index volcano of the Aleutians."

Not until 1935 did scientists again visit Bogoslof, now nicknamed Jack-in-the-Box.

"Knowing the island by reputation as a bad actor, it was with interest and some trepidation that I, with three other men, landed on barren Bogoslof for a 10-week stay," wrote Lt. George E. Morris Jr., elected by USC&GS to chart the area. "As recently as 1926 the volcano was rumbling again and a mass of land 170 feet high was pushed up where the two lost peaks had been. This land is now 140 feet high and a little vegetation is beginning to grow on it.

"A hasty survey of the island after we landed revealed that there was no fresh water. We fancied the old volcano might start activities at any time, so we felt ourselves fortunate in being on the island at the same time as the birds and sea lions. They are uncanny in their detection of approaching danger and if the volcano had been about to erupt, they would have vacated the island 'en masse.' Luckily, there was no sign of impending eruption during our stay."

According to their research, the summit of Bogoslof cone rose some 6,000 feet from the ocean floor and a salt-water pool at the island base registered 68 degrees, providing a fine bathtub.

Vegetation was sparse, "a few small patches of wild rye, numerous tufts of grass and a variety of very short moss," but seagulls utilized the materials for nest building, murres still darkened the skies—an estimated 50,000 of them—and sea lions had moved in in record numbers.

Surveyors also were amazed to discover that the 1,000-fathom curve surveyed four miles north of the island at the turn of the century, had moved a mile farther out into the Bering Sea.

Today the island is still in place, roughly a mile long by half a mile wide and 330 feet at its highest elevation. It remains unstable, however, subject to erosion and still venting hot steam and sulfurous gases. □

The crew of the Revenue Cutter Albatross *bravely pose for pictures on a newly formed section of Bogoslof Island, undaunted by the fact that volcanic smoke and steam still dominate the scene in 1891. This is the south side of the island. The formation disappeared a few years later.*
(National Archives)

. . . mountainous bow of storms . . .

3
Weather

The maritime climate of the Aleutians is characterized by frequent, often violent cyclonic storms and high winds, countered by dense fogs and eerie stillness.

Weather fronts generally move from west to east, but often climatic conditions on the Pacific side of the Chain differ vastly from those on the Bering Sea, thus placing the islands at the center of a continuing weather war with northern shores offering the most clemency.

In October of 1977 the remains of tropical storm Harriet slammed into the Aleutians forcing barometric pressure to the lowest ever reported (27.35 inches at Adak and off the glass at Atka). Waves of 45 to 50 feet were reported off Cape Sarichef, and at Akutan Bay a 100-knot wind indicator peaked several times for several seconds each. Two homes were blown off their foundations at Atka, and a stoutly built camp on an island in Nazan Bay disintegrated, leaving behind only scraps of flooring and a full-sized cast iron cookstove which had been moved several feet.

Some $3 million in damage was recorded at Adak including the loss of two boats in "protected" anchorages, but amazingly no lives were lost.

Luckily the Aleutian temperature is milder than most areas of the state because the Chain is in the southern region. Below-zero readings are rare, occurring only in the extreme eastern Fox group, although chill factors are often low due to extreme winds.

Temperatures range from 28°F to 47°F minimum and 34°F to 52°F maximum at Shemya, known as the "fog factory" of the western Chain; and 24°F to 47°F minimum and 32°F to 55°F maximum on the eastern perimeter at Cold Bay.

Snow accumulation rarely exceeds one or two feet, but an occasional blizzard may prove the exception. The crew shipwrecked on Bering Island in 1743 reported a six-foot snowfall during a single night in April. Atka people recall a hunter died of exposure when a similar storm mired him within sight of the village. Higher elevations of the Chain often retain paralyzing drifts well into the summer months.

There is little or no permafrost, and gardens thrive where soil is rich and rats are few. Measurable precipitation occurs on an average of more than 200 days each year with an annual average of 33.44 inches at Cold Bay and 28.85 at Shemya.

Coastguardsman Dennis Goodwin is silhouetted against angry surf the day after a violent storm at Murder Point, Attu.
(Joe Gruber)

Left
In November of 1978 the 155-foot Northern Aurora *embarked in 100-mile-per-hour winds (gusting to 120) from Chernofski to Dutch Harbor in the lee of Unalaska Island. One of the area's growing fleet of multimillion-dollar fishing-processing boats, it bucked the weather easily, but the view from the decks under night lights was often impressive. Most amazing were hundreds of seabirds, including puffins, that could be seen doing aerial acrobatics and feeding happily in spite of the fury of the seas.*

Below
A low pressure cell is seldom as distinctly visible as this storm front passing by Unalaska. The Chain comes honestly by its nicknames, "Birthplace of the Winds" and "Cradle of the Storms."
(Ted Bank II)

Above
In the fall of 1977 tropical storm Harriet vented her wrath on the Aleutian Chain, bringing with her the lowest barometric readings ever recorded in some areas. At Atka it took one home and a sturdy summer camp from their foundations, and carried off much of Ralph Prokopeuff's home, pictured here. Atka houses were built in 1945 by the U.S. Army for returning Aleuts after our military forces burned the village to keep it from the invading Japanese. Most homes here were renewed in 1978 and new houses are being built.

Left
A cross-country skier enjoys the endless miles of snowy terrain at Mount Moffett, Adak Island.
(Joyce Robinette)

Below
Unimak Pass surf thunders in at Cape Sarichef.
(John E. Sarvis)

Right
Serenity lives at Kuluk Bay, Adak Island. ("Spots" in photo are a star and lights, exaggerated by time-lapse photography.)
(Michael Gordon)

*. . . ships blue-gray at anchor
an orange buoy blazing once
smoke gray fog locking the harbor . . .*

4
Transportation

Aleutian waters are sometimes compared to wild seas of Norway or the Furious Fifties of the Antarctic, and in narrow passages of the Chain where the Bering Sea meets the violent North Pacific and two weather systems collide, there is perhaps no worse sailing in the world.

It is not surprising then, that the Aleut nation surpassed all other aboriginal Alaskans in seamanship, confidently navigating turbulent open waters in *baidarkas*—kayaks designed along the same lines as the sea mammals from whose skins they were crafted.

The design of these boats was such that balance was required, much as is needed by a bicycle rider, and groups traveling in one-, two- or three-man boats would raft themselves together at night so that they could nap safely.

Early Aleuts developed a primitive compass and sometimes marked their way home with inflated sea lion bladders weighted with long ropes of kelp with stone anchors.

Baidarkas were so remarkable in strength, speed and maneuverability, Aleuts used them to hunt whales up to 60 feet in length and did not hesitate to cover great distances in them—even the 400 miles of open seas between the eastern Chain and Kodiak.

By contrast, Russia was one of the most backward of maritime nations in the mid-1700s, yet she was destined to make the last great voyage of discovery on our planet, through Aleutian waters. The sailing ships of her early explorers were often hastily built of green lumber by men who didn't know all the principles of naval architecture, and from early accounts it would seem that many (perhaps more) sank than made the crossing from Kamchatka to Alaska. Yet what the nation lacked in shipwrights, her men overcame with brute courage, and surprising numbers returned home to report on the last great blank on the globe.

As the Chain was colonized, Russia gained maritime skills, but legend is littered with intriguing tales of shipwreck, in at least two cases involving vessels carrying full payloads of gold.

Takeover of Alaska by Americans coincided with the rise in popularity of the steamship which proved far more dependable than sail at bucking the vagaries of Aleutian weather, yet many areas remained uncharted and shipwreck continued to be a way of life.

A good number of ships piled up on Amatignak, southernmost of the Aleutians and

landmark on the Great Circle shipping route. Most spectacular was the loss of the S. S. *Nevada* which cost the lives of 33 of a 35-man crew and left the vessel broken on the jagged teeth of that lifeless shore.

The U. S. Revenue Cutter Service (which became the Coast Guard in 1915) patrolled the Aleutian waters seasonally, saving many stranded vessels and occasionally losing its own.

In 1914 the cutter *Tahoma* hit an uncharted rock 60 miles east of Attu, forcing 80 passengers and crew to take to lifeboats in high seas. Supplies were lost in launching, but crews of five out of six lifeboats managed to row to the island of Semichi 75 miles distant and were rescued eight days later. Passengers of the other boat spent eight days at sea before they were finally saved by a freighter.

Most haunting of Aleutian disasters is the

A close look at this view of Adak Harbor reveals the USCGS Ironwood *tied up at the pier, as well as the many bays of the area— Sitkin Sound, Kuluk Bay, Sweeper Cove—and the relatively small naval station, all against the backdrop of Great Sitkin Volcano.*
(Michael Gordon)

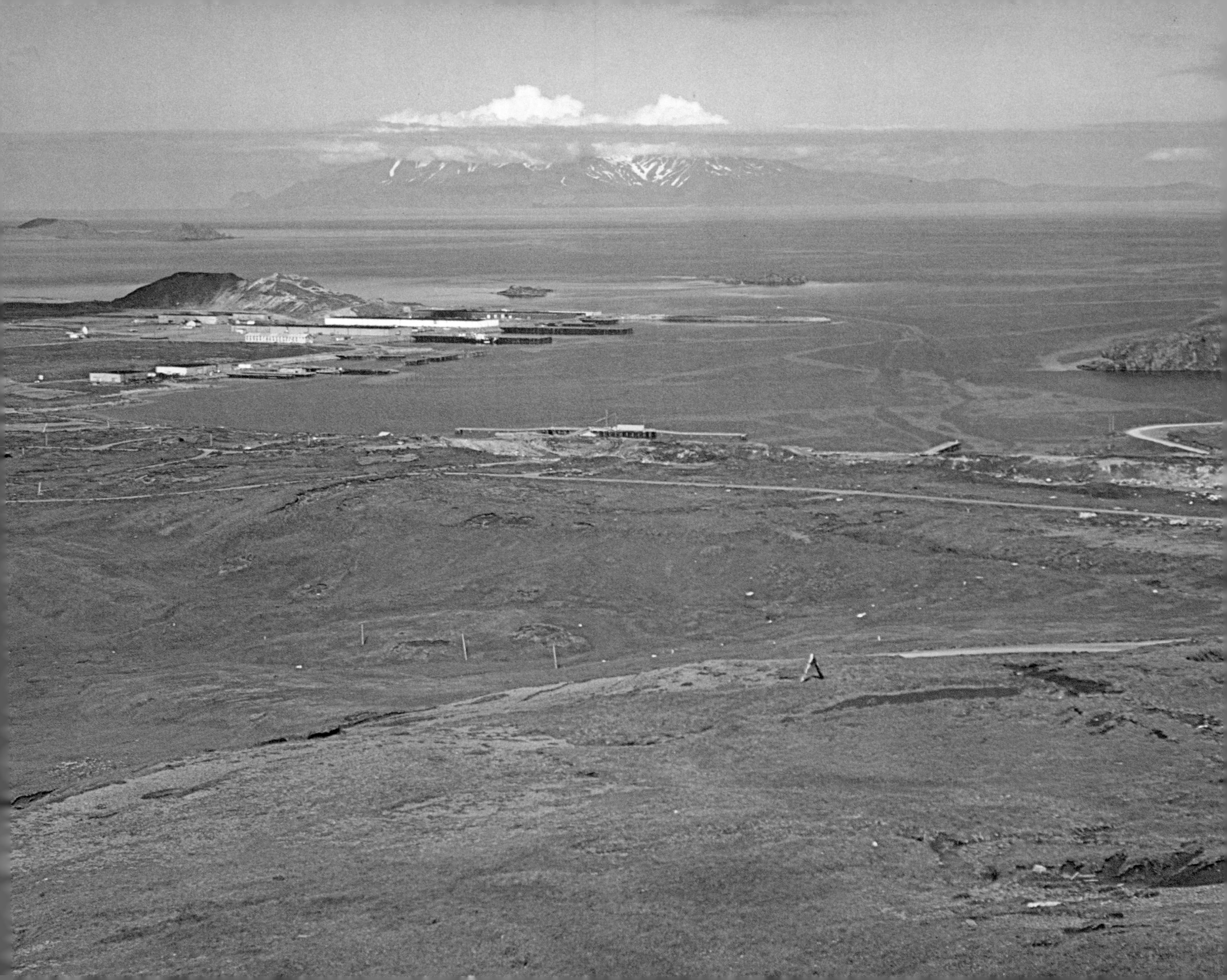

The Race

By Alonzo H. Moser

Modern kayaks now brave the same rough waters traveled by Aleut baidarkas of old. Here members of the British Alaska Expedition of 1978 paddle near Cape Aspid, en route from Kashega to Chernofski.
(George Peck)

Alonzo H. Moser has lived in Alaska since 1934, working as a longshoreman and fisherman in Seward and Kodiak, and traveling throughout the Aleutian Chain with the Army Transport during the latter years of World War II. He wrote many stories and compiled them as a gift for his niece, Lue Rae Erickson of Anchorage. *The Race* is one of these stories. Moser now lives at Clam Gulch on the Kenai Peninsula.

Before the advent of the efficient aeroplane and before there were suitable airfields throughout the Aleutians, that area was serviced by a ship which carried the mail, passengers and freight once a month throughout the year.

The name of the ship which we are concerned with here is the *Starr,* a steamer which had originally been built to be a halibut fisher and had been converted into a freight and passenger ship. It was 125 feet in length, made of iron, and I think the registry listed her at 500 tons. That, of course, is the measurement below deck and doesn't take into account the deck load of lumber, oil drums, cased gasoline, pigs, chickens, cows and machinery and (whisper) dynamite, neatly stowed into a lifeboat. Carrying dynamite on a ship with passengers is strictly a no-no, but if the *Starr* did not haul it, the customer would not get it, and in the case of the Unga gold mine it would have to close down. There was usually never more than 18 cases aboard.

One year in the 1930s the *Starr* came up from Seattle with a new Norwegian captain. Personally he was a jovial and exuberant man, and as a captain he was well liked.

He was always careful in trimming his ship, and when we were loading he always insisted on having heavy machinery and crates towards midship as that stuff should be stored, so he could get 8½

wreck of the *Umnak Native,* which hit the rocks with 13 aboard in 1932. Owned by the village of Nikolski, the trading vessel was en route home with Native fox trappers in seas higher than the pilothouse, and safety had been the subject of bitter debate between Aleuts and the white captain who took charge after accusing the Natives of timidity for not wanting to buck heavy weather. Engine failure and slipping of anchor sealed their fate and only four survived.

The *Iskum,* an old Arctic schooner purchased by the village of Atka in 1931, also sank, less than 24 hours after delivery, under command of a white skipper who refused to heed local advice. En route to Kanaga with a load of lumber, the craft hit an uncharted rock (still uncharted), but seas were relatively calm

knots. The mate, however, wanted the cargo for the farthest port in first, then that for the next farthest port, and so on down the line, which is a proper way to load a ship like the *Starr* because it had one big hold only. So we would load as unobtrusively as possible and mark off with chalk or rope each port of call. Usually when she left Seward she was crammed to her gills.

Well, at Sanak one morning on her return trip, four young Aleut men, ranging from 19 to 24, were on the dock where the *Starr* always tied up and challenged the Captain to a race from Sanak to Unga.

That, said the Captain, was the silliest and most preposterous thing he had ever heard of in his life. Two tiny skin boats racing a steamer for a distance of 45 miles! Whereupon the Aleuts offered to bet $100 that they could win the race.

Now it became interesting. The Captain first gave the young men some fatherly advice about the dangers of the sea—then a sermon about squandering money and especially on some silly bet they had no chance of winning. But that only made the boys want to increase the size of the bet and the Captain, being not averse to making an easy $100, agreed.

The crew and passengers also bet $100. Two of the boys put up $100 and two others put up another bet of the same size and the purser of the *Starr* held the money with the payoff to be in Unga.

The young men put on *kamlaikas*, a sort of parkalike waterproof suit of seal stomach and intestine with a flared bottom with a drawstring which could be fitted over the hatch of the *paliak* (kayak) and drawn tight so as to keep water out and make the *paliak* waterproof.

The race was to start when the *Starr* took her mooring lines aboard. When the dock superintendent gave the signal, a 12-year-old lad fired a musket which almost kicked him flat and scared about 1,000 sea gulls half to death, and the race was on.

Now the betters aboard the *Starr* had expected to see the Aleuts paddling for dear life but they did nothing of the sort. The *paliak* is made from seal or sea lion skins stretched and sewn over a light wood frame and coated with a sort of lacquer made of dissolved sea shells, seal oil and gums. It floats like a feather and responds instantly to the touch of a paddle.

The sea had to set to the eastward on that tide and would continue to run thus for the next six hours so the Aleuts took their time, counting the swells as they rose and fell under them, waiting for the big one they call the "ninth wave." This big swell is a fast traveler

and goes crashing through the smaller waves ahead of it and travels for miles before it is spent.

As this large swell rose under their *paliaks,* the Aleuts caught the top of it and stayed on it, sometimes paddling forward to catch up, sometimes paddling backwards, if they were going too fast, until they had gained the same momentum as the wave. Once this rhythm had been established, it took only an occasional touch of the paddle to maintain it and at this the Aleuts waved a merry bye-bye to the *Starr*, and by the time the trip was only half over the *paliaks* had outdistanced the *Starr* so far that they were no longer in sight.

When the *Starr* tied up at Unga, the Aleuts were standing on the dock waiting to get paid and that was the first thing the purser did. Then the Captain went up to the Aleuts and shook hands with each one of the four and complimented them on their fine seamanship.

Those young men waited in Unga until the tide peaked and then caught the ninth swell, which had now reversed itself and was running west, and got home in time for supper.

There was no such word as hitchhiking in those days when the race took place, but the Aleut has been a master of that art in the sea-wise sense for centuries. A wooden boat, no matter how nimble, is too heavy and too cumbersome to maintain the necessary rhythm to sustain itself properly. □

Opposite page
"Natives Sporting at Unalaska" is the caption on this photo taken by a military signal officer. The gear used by these sea otter hunters is traditional. The paliaks in The Race *were two-hole Aleut baidarkas similar to these pictured.*
(National Archives)

Above
The steamer Starr— *no match for a* baidarka.
(Alaska Historical Museum, Juneau)

A Reeve plane takes off from Dutch. Passenger space is at a premium on the flights that serve Dutch Harbor daily during the height of crab season.
(Tim Thompson)

and all 18 aboard managed to row themselves to safety in a lifeboat.

The most famous boat of this era was the mail steamer *Dora*, launched on the western mail run in 1894 and serving for 35 years. During her career she went on the rocks near Port Sampson, Shelikof Strait, beached at Kodiak and Resurrection Bay and Homer, narrowly escaped the volcanic eruption at Katmai, and was lost 80 days at sea when gales disabled her and carried her south almost to Hawaii. Again and again she was rebuilt and refloated, surviving beyond her usefulness to the postal service and meeting her end at last on Canadian shores en route to Akun with supplies and workers for a sulfur mine.

Alice Nutbeem of Seldovia, who was aboard at the time, recalls ample cargo of whiskey had been loaded at the last stop and that all made it ashore safely to await rescue in an abandoned logging camp.

"They forgot to put the plug in our lifeboat," she recalls. "And I was wet up to here... [gesturing just short of her neck]. The radio man had a wooden leg. Complained his feet were cold and when we gave him a pair of heavy woolen socks he put one on his wooden leg. I tell you, we had fun."

Often survival demanded ingenuity as well as endurance. Henry Wheaton recalls with justifiable pride that he and partner John Taylor once killed a seal and rendered its oil to use in place of motor oil when their engine ran out. "It worked clean as a whistle."

And Robert "Sea Otter" Jones, formerly head of the wildlife refuge attributes his superb dory navigation through fog in the Near Islands to knowledge of the sea lion rookeries and use of their smell as a nav aid.

Because of the watery isolation of the Chain and because traders plied these waters with a substantial fleet, airplanes remained a novelty, especially in the western islands.

In 1923 the U. S. Navy fleet anchored for two weeks in the Shumagins at Dolgoi, launching a floatplane which boggled spectators at nearby Belkofski. Andrew Gronholdt, a youngster enrolled in school there at the time, recalls many children hid in the attic when the craft circled the village.

A year later three Douglas biplanes braved the area, flown by U.S. Army men attempting the first aerial circumnavigation of the globe. A fourth plane of that expedition was forced down April 30 on the peninsula en route to Unalaska, and it took her pilot and co-pilot nine days to walk out to a cannery at Port Moller. The rest of the eight-man team waited at Unalaska for word of them until May 2, when they were ordered on to Japan. They flew without incident to Atka where they were forced to wait five days on account of bad weather.

"Say, when does your season change up here? When does winter end and spring begin?" co-pilot Lt. John "Smiling Jack" Harding asked a local.

"Don't be funny, young feller," came the reply. "We have only two seasons, this winter and *next* winter."

Next they made a 555-mile hop over rough seas to Attu and headed for Japan, only to be forced down in the Komandorskies. Russian authorities were hostile, but luckily the

The Reeve terminal at Dutch Harbor is always crowded at the height of the crab packing season. Often would-be passengers spend days on the waiting list because demand for space greatly exceeds the number of flights. Unfortunately the World War II runway is too short for jets and larger cargo planes and cannot be enlarged without spanning a watery gap to nearby Hog Island.

Colorful pilot Bob Reeve came to Alaska after pioneering mail routes in South America and became an Aleutian legend during World War II when he hauled tons of military freight the length of the Chain with a 14-year-old single engine Fairchild. Army pilots laughed at his craft, called it "The Ironing Board," but they stood in awe of the gutsy flier who managed continually to outwit the world's toughest weather. At the war's end Reeve chose the Aleutians for a commercial venture "because it was the only route left" and parlayed surplus aircraft into the highly successful Reeve Aleutian Airways. Now 80, he has turned the bulk of the company's day to day operation over to his son, Richard, but still keeps a weather-eye on the business and the Aleutians where he knows just about everybody on a first name basis (and vice versa).

Youngsters at Dutch Harbor go to school by boat. Served by the Unalaska School District, the students live on adjacent Amaknak Island and depend on a ferry or family boat to get them across the intervening waters. Their marine "school bus" may become obsolete now that a bridge (below) has been completed. The span would have been built earlier but a valuable archaeological site was discovered where it was to be located and the project had to be reengineered. Now providing easy access between Unalaska and Amaknak islands, it is called simply "The Bridge to the Other Side."
(Photo below—Martin Butz)

USF&WS boat *Eider* was nearby and the fliers were able to tie up alongside to weather the storm.

Finally they crossed the Pacific, the first aviators to do so, and went on to claim the record for a round-the-world flight, although they lost a second plane off Iceland.

In 1932 mountaineering Father Bernard Hubbard chartered Anchorage pilot Frank Dorbandt and mechanic Herb Swanson for a pioneer flight to False Pass with a Yukon dog sled lashed to one pontoon of Dorbandt's Ford trimotor.

"What's the use of killing yourself climbing a mountain for a month when you can do it in an hour in an airplane?" Dorbandt asked, and after a rough assault on Shishaldin, Hubbard saw his wisdom and chartered him to fly Aniakchak crater, the first plane ever to land there.

Harry Blunt, who pioneered the mail run to Unalaska for Pan Am in 1932 and also flew Hubbard, maintains that flying the Chain is no more difficult than other Alaska work. Now a feisty 88, he insists, "If you can last a year up there, you'll get by."

The Navy returned to Aleutian waters during 1933-35 with an aerial survey expedition but was often stymied by storms. Their final report named Unalaska and Adak as the only areas worthy of being considered for a permanent Navy base, and Lt. H. B. Hutchinson, commander of the expedition, recommended Amchitka be made into a national monument and sea otter preserve.

About this time a German pilot with a flying boat made an Aleutian tour. Henry Wheaton recalls gas for the pilot's refueling was shipped a year in advance to Kanaga, but his name seems lost to record.

Occasionally other pilots from Bristol Bay and Anchorage ventured into this area, but those most seen in the western Chain were Japanese who came and went without official sanction.

Pull-out after World War II left a fair number of airstrips where none had existed previously. Bob Reeve, who had covered supply routes on the Chain as the only civilian there under Army contract, inaugurated the first scheduled commercial service in 1946, using surplus military aircraft, maintaining his own runways and ground facilities.

Although the Reeve line readily concedes it has about the most expensive air mile in the United States, it has managed without federal subsidy to service remote communities too small for other airlines to consider, early resorting to a bomb rack to drop the mail.

Military traffic to Adak, Shemya and DEW line sites kept the Reeve airline going initially, and today the naval base at Adak still generates roughly half the airline's revenues, although the fishing boom in Unalaska is making that run more lucrative.

In a petition to the Civil Aeronautics Board in 1979 for route extension from Adak to Seattle, company president Richard Reeve wrote, "It is fair to say that on a year-round basis no U. S. carrier provides regularly scheduled service under weather conditions as bad as those which prevail over Reeve's system. Basically there are two weather seasons—the foggy season from June to September and the stormy season from October until May."

Despite weather hazards, the line has only one serious blot on its record—the crash of a DC-4 into Great Sitkin Volcano in 1958 with the loss of 19 lives—but hair-raising flying stories are legion.

Classic is the one about the late Pat Kelly who radioed Adak tower to turn on its runway lights and was advised to overfly because of a local blizzard.

"I've already landed," he told them. "Just need the lights to taxi to the terminal."

Other lines in the area are Bristol Bay-based Peninsula Airways, and smaller air taxi operations out of King Cove, Sand Point and Akutan,

The amphibious Grumman Goose serves villages which have no airfields. Here one of the sturdy planes unloads on the beach at Akutan.
(Christy Turner)

with an occasional chartered Lear jet out of Anchorage.

It was Orin Seybert, part-owner of Peninsula, who in 1972 dared the 600-mile run from Cold Bay to Atka, particularly risky due to lack of nav aids and the fact that he had to carry enough fuel with him for the return trip.

Atka's airport eroded beyond use in the 1960s, and monthly tug service from Adak, provided by the Navy under contract with BIA, became spotty and was ultimately discontinued, leaving the small community the most isolated in the nation. Charter service averages about $2,500 a trip *if* flying weather is good.

In the easternmost part of the Chain freight

service is becoming more competitive due to the fishing boom. Residents of tiny Squaw Harbor were astonished one morning in the summer of 1978 to see a large state ferry aiming at their dock in a trial run. However, the Chain remains one of the most isolated areas in the state and no one to date seems to have topped the mobility of *baidarka*-paddling Aleuts of old.

The gulls drift
crying crying,
Ivory upon their wings
Wings the color of frost
Flakes of ash on their snowy breasts.

5
Birds

By Elaine Rhode

Elaine Rhode,
free-lance writer and
biologist, spent four
summers in the
Aleutians assisting
with seabird,
Aleutian goose and
sea otter studies.

New life breaks out of its shell all over the islands in summer. Five million seabirds, or one-quarter of Alaska's entire seabird breeding population, flock to the Aleutians to nest.

The isolation, winds, heavy seas and steep volcanic shores that damn the Aleutians in the eyes of man are just what attract and sustain the birds.

The swirling tiderips between islands and the offshore upwellings are nutrient-laden dining tables for these deft divers and underwater swimmers. Some birds, such as the murre, may plunge more than 150 feet after tiny capelin and sandlance fishes and feast as well on an invertebrate soup of euphausiids and amphipods.

On land the sheer sea cliffs, lava flows, caves, rock slides and rugged hillsides offer places to lay an egg—often on bare rock or scraped earth—for this short but vital time that a seabird spends on land.

Their isolated existence is not without dangers: earthquakes split hillsides, volcanoes erupt, storms wash nests from cliffs or drown young in burrows. On top of natural catastrophe, man has added his own: introduced predators such as foxes and rats, fishing nets, oil spills and bottomfishing competition.

Aleutian birds have proved they can cope with nature's tumult; in fact, they often capitalize on the results.

Auklets in particular favor rock slides and rough lava outpourings for raising young. Their nurseries are cracks between rocks and interior cavelike chambers. The growls, wheezes, barks and staccato grunts that come from these crevices make the rocks seem bewitched. The "meow" of the elusive whiskered auklet is as shy as the bird. In all the world, the Aleutians are its only home.

Morning and evening above the lava flows a new nonsulfurous smoke wafts out to sea. Tens of thousands of auklets hurl themselves from rocky launching pads into flocks so dense that it looks like dark smoke being blown by a capricious wind as they circle back over the slope, dip, climb, swerve and head out to sea to feed.

Murres and kittiwakes inhabit the staircase cliffs of Amak Island near Cold Bay.
(John E. Sarvis)

The sound of those torpedo bodies and whirring wings rushing past is awesome. Olaus Murie, pioneer in cataloging Aleutian wildlife, watched the colony on Semisopochnoi and wrote: "There is a storm about our ears—the air is full of auklets. . . ."

The Aleutian Islands form the stronghold of small auklets: least, crested, parakeet and whiskered. Kiska Volcano's Sirius Point lava flow houses more than 1.3 million least and crested auklets—the world's largest known colony. Below Gareloi's smoking cone nest at least 800,000 auklets.

I have sat on the giant boulders of the auklet colony on Buldir Island and had crested and least auklets land within two feet of me. Whiskered auklets just peeked over the top of more distant rocks, and a parakeet auklet sat calmly by its burrow. Two least auklets were so intent on getting back to their crevices with food that they simultaneously landed on the shoulder and head of one of the other biologists instead of a nearby rock. Realizing their error they reversed themselves, but not before regurgitating their meals—into his jacket pocket.

No less crowded or noisy are the cliff colonies of murres and kittiwakes. The penguinlike common and thick-billed murres nest almost wing to wing on narrow ledges above crashing surf. If their single eggs—laid directly on the rock—survive the jostling to hatch and grow for several weeks, the murre fledglings will simply jump off the ledge into the water to join the waiting adults for a life at sea.

Black-legged and red-legged kittiwakes take time to build nests of grass and mud for their one or two eggs, but they too hang precariously on sheer sea cliffs. All the world's

Left
Of the state's three ptarmigan species, the rock ptarmigan (female shown here) is the most abundant in the Aleutians.
(Dr. Forrest Lee, USF&WS)

Below
The tufted puffin, a colorful member of the Aleutian seabird population, builds its nest in burrows. Kaligagan Island in the Krenitzin group supports the largest colony of this species in Alaska.
(Tom J. Ulrich)

Among the more numerous seabirds of the Aleutians is the murre. The common murre (shown here) and the thick-billed murre feed on small fish and usually lay a single egg on bare rock ledges.
(Tom J. Ulrich)

population of red-legged kittiwakes nest here and on the Pribilofs.

Both murres and kittiwakes ring the steep shores of tiny Bogoslof Island and companion Fire Island in such great numbers (100,000) that it was among the first areas named a wildlife refuge in Alaska and the nation. Bogoslof's thorough colonization by marine birds and sea lions in less than 150 years after rising from the sea demonstrates the remarkable richness of the Aleutian corner of the Bering land bridge.

The richness of the Aleutians cannot be judged in the daylight alone. The islands boast their own special night life filled with raucous music and wild stepping.

The music comes from nocturnal seabirds returning from ocean feeding to change egg-sitting duties with their mates or to fill the open bills of hungry young deep in a nesting burrow. Their calls may help them locate their own tunnel apartment in a seemingly look-alike hillside bedroom community.

Buldir Island's storm-petrel community has one million residents, North America's largest colony. From midnight to the predawn hours the air is filled with the twitterings and strange laughing calls of fork-tailed and Leach's storm-petrels. That sound is thrilling—unless, as happened one season, a petrel burrows under the research cabin. The bird began his repetitious call, like a motor being primed but never igniting, after the tired biologists crawled into their bunks. Mercifully, he never attracted a mate and moved away after a few nights.

A sky full of petrels usually drowns out the "follow me" call of the ancient murrelet adult leading its two-day-old offspring to sea. This tiny black and white puff, blessed with innate survival mechanisms, is wound up like a perpetual jumping toy for propelling itself over and through tufts of dense grass, hummocks and beach boulders on its journey from burrow to sea.

These downy ancients must be far offshore

Effects of Man's Activities

Adaptation by *Elaine Rhode* of
Interrelations Between Seabirds And Introduced Animals,
by *Robert G. Jones Jr.* and *G. Vernon Byrd*

Robert D. Jones Jr. liked what he saw of the Aleutians during World War II and returned in 1948 as refuge manager in Cold Bay. He is now wildlife biologist in the Anchorage office of the U.S. Fish & Wildlife Service.

G. Vernon Byrd initiated intensive biological investigations of seabirds and the Aleutian Canada goose as manager of the Aleutian Islands National Wildlife Refuge when the headquarters were moved to Adak.

Aleutian bird populations have experienced many drastic changes since man first entered the islands. Ironically, the greatest impact came not from what he took away, but from what he added.

On a majority of the islands birds evolved a life cycle without needing to incorporate defense behavior against land mammals. There weren't any. Ptarmigan, geese and songbirds could nest on the open ground, adopting caution only for predation from above—by eagles, peregrine falcons, gulls or jaegers. Puffins, petrels, auklets and murrelets needed only to dig shallow burrows for their eggs to be safe. Cormorants, murres and kittwakes that prefer rocky ledges for raising their young could choose any suitable cliff face.

Man tipped that delicate balance, not suspecting the Pandora's box he would open by introducing new species either accidentally or deliberately for food or profit.

Russian ships brought the first rats; trading vessels spread them to other islands as the human inhabitants dispersed; and World War II troop and supply carriers enlarged the rats' domain. In recent times rats have even been seen disembarking from aircraft.

Their size and sinuous shape allows rats to enter most burrows and crevices in search of birds, eggs or young. They also destroy ground-nesting birds and probably prey on cliff-nesters as well. On Amchitka, researcher Clayton M. White one year found that rats had ravaged all of the 16 peregrine falcon eyries that he checked.

Rats were only the beginning. With an eye solely on profit, man deliberately dropped off pairs of foxes on nearly all the Aleutian Islands between about 1836 and the 1930s with the biggest push occurring in the early 1900s. An island's bird colonies made it all the more attractive to the fox farmer: the birds would serve as free-for-the-grabbing fox food.

The Aleutian Canada goose, now endangered, is the best-known victim of the fox introductions. In 1906 Austin Clark walked among geese breeding "by thousands" on Agattu Island. In 1923 the Attu Native Community leased the island for fox farming and by 1930 had released at least 32 arctic foxes. They took a total of 1,135 pelts by 1936. When Olaus Murie and his biological survey crew visited Agattu in 1937, they found less than six nesting pairs of geese. His group was the last to find Aleutian Canada geese breeding on Agattu until the USF&WS initiated a reintroduction program in 1974.

Less publicized but perhaps even harder hit by hungry foxes were the nocturnal burrow-nesting storm-petrels, ancient murrelets and Cassin's auklets. Many colonies or entire populations, including the northern fulmar colony of Amukta, disappeared without man's realizing what was happening. Ptarmigan, ducks and songbirds fell prey also. Even some of the cliff-nesting birds found the nimble-footed foxes invading their sanctuaries.

Today the remaining seabirds concentrate on tiny offshore islets or sea stacks in defense against foxes. Onshore, auklets find the deepest crevices available and some cormorants and puffins choose damp sea caves as nesting sites. On the few islands where refuge biologists have managed to eliminate the introduced foxes, bird reaction is encouraging: within the year, terns and gulls come back to nest and songbirds begin to recover; soon ptarmigan increase and perhaps in time the murrelets, petrels and geese will return.

Perhaps for fox food, Samuel Applegate released ground squirrels on Unalaska in the 1890s and Nick Bolshanin captured a few of those and placed them on Kavalga Island in 1920. However, during the critical winter food shortage time for foxes, ground squirrels hibernate. Today Kavalga's foxes are gone but the ground squirrels remain fat and sassy.

Sheep, cattle, reindeer and caribou introduced since 1900 for profit or experiment have varying effects on island bird populations but all crop the naturally protective vegetation where birds might hide their nests. Their hooves may collapse some birds' burrows or cause landslides of nesting slopes. Some eagles, in turn, may shift from hunting fish and seabirds to dining on wool, causing the sheep industry to demand that eagles be destroyed. The rabbits now established on Ananiuliak Island are sometimes eaten by glaucous-winged gulls, uncontested.

Robert Jones, former refuge manager, detected the most recent introduction—the black fly, which reached Adak by 1958, Shemya by 1964, and Amchitka in connection with activities of the Atomic Energy Commission in 1968, all apparently transported by jet aircraft. The female black fly sucks blood from warm-blooded animals and in the process becomes the vector of a blood parasite of birds that can cause reproductive failure.

Although this latest accidental introduction is irreversible,

Monofilament nets used by foreign fishing vessels wash ashore in the Aleutians and become fatal traps for birds, sea otters, sea lions and beach-grazing reindeer. Here, at Sergief Bay on Atka Island, the skeletal remains of 34 reindeer were counted in one five-mile stretch of shoreline. (Kevin Hekrdle, reprinted from ALASKA® magazine)

Aleutian winds may come to the rescue and control the severity of the problem by keeping the flies grounded.

Introduced species have extracted a toll on breeding seabirds during the short, but critical breeding season on land. Man's latest activities threaten to charge an even higher toll year around while the birds are at sea.

Already tens of thousands of seabirds drown each fishing season, entangled in gill nets on the high seas as they dive for their own tiny food items. Shearwaters, murres and tufted puffins suffer the highest mortality from the monofilament nets used by foreign fishing fleets. Pieces of net, either broken away or deliberately tossed overboard, litter Aleutian beaches with blue mesh and trap more birds. Mammals too are ensnared at sea; carcasses of sea otters and choked sea lions wrapped in netting wash up with increasing frequency on the beaches; beach-grazing reindeer are frequent victims.

Oil tankers and increasing ship traffic along the Chain threaten oil spills in fish-rich waters and against beaches where fog, fierce waves and lack of observers, runways or docks would defeat cleanup attempts.

No one can predict the impact bottomfishing will have on seabird populations. Direct effects of competition for Pacific herring, capelin and sandlance will combine with the more subtle changes in the food chain that could lead to a gradual population decline for birds. Lacking the dramatic visibility of oil spills, the decline may continue unheeded until suddenly a point of no return is reached and a bird population is wiped out.

The chapters of man's greatest impact on Aleutian birds may only be opening. □

Bald eagles are common in the Aleutians. This magnificent adult (three to four years elapse before bald eagles reach full adult plumage) was photographed on Adak Island.
(Michael Gordon)

startling blue-white eyes, stay in the home burrow until they grow nearly to adult size and are ready to begin their life at sea.

When gale-force winds ground all other marine birds, Laysan and black-footed albatross will still be gliding in suspended animation on fixed wings for hours at a time, combing the crests and troughs of waves. From on board a ship, glimpses of these huge, stately birds with seven-foot wingspans provide moments of calm in what otherwise usually is turbulent sailing.

Dipping more rapidly across a ship's bow, the sooty and short-tailed shearwaters also glide the wave crests, but typically in flocks rather than singly as the albatross.

Robert Jones, former refuge manager, has seen shearwaters blackening 50 square miles of the nutrient-rich waters of Unimak Pass. He gave up counting when he realized no one would believe his 150 million estimate.

Shearwaters and albatross represent a tourist invasion from the south—some from as far as New Zealand, Australia and Antarctica where they nest. Their vacation from the austral winter reflects the international importance of the Aleutians.

Strengthening multinational ties are the whooper swans from Russia that stop for a visit in the winter; Aleutian nesting shorebirds that migrate to the South Pacific for winter; and numerous shorebirds and songbirds that make regular migrations between points in Southeast Asia, the western Aleutians and eastern Siberia.

Only within the past four years have studies determined that what had appeared to be totally accidental sighting in North America of such birds as the Mongolian plover, brambling, or Polynesian tattler had actually been the recording of annual visitors to this island crossroads.

While Asian birds such as greenshanks and long-toed stints merely pass through the Aleutians, other land birds are more faithful. The

winter wren, an elusive beach songster who belts out melodies bigger than its tiny size, braves the winter's snow and gales to stay year-round.

Rock sandpipers that begin life as long-legged chicks sprinkled with spots also manage to hang tight through the 100-knot winter winds. Ravens who love to play and soar on thermal updrafts may perform incredible acrobatics during these storms.

Flashily dressed harlequin ducks ride plunging, frothing storm crests without being smashed against the rocks. Unlike the common eider whose ducklings bob in the surf each summer, the harlequin is not known to breed in the Aleutians.

Another permanent resident, the gray-crowned rosy finch, uses barren shelves in World War II Quonset huts for its nesting platform. Here the young finches are protected somewhat from the rats that might raid a nest on a sea cliff and from avian predators such as peregrine falcons and jaegers.

The Peale's peregrine falcon of the Aleutians is unique in two ways: it doesn't migrate south and, because of that, its population is stable and not endangered as peregrines elsewhere are. In late summer the young peregrines practice their aerial acrobatics—often by dive-bombing and bedeviling awkward young gulls—"glorying," as Olaus Murie observed, "in their new-found power of flight."

Roughly every five miles of Aleutian shoreline has one bald eagle eyrie, except in the islands west of Buldir where there are none. This lack of bald eagles in the Near Islands may be linked to changes in the near-shore community of kelp, sea urchins, fish and sea otters. Since at least 1977 a pair of white-tailed sea eagles, common in the Komandorskies, has taken up residence on Attu.

Some birds only come to the islands for the winter. The most conspicuous is the emperor goose whose entire world's population forages on the beaches of the Aleutian arc from the

by dawn to avoid becoming a quick gulp for a hungry glaucous-winged gull or scavenging jaeger. The successful murrelet chicks grow up at sea; they will not set webbed foot on land for several years until they too are old enough to nest and lead another generation to sea.

Cassin's auklets, more numerous in the eastern part of this region, especially on fox-free islands in the Sandman Reefs and Shumagin Islands, also perform the nocturnal rituals of incubation shifts and night feeding flights. Cassin's chicks, gray-feathered with

Komandorskies east to Sanak. They depart for their Yukon-Kuskokwim Delta and Siberia breeding grounds by May.

One of the few Aleutian birds not oriented to the sea or fresh water is the rock ptarmigan. Several islands have their own subspecies, all darker than those from mainland Alaska. Introduced foxes reduced some of the populations, but the ptarmigan's preference for interior, mountainous terrain helped save brood stock on many of the islands.

The Aleutian Canada goose was not as lucky. Once abundant from the Islands of Four Mountains westward, the goose had only one sanctuary after fox farming became widespread in the Aleutians: fox-free Buldir Island.

Biologists are now working nationwide to help the goose recover by studying and protecting the wild Buldir flock, by removing foxes from selected islands, and by raising birds in captivity to release on these former nesting islands such as Agattu.

In 1976 the refuge staff turned Amchitka Island into a holding station to acclimate Lower 48-raised geese to the Aleutians and began hatching its own goslings under the guidance of Forrest Lee, USF&WS biologist.

Meanwhile, G. Vernon Byrd, acting refuge manager, led his biologists to Buldir to band this small, dark goose and discovered, through tracing the bands, where these birds flew each winter: California.

Next season hunting closures followed the geese as they moved around their wintering grounds. Since the first spring count in 1975 of 800 birds on Castle Rock in northern California, that figure has doubled.

With the doubling, hopes are high that a way will be found to successfully start geese breeding in the wild on three more islands, removing the specter of extinction from over the Aleutian Canada goose.

Biologists should find encouragement from the success story of another near-extinct Aleutian resident, the sea otter.

The Aleutian Canada goose is the only endangered bird species in the Aleutian Islands. A team of biologists has worked to restore the species' population and breeding pens and hatching facilities are maintained on Amchitka Island where this 15-minute-old gosling (below) *was hatched. The 30-minute-old gosling* (right) *weighs 75 grams (about 2.65 ounces).*
(Both by Forrest B. Lee, USF&WS)

Above
Charles Craighead herds a band of Aleutian Canada geese on Agattu Island in the western Aleutians.
(USF&WS)

Left
Dr. Forrest Lee and Craig Beauduy watch Aleutian Canada geese at the holding pens on Amchitka. The geese are confined on the island until they are strong enough to migrate to their wintering grounds in California.

. . . The sea blood-stained, sealion and seal,
Fowl's flesh now rose and salmon . . .

6
Mammals

The sea otter is synonymous with the Aleutians. This smallest marine mammal has prompted the worst and the best in man—all deeply ingrained throughout the turbulent history of the islands.

Hunted almost to extinction, the sea otter received a reprieve from slaughter in a 1911 international treaty and a protected refuge in the 1913 designation of the Aleutian Islands Reservation. Yet many scientists predicted the otters had been too drastically reduced to expect survival of the species.

Remnant populations did hang on, however, along the most forbidding coasts where offshore reefs and no safe anchorages made poaching hazardous. The habitat had remained unimpaired so that with time the sea otters began to increase in number and expand their territory—first around the initial "seed" islands and then slowly to other nearby islands. That gradual expansion and migration is continuing today.

Amchitka, major center for sea otter recovery and study, even provided excess otters for transplant elsewhere in Alaska and to the coast of the Pacific Northwest. California colonies have also burgeoned to the point that abalone and crab fishermen are protesting bitterly that otters are eating them out of business.

Steller sea lions are the most abundant marine mammal in the Aleutians today. The roar from their breeding colonies can be deafening. The 2,000-pound bulls attempt to reign over a loose harem of cows as they come ashore to deliver their pups. Bachelor bulls linger near the fringes or haul out in colonies of their own on separate islands.

Aleuts covered their *baidarkas* with sea lion skin, depleting the population until 1914 when canvas *baidarka* covers began to be used.

After rising to a population of about 100,000, the Steller sea lion may have reached a maximum and is declining in the eastern Aleutians. However, recent surveys indicate new and growing colonies in the western Aleutians: whether or not this indicates a shift in territory has yet to be determined.

Harbor seals, while numerous, are much more elusive than either the sea otter or sea lion. At the least sign of danger the females slither from their sandy beach resting areas and slide into the water with their wide-eyed pups. Once in the water they observe surface goings-on as cautiously and silently as a submarine periscope.

In the waters off the islands are some of the largest marine mammals—whales. The list includes minke, sei, finback, gray, blue, right and sperm whales. Rare specimens of the deepwater Stejneger's beaked whales have washed up on Aleutian beaches. Pods of killer whales are the most visible offshore residents due to their tall dorsal fins.

Unimak Pass serves as a whale corridor in spring and fall as species such as the gray whale migrate to and from feeding grounds in the Bering and Chukchi seas.

Dall porpoise often play alongside ships. They can cut across a ship's bow with lightning speed. Sightings of both whales and porpoise are less frequent today than in years past and observers worry that heavy hunting or harassment by foreign fishing fleets may have caused the decline.

Two occasional marine visitors to the islands of the Chain are the fur seal and walrus. Fur seals breed in the Komandorskies and the Pribilofs and migrate in waters adjacent to the Aleutians and through Unimak

A herd of Steller sea lions takes to the sea at Pochnoi Point, Semisopochnoi Island.
(John E. Sarvis)

52

Pass. Walrus once hauled out regularly on Amak Island, but ivory hunters exploited them so heavily that only recently have they begun to return to the area.

Elephant seals occasionally wander into this territory, but the event is so rare they seldom appear in refuge listings. Hunted almost to extinction by 1890, the elephant seal now numbers about 45,000, but most prefer warmer climes.

The Aleutian's record range of sea mammals overshadows its terrestrial counterparts. In fact, on most of the islands between Unimak and Attu, no land mammals are native.

Unimak Island, barely separated from the Alaska Peninsula, is the natural western limit of caribou, brown bear, wolf, wolverine, ground squirrel and weasel. Almost all land animals to the west were introduced by man.

The arctic fox, indigenous to the Komandorskies and Attu, might well have found its own way to the other islands of the western Chain, but mice, rats, rabbits, reindeer, wild horses, cattle, buffalo and caribou are all imports.

Abundant forage and scarcity of biting insects allowed caribou transplanted to Adak in 1958 and 1959 to reach record size. Despite an executive order in 1930 to protect Unimak caribou from domestic dogs, the once-numerous herd there disappeared after military occupation in the mid-1940s. In 1955 a small herd was spotted and today it numbers in the thousands.

In 1891 Sheldon Jackson purchased 16 reindeer from Siberia and established them without herders on Amaknak and Unalaska islands, the first Alaska transplants. Two years later all these animals had vanished, and 21 more landed in 1913 also disappeared. However, 36 deer transplanted in 1913 on Umnak survive today in the form of a substantial wild herd, and a scant two dozen deer moved to

Caribou wander on Unimak Island. Because of high winds, these animals are spared some of the torment of flying insects that plague their species elsewhere in the state.
(Palmer C. Sekora)

Atka a year later have multiplied to a herd of about 1,500.

Horses, cattle and sheep, left unattended on several islands, have become tough, hardy breeds, as have buffalo, originally imported to Popof Island to be mated with cattle. The cattle died here, but a small number of buffalo continue to survive by keeping a healthy distance from the island's main settlement of Sand Point.

The red fox and blue fox, transplanted by fur traders during the Russian period and in the 1920s, populated the Chain in such devastating numbers that they wiped out

Right
A silver fox casts a wary eye on the photographer on Umnak Island.
(Douglas W. Veltre)

Center right
A herd of bull walrus compete for space as they haul out on Amak Island near Cold Bay.
(John E. Sarvis)

Below
Steller sea lions fascinated and amused divers who photographed them underwater at Cape Morgan, Akutan Island. Gulping air at the surface and then emitting bubbles as they submerged, the animals seemed to enjoy imitating the divers. Some of them moved in close enough to touch the men; several took divers' arms tentatively in their mouths, perhaps wondering if they'd come across some new and delectable food source. Gentle, graceful, they lingered without fear or aggressiveness, sharing their watery space.
(Ted Bank II)

Top
A harbor seal rests on a sand bar at low tide at Izembek National Wildlife Range, Cold Bay.
(John E. Sarvis)

Above
Umnak has been the site of one of the largest ranching ventures in the Chain. Wild sheep that roam unattended on some parts of the island appear to fend fairly well despite rigorous terrain and climate, and are too wild to be approached on foot.

whole bird colonies, and attempts to restore bird life by eliminating them have proved highly frustrating.

Norwegian rats, first landed on the islands in early Russian times, now sustain themselves in the wild. However, you may disregard reports that the creatures often reach a weight of 35 pounds. When the Atomic Energy Commission took over the old military base at Amchitka in the late 1960s, it inherited a number of cases of C rations (35 pounds each), which staffers casually referred to as "35-pound rats," and Outsiders, hearing the expression, spread rumors of this remarkably large rodent.

The crew of Vitus Bering, discoverer of Alaska, reported wolf tracks on Nagai in the Shumagins, but no sign of this animal has been seen there nor in the western islands since; nor did the aboriginal Aleuts appear to have domesticated dogs.

Collared lemmings have been reported as far west as Umnak, sometimes in great numbers. Ground squirrels, found naturally at Unimak, were introduced to Unalaska by Sam Applegate in a quest for fox food and have also gained considerable range. The tundra vole is found in the Shumagins and the eastern Aleutians to Umnak.

Old-timers recall that for some years a large brown bear roamed Unga Island, abandoned there by youngsters who kidnapped it from the mainland but found it hard to handle in a small boat. The sight of it sent unwary travelers into shock, but the creature finally disappeared, probably dying of old age or sheer lonesomeness, which leaves Unimak as the only bear-bearing Aleutian island.

There are no reptiles on the Aleutians, no frogs or amphibians, despite the considerable rainfall. One reason may be that flying insects, a usual food source, have a tough time surviving high Aleutian winds. Black flies and white sox were inadvertently imported by the military, and mosquitoes appear occasionally, but none in great number.

The Historic Role of the Sea Otter in the Ecology of the Aleutian Islands

By Charles A. Simenstad
and James A. Estes

Charles A. Simenstad and James A. Estes both began Aleutian research on Amchitka Island in biological monitoring of the Cannikin test by the Atomic Energy Commission. Simenstad is now at the Fisheries Research Institute, University of Washington; Estes is with the Center for Applied Coastal Management, University of California.

Recovery of the sea otter in the Aleutians from near extinction less than a century ago apparently caused more changes in that foggy, windy seascape than one might imagine. It took but 170 years for European and American fur hunters to all but eliminate the sea otter from the entire northeastern Pacific Ocean. But the resurgence of otter populations at some island groups, while other island groups remain unoccupied or sparsely populated, has revealed dramatic differences in the nearshore ecology which can only be attributed to the sea otters' presence.

After the cessation of sea otter exploitation in 1911 and the creation of the Aleutian Islands National Wildlife Refuge in 1913, wildlife biologists monitoring those misty isles noted differences in the islands' shoreline character. However, those early biologists—Olaus Murie, Victor Scheffer, Robert Jones and Karl Kenyon—did not have access to either quantitative or comprehensive information on the structure of the nearshore community, and it was not until the Atomic Energy Commission occupied Amchitka Island for underground nuclear testing in the mid-1960s that such in-depth studies of the Aleutian nearshore community took place. Ecological investigations supported by the AEC to document the effects of testing on the island's ecosystem indirectly led to an intriguing discovery about the ecology of the temperate North Pacific. Marine biologists from several universities and state and federal agencies spent some six years, from 1967 to 1973, meticulously studying the algal, invertebrate, sea and shore bird, and marine mammal populations which characterized Amchitka's marine environment. What they described was a nearshore community which had been under the influence of a sizable population of sea otters for over 30 years, because Amchitka appears to have maintained a small remnant population throughout the period of exploitation by fur hunters, and hence was one of the first islands to show significant recovery of its otter population. By the time Amchitka researchers began work on the population in 1968, the total number of otters was estimated to be 4,000; with refined techniques that estimate rose to almost 7,000 otters by 1972, or approximately 63 otters per square mile of near-shore waters.

More interesting to marine ecologists in the group were the extensive and dense kelp beds surrounding the island. This lush habitat harbors a rich variety of fishes and invertebrates which utilized the kelp beds for protection, spawning habitat, and food. When the first results of detailed studies emerged, it became obvious that the near-shore food web—i.e., the complex sequence of energy and nutrient flow from plants to herbivores to carnivores—was based to a great extent on the yearly decomposition of the algae and kelp into detritus.

But the key to the discovery rested in the diet and feeding efficiency of the sea otter. Observations of sea otters and analyses of their stomach contents indicated that their primary food items were sea urchins and other invertebrates such as limpets and chitons which eat algae and kelp. Because 4,000 to 7,000 sea otters, eating approximately 25% of their body weight per day, consumed a lot of these herbivores, the kelp and algae flourished. This was further confirmed when the biologists dived to the bottom of nearshore waters and found that sea urchins were sparse and typically very small. Thus, the presence of high densities of sea otters appeared to be the reason that the nearshore environment was so dominated by algae and kelp beds. This, of course, posed the hypothesis that sea urchins and the other herbivores were abundant during the period of few sea otters and the algae and kelp beds were severely reduced as a result.

Such a hypothesis had to be verified by means other than historical records of the numbers and sizes of sea urchins, since none existed for Amchitka before the sea otter population began its recovery. The obvious solution was to go to some of the other Aleutian Islands which still had few or no sea otters. Thus, two islands 250 miles west of Amchitka at the far western extreme of the Aleutian Chain—Shemya Island in the Semichi group and Attu Island in the Near Island group—were chosen because Shemya lacked sea

A sea otter enjoys a leisurely seafood dinner.
(Paul Arneson)

otters and Attu had only a few, and because they offered easy access through their military installations.

When the biologists visited these islands their hypothesis was almost immediately verified. Instead of the virtual forest of kelp and algae which occurred at Amchitka, there were only a few scattered kelp beds and the algae were largely restricted to the high intertidal zone. A dense green carpet of large sea urchins covered the bottom and created a translucent emerald-green sea, very different from the dark brown waters of Amchitka. These observations and subsequent detailed measurements and experiments indeed illustrated that, through their constant grazing of the algae, the sea urchins had rather strikingly altered the character of the nearshore community at these islands.

As two of the biologists involved in initial research on the relation-

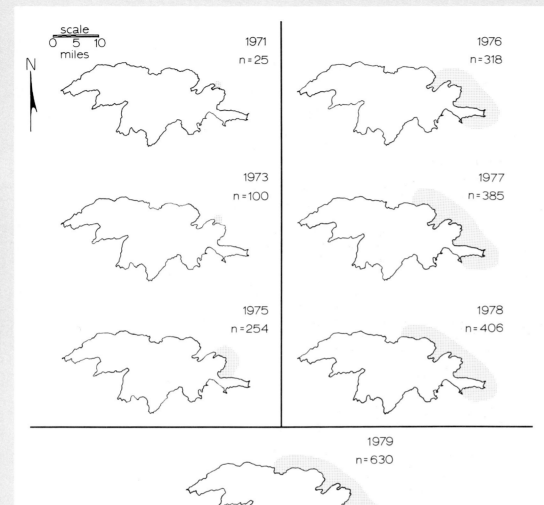

scale
0 5 10
miles

N

1971
n=25

1976
n=318

1973
n=100

1977
n=385

1975
n=254

1978
n=406

1979
n=630

Growth and expansion of sea otter population at Attu Island as documented by visual surveys between 1971 and 1979. Estimates of abundance (n) may also vary according to weather conditions, otter behavior and other factors affecting their distribution within the nearshore region.

ship between sea otters and the nearshore community, our interests remained close to the Aleutian Islands. There were still many unanswered questions. One problem with the early study was that it was a short-term comparison of areas that may have differed in other ways unknown to us. Casual descriptive anecdotes of the Amchitka nearshore region during the early 1900s, before the recovery of the otter population, suggested that the biological community was similar to the community presently seen at Attu. It appeared that there had been many changes since then. However, to really understand the relationships among sea otters, sea urchins, kelp and algal assemblages, nearshore fishes, and benthic invertebrates, we needed to study a system in the process of changing from one community state to another. No island could have fit this situation any better than Attu. Sea otters probably had been absent from Attu since the late 1800s or early 1900s and were not reported again until 1959. In 1965 USF&WS biologists observed 13 otters at Attu, suggesting that a population was again established. When we first visited Attu in 1972, only about 25 otters were counted from shore, and these were restricted to the northeast corner of the island. So, on one side of the island a sparse population of otters had existed for about a decade, whereas they had been essentially absent from the rest of the island for a century or longer. Here then was a situation that enabled us to identify changes that had occurred during the ten-year history of sea otters at Attu, as well as to precisely document changes in species composition and abundance of algae, marine invertebrates, and fishes as the otter population grew and expanded into new habitat. A long-term research program also provided the opportunity to conduct various ecological experiments and collections designed to delineate mechanisms of change observed in the community, something we had been unable to do at Amchitka.

Since 1975, with support from the USF&WS and the cooperation of the Aleutian Island National Wildlife Refuge, we have been conducting such studies.

The sea otter population at Attu has grown from about 250 in 1975 to about 450 in 1978. Its range also has expanded around the east end of the island and along the north coast, until now it occupies about one-third of the shoreline. (See chart.) Although it apparently is too early to see some anticipated changes in the community, the average sea urchin size has certainly declined in the area where otters have been feeding. We are also studying the sea urchins' foraging response to different species of algae in different habitats—i.e., at different depths and exposure to wave action—in an attempt to explain why small populations of algae and kelps, that we know are consumed by sea urchins, persist amongst sizable densities of urchins. Knowing this will give us some idea of how rapidly, in which habitats, and through which mechanism the kelp beds will begin to expand with decreased grazing by the exploited sea urchin population.

Nearshore fishes, especially the abundant rock greenling, appear to be closely linked to the distribution and abundance of kelp. Kelp may serve fishes as a refuge from predators such as seals and otters, as a habitat for laying their eggs, and as a source of algal detritus which it utilizes by their prey organisms. Sea otters at Amchitka rely on fish as a major component of their diet, principally because availability of large sea urchins has declined under intense otter predation. The consequent reduction in grazing by sea urchins has caused kelp beds to flourish, increasing production of an alternative prey for the sea otter, the rock greenling. Thus, we believe that the sea otter, through its activities as a predator, helps maintain a productive nearshore ecosystem.

We have also taken part of our research program from the Aleutians to the laboratory in order to carry out studies otherwise limited by uncontrollable field conditions and severe winter weather. We have been maintaining sea urchins from Attu in experimental aquaria at the Seattle Aquarium for almost a year at various population densities and food sources while we record their growth and egg production (fecundity). Results from these experiments, which would be impossible to maintain on Attu, are already verifying our impression that the dense, unexploited populations of sea urchins at Attu are characterized by low growth and fecundity. Thus, the production of sea urchins in communities without otters probably is less than it would be with some degree of sea otter predation.

Results from the study at Attu carry implications to areas beyond the Aleutian Islands. Through either natural expansion or translocation the sea otter is now reinhabiting regions where it had been exterminated at the beginning of this century, including Southeast Alaska, British Columbia, Washington, Oregon and California. Man and the sea otter will come to co-occupy and exploit more and more of those areas. Such research will enable us to anticipate, and perhaps allow for, the consequences of this situation. □

A sea otter feeds on greenling at Amchitka.
(Charles A. Simenstad)

A sea otter, grooming her pup, pauses to inspect the land-bound photographer.
(Michael Gordon)

7
Extinct Species

The coming of the white man to the Aleutian Chain brought extinction for at least two unique species which had already been pushed to the brink by Native subsistence hunters. The placid Steller sea cow lasted only 27 years after discovery and the great Spectacled Cormorant became extinct within 100 years.

Unfortunately nature designed both creatures with built-in obsolescence, in that they had scant means of protecting themselves, moved slowly, and were good eating. A sea cow bone dating back 130,000 years was found on an interglacial beach at Amchitka. The final sighting of the species occurred in the westernmost Komandorskies which, until the coming of explorers, were uninhabited.

In 1742 Vitus Bering's shipwrecked crew—weak from hunger, exposure and scurvy—were overjoyed to encounter a mammal of 30 feet, weighing some 8,000 pounds, that was not only palatable but delicious. Even George Steller, the ship's naturalist and the only scientist ever privileged to study the sea cow alive, waxed lyrical over its flavor.

"Melted, [the fat] tastes so sweet and delicious that we lost all desire for butter," he reported. "In taste it comes pretty close to the oil of sweet almonds . . . the meat, when cooked, although it must boil rather long, is exceedingly savory and cannot be distinguished easily from beef."

Thus happily well fed, he settled down in the midst of disaster to study this heretofore unknown species with professional detachment, taking notes in concise Latin.

The sea cow *(Hydrodamalis gigas)* was most like the manatee we know today, but different in that it had no phalanges or finger bones in its considerably shorter forelimbs.

Nature had apparently cruelly limited the scope of its hearing and sight.

"I do not venture to confirm that they could definitely see and hear and since the head was repeatedly submerged in water it seemed that the animal itself neglected and scorned the use of these organs," Steller speculated.

Brainpower may have been equally dim, but nonetheless, the sea cows managed to fend for themselves when left undisturbed.

"These gluttonous animals eat incessantly, and because of their enormous voracity keep their heads always under water with but slight concern for their life and security, so that one may pass in the very midst of them in a boat and single out from the herd the one he wishes to hook," wrote Steller, who had a chance to observe the creatures for 10 months before crewmen built the wreckage from their ship into a small boat.

"All they do while feeding is to lift the nostrils every four or five minutes out of water, blowing out air and a little water with a noise like that of a horse snorting. While browsing they move slowly forward, one foot after the other, and in this manner half swim, half walk like cattle grazing. Half the body is always out of the water. Gulls are in the habit of sitting on the backs of the feeding animals, feasting on the vermin infesting the skin.

"Where they have been staying even for a single day, there may be seen immense heaps of roots and stems. Some of them when their bellies are full go to sleep lying on their backs, first moving some distance away from shore so as not to be left on dry land by the outgoing tide."

In dissecting one of the creatures, he found the stomach stretched six feet by five, so stuffed with seaweed that four men with a rope attached could scarcely move it.

And the animals had considerable appetite for romance, he noted. "In the spring they mate like human beings, particularly towards evening when the sea is calm. Before they come together many amorous preludes take place. The female, constantly followed by the male, swims leisurely to and fro, eluding him with many gyrations and meanderings, until, impatient of further delay, she turns on her back as though exhausted and coerced, whereupon the male, rushing violently upon her, pays the tribute of his passion, and both give themselves over in mutual embrace."

Although sea cows were capable of bearing young in all seasons, the majority were born in autumn. Steller concluded that the gestation period was over a year and that the animals were not capable of producing more than one calf at a time, a fact that hastened their doom.

Leonhard Stejneger, who researched the sea cow for the National Museum just before the turn of the century, observed that the animal played the same part in the exploration of the northwest coast of America as did the buffalo in settlement of our western plains.

Ill-provisioned Russian fur hunters stopped at the Komandorskies en route to the eastern Chain to put in a supply of fresh meat and they came in such number that by 1754 the sea cow was extirpated on Copper Island.

A year later Peter Jakovleff, a mining engineer, requested authorities at Kamchatka to restrict sea cow hunting, but it was too late. Authorities generally conclude the animal died out about 1768.

Professor A. E. Nordenskiold, a Norwegian explorer who visited Bering Island for five days in 1879, reported Natives had seen the creature there as late as 1854, but Stejneger, who spent a year and a half on the Komandorskies, presented "conclusive evidence" the statement was untrue, and recent Russian reports that the animal still exists have likewise been challenged, even by Russian scientists.

The Spectacled Cormorant *(Phalacrocorax perspicillatus)* was, according to Stejneger, the "largest and handsomest of its tribe, and so little has been known of it that there is not yet [1889] printed a detailed and good description of it."

Again Steller seems to have been the only naturalist ever to have viewed a live specimen. He was awed by the great bulk of body—12 to 14 pounds—and observed that its disproportionately small wings were entirely deprived of the power of flight, making it an easy mark.

Its head was dark greenish-blue with two green-blue crests and a bare forehead. Long,

hairlike features of pale yellow ornamented the head and upper neck; it had large patches of white on its flanks and a bit of black on the tail.

Ever the gourmet, Steller also observed, "It was particularly palatable compared to the rest of its species" and that "one single bird was sufficient to feed three starving men" of his shipwrecked crew. He even passed on a recipe in which one encases the bird, feathers and all, in a mold of damp clay and bakes it in a heated pit until tender.

Komandorsky Aleuts told Stejneger they had seen and eaten this bird 30 years before his visit (1882) and that the bird was considered a delicacy by employees of the Russian American Company.

In 1837 or 1838 Capt. Edward Belcher of the *Sulphur* presented a specimen of the Spectacled Cormorant to Kupreanoff, Russian governor in Sitka, noting only that it came from Bering Island. This prize may have gone to the museum at Leningrad. Today only three other complete specimens of the bird are known to exist (in Holland, London and Helsinki); however, Stejneger did bring home a skeleton to the National Museum.

Stejneger paralleled the demise of the Spectacled Cormorant with that of the last Great Auk which disappeared about the same time. He speculated that, like the sea cow, the cormorant once inhabited other Aleutians, adding it is likely volcanic eruptions as well as predation by man and other beasts may have caused its demise.

Also on the list of missing species is Steller's sea monkey, reported in the southern Semidis. According to his description, it weighed about two Russian pounds, had a head like a dog with pointed ears and whiskers that "hung down like a Chinaman's." It was covered with gray and reddish fur, white on the belly and its tail was divided into fins like a shark. The naturalist wrote that he was intrigued by its wonderful antics and, with the crew, watched

Nature designed the placid sea cow (Hydrodamalis gigas), *first described by naturalist Steller, for inevitable obsolescence. The creature had no means of protecting itself, moved slowly, and made good eating, as Bering's shipwrecked crew discovered during their enforced stay on an island in the Komandorskies.*
(T. Walker Lloyd photo of painting by Richard Ellis)

it admiringly for two hours, yet nothing that exactly matches his description has ever been reported again. Stejneger confessed to doubts about Steller's impressions of the creature, suggesting that in all probability it was indeed a sea otter.

However, there are some—even men of science—who still hold out hope that these misfits of the past may yet survive and, because of the isolation and unexplored nature of the Chain, such speculation may not be as silly as it sounds. Currently a group is planning to reenact Bering's voyage with ships of exact replica (hopefully spared the shipwreck and loss of life), and another expedition is forming on a more modest scale in quest of the tasty *Hydrodamalis gigas*.

. . . I found sleeping shoots of rye pale
green sunken under
the white yellow slender stems and
blades of broken Autumn . . .

8
Plants

While the flora of the Aleutians is relatively simple—only 600-700 species—the islands contain newly introduced plants and also relics of the past.

"There have been only two places in the world where botanists have had a chance to watch plant invasions of islands created anew," botanist Edward Clebsch, University of Tennessee, points out. "They've kept extremely careful track of plants on an island off Iceland, but about the Aleutians we have much to learn."

Some researchers have held that the Chain was covered by the continental icecap as recently as 10,000 years ago. Clebsch speculates glaciation was regional with only a few local glaciers and that the central islands may have escaped the scouring, creating a plant refuge.

It is obvious that the western Aleutians belong to the same floral and vegetation province as the Kamchatka Peninsula of Siberia while eastern islands are most closely related to the Alaska Peninsula, so it would seem the islands serve as stepping stones for continental plant migration.

"If this is the case, the center of the Chain should have fewer species than the ends," reasons Clebsch, "but the longer I'm here, the less the theory seems to hold water." If the center islands served as a refuge, however, that would explain the number of unique plants in this area.

Usually botanists have pollen analysis to chart plant history, but pollen grains are generally destroyed by oxidation in the ash soil of the Chain, leaving investigators with little to go on.

Nor have there been many investigators. Although George Steller, the naturalist who first saw the Chain in 1741, made notes on flora, the samples he collected were lost through shipwreck. One D. Nelson, traveling with Captain Cook in 1779, sent a small number of specimens from Unalaska to the British Museum, and C. Merck of the Billings Expedition of 1786 likewise forwarded small collections to England, Berlin and Russia.

Not until 1866, however, was there a serious effort to examine vegetation. At that time Adalbert von Chamisso, working at Unalaska, gathered a wide range of specimens for Leningrad and Berlin museums and until recently his work was the major source of our knowledge.

In 1929-1930 Misao Tatewaki and Yoshio Kobayashi made botanical investigations supported by a Japanese newspaper and, although there was speculation the expedition was a cover for espionage, their listings were the most complete available until Eric Hulten, working with J. F. Eyerdam, explored the area for the Swedish Academy of Science in 1932.

Isobel Wylie Hutchinson collected additional material for the British Museum in 1936, and P. P. Anderson's investigations for *Flora of Alaska and Adjacent Parts of Canada,* 1947, are also valuable, but Hulten's book remains a classic.

The Atomic Energy Commission initiated an extensive American study in the early 1970s, commissioning Clifford Amundsen, University of Tennessee, to supervise restoration of ground cover after atomic testing at Amchitka. And Amundsen has continued this research, broadening his field of study and encouraging other botanists.

In its natural state the Aleutian Chain is essentially treeless, vegetated by arctic-alpine species, dominated by heath, grasses, sedges and composite families. Despite poor soil,

Ted Bank II, research expedition leader, and student John Wasiuk collect plants in a meadow at the head of Captains Bay, Unalaska Island. Flowers include lupine, white bog orchids, bistort, geranium, and Mimulus. The grasses are short bog grasses and sedges.
(Courtesy of Ted Bank II)

Right
Botanists Mike Williams, Ed Clebsch and Cliff Amundsen scout the hills of Adak for new plants. A species of fern (Polystichum aleuticum) was recently found here that exists nowhere else in the world. Studies are far from complete, but it is known that while Aleutian species are limited they vary considerably from one end of the Chain to the other.

Below
Jeanne Culbertson of Adak gathers edible seaweed near the tideline. She reports that "a quick and invigorating trip to the shore provides five or six varieties for all types of dishes and plenty for friends and neighbors too."

heavy moisture and comparatively mild summers encourage lush growth below 1,000-foot level, but plant life is severely limited in the wind plane, while lack of solar radiation limits species.

On many islands crowberries, cranberries, blueberries and salmonberries provide welcome variation of diet along with wild celery, which has long been a staple.

Vast fields of lupine, yellow monkey flowers, monkshood, orchids, rhododendron, primrose and marsh marigolds brighten summer landscapes. Occasional maidenhair ferns turn up to baffle botanists, for the climate is supposedly not right for them, and another fern, *Polystichum aleuticum*, is found nowhere else on earth.

Among the hardiest and most fascinating common species is rye grass, *Elymus arenarius mollis,* on which aboriginal Aleuts depended for woven baskets, matting, even clothing. Amundsen, who has done the bulk of his research on this species, reports it is superb ground cover, requires no fertilizer and transplants easily even in the face of severe weather. He suspects early Aleuts may have transplanted it to prime locations to improve the species, but there is no way to prove his theory.

Botanists also suspect that a large number of edible plants on which Aleuts have long depended may have been imported—wittingly or unwittingly—by early Siberian hunters who stored bulbs, roots and seeds as emergency rations.

Mushrooms, which thrive in the Chain, arrived there as airborne spores or with shipments of lumber; and earthworms, another import, may have come with shipped materials.

Aconitum, utilized by Siberians as poison, may also have been discovered by Aleuts, who were known to have used poison lances for whale hunting, but again scientists disagree on origins.

Many of the world's most edible seaweeds—red dulse, alaria, laminaria, ulva—grow thickly throughout the Chain, and Aleuts long used them to supplement diet. Tough, ropelike kelp served as fishing lines, and other sea plants were used as bases for paints.

Sea urchins, an important part of the Aleut diet, feed on algae, which inhibits seaweed growth, and when urchin populations are low, dense beds of seaweeds flank the Chain where the sea bottom is rocky, encouraging vast flocks of birds and other sea life.

Russian colonists, who generally disdained Aleut subsistence fare, cultivated gardens with varying results. Outlines of their huge vegetable fields can still be seen at Old Harbor, Atka, yet it is remembered that one winter priests and their dependents actually starved here because crops failed. Unalaska residents recall that turn-of-the-century gardens, cultivated by Russian-Aleuts and by the orphanage, were exceedingly productive. But introduction of Norwegian rats made gardening impossible in many areas.

Lupine (Lupinus nootkatensis) *is one of the many flowers that grows abundantly throughout the Chain.*
(Michael Gordon)

Locally, this abundant weed is called wild celery and parts of it are edible at certain times of the year. The field guide calls it cow parsnip (Heracleum lanatum)— *Aleuts call it* putske. *In the background are the Adak Naval Station and Mount Moffett (3,924 feet).*
(Michael Gordon)

Millie Prokopeuff picks grass to make baskets in a field near Atka. Picking must be carefully timed so that there will be sunshine for drying and bleaching the grass. Locations away from salt water are favored.

Purple orchis (Orchis aristata), *Amchitka.*
(Forrest B. Lee)

Lichens are woven into the colorful groundcover of autumn near Unalaska.
(Richard Eggemeyer)

Violet (Viola)
(Forrest B. Lee)

65

Top
Eschscholtz Buttercup (Ranunculus Eschscholtzii)
Above
One-flowered Cinquefoil (Potentilla uniflora)
Right
Fireweed (Epilobium angustifolium)

Top
Cranesbill or
Wild Geranium
(Geranium erianthum)
Above
Wild Iris (Iris setosa)

66   (All by Michael Perfit)

Aleutian Trees

Before the coming of the white man, according to Umnak legend, a tree grew at the village of Nikolski. Without branches or leaves, its twisted trunk grew into the sky where its top was enshrouded in fog. For some it symbolized the Aleut race, but although local people tried to protect it lest their lineage die, the tree was felled by Russians who used it to build shelter and who were cursed to death for their sacrilege.

Today the remains of this tree are carefully housed by the village, and men like Sergie Sovoroff, who heard the story from their fathers and grandfathers, value the relic highly.

The Aleutian Chain is one of the most extensive treeless zones in the world. Its lack of forests puzzled early explorers, because the climate and soil seemed right and rainfall was most certainly sufficient. High winds proved a hazard to seedlings, but weather was not much worse than that of forested mainland some 550 miles distant.

Before the ice ages, trees appear to have thrived here. Scientists working for the Atomic Energy Commission on Amchitka found large petrified trunks; Atka also has petrified wood; and Unga Island boasts a great stone forest which, experts claim, rivals those of America's national parks.

Unga's petrified stumps of black, yellow and gray cover some 150 acres of beach on the northwest side and measure two to four feet in diameter. These are angiosperms rather than cone-bearing evergreens (gymnosperms), which are the trees that do well today, and scientists estimate they lived from 11 to 25 million years ago, encouraged by the warm humidity of the Miocene period.

In 1945 David Bruce and Arnold Court, writing on Aleutian trees for *Geographical Review of Geological Science* of New York, reported evidence of "slow outward spread" of tree growth in the region, a phenomenon that had been building since the last ice age. The report noted that old-timers on Kodiak remembered only bushes where forests now grow. Man has produced a similar renaissance in the Aleutians.

In 1805, by order of the Russian chamberlain, one Nicolai Petrovich Rezanov imported two- and three-year old spruce from Sitka and planted them at Unalaska village, making it the oldest afforestation site on record in North America.

Twenty-six years later Father Veniaminov reported 24 of the transplants had lived, and had grown to about 8 feet, 6 inches high and 5½ inches in diameter.

Above
The oldest living trees in the Aleutians were planted by the Russians at Unalaska in 1805 and, after a barren century and a half, are finally beginning to reproduce. Here the Russian "forest" serves as a backdrop for the busy harbor.
(Martin Butz)

Left
Blue light reflects from a quartz lens in a piece of petrified wood on Unga Island. Along a five- to eight-mile stretch on the northwest coast of this island are the petrified remains of many metasequoia trees, thought to be an ancestor of the redwood trees of the western United States, and estimated to be 30 to 50 million years old.
(Andrew Gronholdt)

Right
Homesick military personnel at Atka Air Force Base during World War II planted trees and then hopefully installed a park bench to go with them. Despite three decades of bad weather, the bench is still sturdy and the trees have grown—one so large that an average-sized man has trouble getting his arms around the base.

Below
Soldiers stationed at Adak during World War II started this forest, and the Navy personnel who took over the base after the Army and Air Force pulled out honored the woods with a sign which amuses people on this naturally treeless island.

Bernard Fernow, probably the first professional forester to view them, in 1899 wrote that one group of 12 and another of 7 trees had survived, with the largest among them being 25 to 30 feet tall and 24 inches in diameter. He also noted two seedlings had apparently taken root.

By 1943 there were 13 trees, the rest laid waste by military construction, according to local memory. E. P. Walker of the Smithsonian, who inspected them at the time, recorded a height of 30 feet and a diameter of 21 inches for the hardiest.

Bruce and Court reported the little forest still standing in 1944 but that it had not spread; also noting that trees on Kodiak required 20 to 50 years to produce enough seed for second growth.

Bernard Fernow noted that cones of spruce and hemlock must be dry to release their seeds and the months when they generally do this (May through September) are usually wet in the Aleutians.

"During these months, a constant succession of southeast and south winds [blow] and the air is heavily charged with moisture," he theorized. "For this reason the spread of forests is at least retarded, and only when, as may occasionally happen in many decades, favorable wind direction at the right time coincides with a seed, is progress possible."

Biologist Robert Jones sees the problem as lack of sun. The rainy

Chain has the lowest level of solar radiation in North America; generally not enough to allow for the germination of trees. One exceptional summer in a hundred could make a difference, he allows. Perhaps the explanation for the rare reseeding of Aleutian transplants.

Richard W. Tindall, inspecting the Unalaska stand for the Bureau of Land Management in 1976, found six of the original Russian trees still living. Their average diameter was 23.1 inches, their average height 35.7 feet. And in addition, over 1,000 seedlings flourished, many exceeding four feet in height and the tallest six feet, three inches. They had taken root, he observed, in soil exposed through military construction efforts.

The site, which is within the holdings of the Unalaska Native village corporation, has been designated a National Historic Landmark and was placed on the National Register in June 1978.

Other attempts at reforestation have also been successful. Just after the turn of the century, well-heeled citizens of Unga enjoyed high success in landscaping with Sitka spruce and, although today the site is a ghost town, these trees have grown on a magnificent scale and are reseeding to the point that a forest will soon replace toppling buildings.

At neighboring Squaw Harbor, private citizens not only rooted spruce but succeeded in cultivating the only large deciduous tree yet reported well established in the islands—a cottonwood, which stands in the sheltered spot shedding its yellow leaves in fall on the cannery boardwalk.

From 1920 to 1941 the U. S. government, Indian Service and Coast Guard experimented with several varieties of trees, but did not plant systemically or on a large scale. A few successes were recorded at Nikolski, although they have since died off. Trees failed at Atka and Attu, although small mountain ash of an Asiatic variety and willow grow naturally on the westernmost islands of Attu and Agattu. However, spruce planted at Akutan some 80 years ago are still vigorous.

During World War II the military also concerned itself with the Aleutian barrens, planting trees to provide a morale boost for the tens of thousands of GIs isolated there. Early, Alaska Air Defense Commander Lt. Gen. S. B. Buckner Jr. encouraged the shipment of trees down the Chain, and before he left established official tree-planting programs for the islands.

Of some 2,000 spruce set out on Adak in 1943, only six survived, but by 1944 a 90% survival rate was reported for 1,000 imports.

GIs also succeeded in rooting trees on Attu and Atka and their mini-forests stand today in sheltered valleys and ravines, weathered, often somewhat bonsaied, but still growing.

By 1976 botanist Clifford Amundsen had supervised the planting of 2,000 trees on Adak as a bicentennial project and a high survival rate has been reported.

Randy Caldwell planted several types of dicotyledons including lilac when he worked as cannery manager at Squaw Harbor in 1978, and several private citizens throughout the Chain continue to take an interest. A highly grafted cherry tree, planted at Unalaska by Jenabe Caldwell, survived six years and produced one cherry before a strong November storm sent part of a neighboring roof down on top of it.

Although no official count has been made recently, it seems safe to guess that at least 2,000 trees are now firmly established in the Aleutians and that many, like the old Russian forest at Unalaska, may be reproducing.

It is also a good guess that their offspring, protected by original transplants that now serve as windbreaks, have a far better chance of survival than did their parents, and that the dream of Aleutian forests may one day come true. □

The only dicotyledon tree in the Aleutian region (besides alders and dwarf willows) known to have reached maturity is a cottonwood which overshadows the boardwalk at Squaw Harbor. No one recalls who planted it, but the port has long been a cannery town and several cannery superintendents have been interested in introducing trees to this region.

. . . now see . . .
in the ocean thin pins of fish.

9
Fish

Aboriginal Aleuts fished enthusiastically with spears, kelp lines, sinew nets and bone hooks, often of two pieces and intricately carved.

Shellfish were also heavily utilized, the staple being sea urchins, or sea eggs as they're called; chitons or gumboots, clams and blue mussels easily available at low tide if the sea otter populations were not too heavy. Octopus also served as food and its ink for dyes.

Sailors aboard Bering's ship on the first voyage to the Aleutians found easy fishing, and the ship's naturalist, George Steller, was excited to discover two unknown species of sculpin in the catch. He also reported cod fishing excellent and, when finally allowed to go ashore briefly on Nagai, he noted that "every stream and pothole" was full of red sculpins and Pacific brook charr, later called Dolly Varden.

In 1778 Captain Cook marveled at halibut fishing off Sanak where his men landed 100 fish weighing from 20 to 100 pounds, and he named the nearby land mass Halibut Island.

Aside from subsistence use, Russian colonists were slow to profit by the vast seafood resources of the Chain and not until just before the sale of the territory to the United States did they undertake even limited commercial fishing.

Americans were quick to establish herring and cod salteries and, when canning was perfected, went for salmon in the Shumagins, False Pass, King Cove and Unalaska.

Pink salmon migrate through Aleutian waters from East Kamchatka and northwest Alaska. Chum are thought to come from the coast of Asia, Kotzebue Sound and the Yukon River to Unimak, while sockeye appear to migrate mostly from Bristol Bay through the Aleutians and into the Pacific, then return.

Pink, sockeye and chum salmon are most common, coho (silver) much less so in salt water surrounding the islands, and chinook occur offshore, but there is no recent record of Aleutian spawning. Four silver salmon, tagged south of Atka and Adak, were reported in the Kamchatka River, a distance of 900 miles away, and one chinook, tagged off Adak, was recovered in the Salmon River, Idaho, a year later, having come via the Columbia River, a distance of 2,400 miles.

Steelhead common in salt water surrounding the islands also travel long distances. One, tagged off Atka, was recovered in the Chehalis River, Washington, some 2,000 miles away.

Halibut, once found in great abundance, are fewer today because of commercial fishing,

Harold Bendixen weighs in salmon on tender at False Pass. A cannery was established here in the 1920s, then closed in the 1970s. Today the False Pass cannery has reopened, giving a new boost to the local economy.

including a large incidental catch by crab fishermen and those seeking other species.

Cod, once so thick a man could fill a dory with them in half an hour, disappeared in the 1950s but are making a strong comeback. Scientists note that crab feed heavily on cod fry and tend to deplete cod stocks until their own numbers begin to decline, as is currently the case in some heavily fished areas. Well offshore, however, Bering waters still teem with valuable shellfish, especially tanner and spider crab for which a market is just beginning to open up. And biologists maintain escapement for king crab is still good in this area, despite the high price it has recently brought.

Recent surveys show good potential for deep sea clam industry. Shrimp may have been overfished in some areas but appear to be thriving in remote reaches. And oysters also exist, although their reddish color makes them unappealing for commercial trade.

For subsistence Aleuts have long enjoyed pogy fish, which are startling in that males have mint green-colored flesh until cooked. This bottomfish—technically kelp greenling *(Hexigrammos supercilious)*—is delicious and easily preserved by salting. Atka mackerel *(Pleurogrammus monopterygius)* are also a fine staple and, in addition, bottomfish such as Pacific pollack, ocean perch, sablefish, flounder and sole are available in marketable numbers.

Fresh-water fish are few with the exception of Dolly Varden and dwarf Dollies which are common throughout the Chain. There are occasional reports of trout found in crater lakes, Tulik on Umnak in particular, which appear to be dwarf Dollies. Kokawaa, land-locked red salmon, are also found in some areas.

An ambitious stocking program was undertaken on Adak in the 1950s to provide rainbow trout, but it was not roundly successful.

Left
Crab is definitely "king" at Unalaska!
(Christy Turner)

Lower left
At the height of the crab season, every available docking facility is in use at Unalaska.
(Martin Butz)

Right
Dozens of cannery operations keep Unalaska humming during the crab season. This is the floating processor Unisea, *docked at Dutch Harbor.*

Right
Bow of the processor Vita *presents an interesting study at Dutch Harbor.*
(Terry Domico, Earth Images)

Opposite
The promontory known as Haystack provides a good vantage point for photographing the impressive Pan Alaska plant on Unalaska Island, with Mount Ballyhoo in the background.
(Martin Butz)

Startled by the photographer, who surprised them underwater, small king crabs scuttle for cover.
(Bob Nelson)

Crew members watch as the crab catch is weighed at Akutan Bay. This photo was taken aboard the Gemini, *a 110-foot crabber out of Seattle. On January 15, 1980, heavy winds and severe ice conditions sank the* Gemini *about 150 miles east of Cold Bay. Three fishermen survived; two were lost.*
(David W. Shapiro)

Exploring the Bering Sea

Top
Sue Chase Hall of Alaska Department of Fish & Game checks a crab boat at Unalaska for deadloss and to make sure the catch is legal.

Above
Fisherman Ben Paz is shown testifying at a hearing at Unalaska in 1978 on the Fishery Management Plan for Bering Sea groundfish, held by the North Pacific Fishery & Management Council. Paz and two other fishermen were lost in early February 1980 when his boat, Pacific Trader, *originally a tugboat, rolled over in heavy seas.*

Although Russians and Americans have been plying Bering Sea waters since the mid-1700s, the area has been sadly neglected by scientists. Yet few oceans equal and none exceed its cold, stormy depths in abundance of fish and marine life. Some 170 plant and 300 marine animal species flourish here. Zooplankton, tiny marine animals vital to the food chain, have been found to average 10,000 per cubic centimeter of water, while the United States and the Soviet Union, which share this rich bounty by treaty, annually harvest more than a million metric tons of pollack, sole, cod, halibut, perch and salmon as well as ever increasing quantities of crab and shrimp.

In 1977 a joint scientific expedition was finally launched by the United States and Russia to better understand this unusual sea; the Soviets expending more than a million dollars to furnish the 300-foot ship *Volna* and a 100-member crew including 18 scientists, while Americans provided advanced technology, a sea probe system, computer and nine scientists at a cost of $300,000.

During the two-year investigation, which began at Dutch Harbor, researchers discovered the rich quality of Bering Sea life stems from a heretofore uncharted current that flows northward from the depths of the Pacific, providing a constant source of nutrients from outside areas. This results in seafood production at a much higher rate than in oceanic areas that must regenerate nutrients within their own boundaries.

The most productive area appears to be the upper layer of this sea which contains large quantities of nitrate and phosphate, the principal nutrients of phytoplankton, which are distributed over the Bering continental slope by upwelling currents.

Researchers also observed that large land areas bordering the sea, as well as the sea floor itself, contain extensive undeveloped reserves of oil and minerals, and warned that once these resources are developed, pollution in the form of chemicals and heavy metals will greatly endanger the present purity of the sea.

Dr. John J. McLaughlin, director of Fordham's Calder Center, who headed the American exploration force, pointed out that the Aleutian Chain makes the Bering a much more enclosed sea than it appears on the maps and that the coldness of the climate here would cause severe problems with pollutants. Because water temperatures are often near freezing, the Bering's chemical oxidation process that would naturally degrade pollutants is slower than average.

Americans and Russians are now hoping to establish ecological monitoring systems to protect the integrity of their remarkable ocean, and further study is also planned. □

*. . . Pass on
to son and daughter
what you shared with the islands . . .
grass woven baskets as fine as cloth . . .*

10
Art Among the Aleuts

By Raymond Hudson

Unalaska teacher, artist, writer, scholar
Raymond Hudson takes a break with friends
Joshua and Clancy during a hike at Beaver Inlet,
Agamgik Bay, on Unalaska Island. Hudson learned
Aleut basketry from the late Anfesia Shapsnikoff;
under her tutelage wrote a paper on basketry
published by the University of Alaska, and is
recognized as an authority on this classic art. His
Stories Out of Slumber, printed last year, retells
many ancient Aleut folktales.
(Michelle Drake Hudson)

The disappearance of Aleut art is due, in large part, to the fact that wood and grass, the primary materials used by Aleut artisans, disintegrate in the perpetually wet Aleutian climate. The deep and permanent alterations of Aleut life in the 18th and 19th centuries, of course, contributed to the near extinction of original styles and techniques. With the possible exception of coarsely woven utilitarian baskets there has been no continuous artistic tradition among the Aleut. This exception may not be an exception at all if it is true that these coarse baskets were last produced for local use prior to World War II.

Nevertheless, among Aleut people there are sensitive and skilled artists. What are the roots of their art?

The Aleut of pre-Russian and early Russian times carved in bone and ivory. No systematic study of these archeological remnants has been made. Excellent, finely executed birds, animals and abstract incised designs testify to a firmly established craft.

An art form which originated before the Russian arrival and which continued into the first decades of the 19th century was the production of wooden hunting hats. Carved and bent from wood, these conical hats became famous for their painted surfaces. Elaborate geometric patterns, swirling and intersecting across the volcanic shaped surface of the hat, were occasionally interspersed with representational figures of men, whales, land animals and birds. The quality of painting on Aleut hats was never equalled in Alaskan Native art. S.V. Ivanov, writing of the Aleut paintings on these hats, said: "Their unusually rich art worked out new motives, a special Aleutian style, and was on the road to great artistic achievements (polychrome art), which unfortunately was shattered by the arrival of Europeans and soon disappeared."

*Mrs. Vasha (Innokenty) Golodoff of Atka
works on a traditional basket. Pliable
weaving strands are produced from blades of
wild rye grass that grow in profusion on
Aleutian hills. Collected in midsummer, the
cut grass is cured to a white creamy
color, dried and later split into strands for
fine weaving.*
Inset
*Fine examples of Aleut basket weaving are
in the State Museum in Juneau.*

Only a few of these hats exist today, primarily in Soviet and European museums. There are none in Alaska.

Wooden masks were carved by the Aleut and used in ceremonies. Because of their religious and non-Christian associations, masks were early suppressed. A few early drawings of masks exist. A few masks have been recovered intact or in part from Aleutian caves, but as with the hats the number of existing Aleut masks is few. Scattered across the world in museum collections—notably in France, the Soviet Union and the United States—the masks as an Aleut art expression have not been studied.

The Aleut artists of the 19th century were quick to adopt European techniques and styles. In the 1820s the Aleut Vassiliy Kriukov painted several icons for the Church of the Holy Ascension at Unalaska. A few of these survive in the church today. In 1870 William H. Dall confirmed Veniaminov's assessment of artistic ability among the Aleut. He quoted Veniaminov as follows:

"It is to be regretted very much that their talent for drawing and painting has never been promoted. I am convinced that they would become artists above mediocrity. They are very skillful workers in ivory (walrus tusks) without instruction. I saw in the possession of Baron Wrangell a number of characteristic representations of animals. They are very fond of cutting caricatures of the Russians, and often make an excellent likeness of the person intended, though very grotesque. This shows that they have vivid imaginations and faithful memories."

Upper right
An Aleut hat of carved ivory and wood, decorated with feathers, is one of the ancient treasures now at the Smithsonian Institution, having been given to the British Museum by the Alaska Commercial Company in 1889.
(Smithsonian Institution)

Right
Wooden hunting hats originated before the Russian arrival. Carved and bent from wood, these conical hats were famous for their richly polychromed surfaces, with "elaborate geometric patterns, swirling and intersecting across the volcanic shaped surface of the hat." This colorful example is at the Smithsonian Institution.
(Smithsonian Institution)

Far left
John Hoover specializes in polychromed, carved red cedar triptychs based on Aleut themes. This one is titled Puffin Lady.
(From personal collection of Lael Morgan)

Center
Michael Dirks of Atka creates block prints depicting the environment of his home at Atka.

Left
Fred Anderson's masks have personalities of their own. This one is made of wood, leather, hair and paint.
(Photo by Sam Kimura, Courtesy Anchorage Historical & Fine Arts Museum)

80

Whereas the art expressed in hats and masks, produced by men and used primarily by men, died out, the art practiced by women survived and flourished. Aleut basket weaving became world famous. It is generally considered the finest grass weaving in North America.

From the blades of wild rye grass that grows in profusion on Aleutian hills, soft, pliable and thin strands are produced. Collected in midsummer, the cut grass is cured to a white creamy color. Dried and later split into fine weaving strands, the grass must be dampened when used.

The predominant form of Aleut basketry is the small, cylindrical covered basket, although flared "May baskets," flat wallets, covered bottles and circular mats are also woven. The covered baskets, according to the well-known Aleut weaver Anfesia Shapsnikoff, had three major styles. These she named after the weavers living on Unalaska, Atka and Attu. Each style had distinctive design patterns and shapes.

The designs in Aleut basketry showed the influence of Russian and American traders as the work began to depict roses, eagles, harps and even Greek vases.

Grass was also woven into matting of various grades. The finest matting has been recovered from burial caves where it was used to wrap mummified bodies. The open work used in mat production was also utilized to make utilitarian baskets. These "fish" or "pack" baskets were used to carry berries and shellfish. Fine fish baskets were also made as trade items and some of these reflect an astounding level of technique. Produced by Aleuts for use by Aleuts, some of these baskets may contain design ties that reach directly back to the pre-contact period.

Today Aleut art is as diverse as contemporary Aleut life. Basketry is the only art form common throughout the Aleutians.

Graphic arts and woodcarving are practiced

The late Anfesia Shapsnikoff of Unalaska was one of the most accomplished basket weavers of the Chain, producing works of art described by Hudson in his poem Summer's Bay *as ". . . grass woven baskets as fine as cloth." The chair pictured was made by Aleut Chief Alexei Yatchmenoff.*
(Ted Bank II, Courtesy of AEIDC, Anchorage)

by a few artists with Aleut background. Michael Dirks of Atka has created block prints that depict the scenes and concerns of life in that village. The two most prominent artists with ties to the Aleutians are Frederick Anderson and John Hoover. Both are of Aleut descent but neither has resided in the Chain. Anderson, although employing techniques which were not learned from Aleut elders, has derived inspiration from the recorded

literature on Aleut masks and from the existing masks in museums. His masks, of course, as works of art go beyond imitation and achieve expressions of their own. Hoover, a nationally acclaimed carver and painter, draws much from the Russian-Aleut traditions and spirit of his Unga-born mother. A third woodcarver, Philemon Tutiakoff of Unalaska, works on a far smaller scale than either Anderson or Hoover. His numerous productions, frequently carved from driftwood collected on Unalaska's beaches, include sugar spoons, letter openers, hair-pieces, rattles, bud vases, tobacco boxes, and occasionally bowls and animal figures. They are tied to more traditional Aleut art in two ways. First, they are primarily objects of use. Second, their lines, curves and design elements have direct echoes of an earlier art: the rise and fall of graceful curves in Aleut hat designs.

Aleut basketry, like the Aleuts themselves, has survived the myth of disappearance. Today the weaving is as strong as it has ever been since the 1919 flu epidemic took the lives of many accomplished weavers. The finest weaving is done at Atka, but excellent weavers also live at Nikolski and Unalaska. Young people in these villages are learning to weave, and classes in Aleut basketry have recently been given in the Pribilof Islands. A price from $100 to $300 is not uncommon for a small Aleut basket today.

Perhaps the time is gone when there could be a living, unified, distinctive expression of Aleut life through art. The percentage of artists in any population is low. When the population is small, as is the case with Aleuts, the possibility of developing a strong artistic tradition is slight. Yet in each Aleut village there are artists at work deriving their inspiration from these wondrous, infinitely various islands. With today's improved means of communication and the increasing pride in and identification with things Aleut, the day for an Aleut expression in art could just be dawning.

*I could remember
the shattered history of these islands . . .
. . . The slow dance of your beginning*

11
Early History

By Lydia T. Black

Lydia Black was born and educated in Russia and as a girl she read accounts of early explorations of the Aleutians by her countrymen as American girls read fairy tales. She has long had access to materials not easily obtainable by other researchers, and her work, although only recently known in Alaska, has opened doors in Russian American history.
Associate Professor of Anthropology at Providence College, and an ethnohistorian, Black is currently on leave through a grant from the National Endowment of the Humanities to pursue translation and publication of the journals of Yakov Netsvetov, a 19th century Atkan Aleut who was a priest of the Russian Orthodox Church and traveled widely throughout the Chain.
Black says that a definitive history of the Aleutians remains to be written, that research in this area is just in its beginning, and quotes Frederica de Laguna, a great American anthropologist:
I . . . conceive of the Aleutian Chain not as a cul-de-sac, . . . but as a port from which, and to which, intrepid voyagers sailed across the North Pacific, mingling the cultural achievements of two continents.
Black's work has appeared in *American Anthropology, Arctic Anthropology, Ethnohistory* and *Studies in Soviet Thought,* which is published in Europe. Her book, *The Atka Years: 1828-1844,* volume I of a larger work, will be published this year by Limestone Press, Kingston, Ontario, Canada.

I. ORIGINS

They call themselves *Unangan,* or *Anĝaĝin,* and on Atka *Anĝaĝinas,*—roughly, "We, the People." They tell their children that they lived in the Aleutian Islands since time began, that they used to be many and now are few, and that they are one people.

Before the Europeans came their island world was divided: in the West, on Attu, Agattu and Shemya, lived the people who called themselves *Alait* or *Aleut,* but by others were called *Sasix̂nan,* which meant, perhaps, "The exiles from the Islands," "The Strangers." In the Islands between Amchitka Pass and Buldir Island lived the *Qaĝun,* related to the Attuans. They were not very numerous and not much feared by their neighbors. East of Amchitka Pass lived the warlike and powerful *Niiĝun (Niiĝuĝis* and *Naamiĝus)* who held the islands between Amukta and Kanaga passes and who once almost exterminated the *Sasix̂nan* of Attu. Eastward of Amukta Pass were their enemies, the *Qawalangin,* Sons of Sea Lions, who held the large Islands of Umnak and Unalaska, and still farther east, in the Krenitzin Islands, were the allies of the *Qawalangin,* the *Slukalingin,* Sons of Sea Gulls. The *Qawalangin* had pushed another group, whom they called by a name roughly meaning "The Locals," "Those over there," into the inhospitable Four Mountains Islands and they raided the Four Mountains people for women and loot. The people of Umnak and Unalaska knew that *Unangan* lived in lands even farther east: the *Quaĝaĝin* on Unimak and Sanak—"The Easterners," to be feared, who came in large flotillas to burn and pillage; and beyond them, on the great Land, on *Alaxshaq* (the Alaska Peninsula), the *Alagsgin,* who fended off *Qanaĝin*—"The Fishermen" of Kodiak and the people of Bristol Bay, and beyond the *Alagsgin,* in the Shumagins, were the *Qawaqngin*—"Those Beyond the Easterners."

Each village had its own peculiarities of speech, so that one knew right away where a person came from, but throughout the Eastern Islands, from Shumagins to the Four Mountains, people understood each other. Beyond Amukta Pass, in the Andreanof Islands, the Atkans did not understand the Eastern speech, but the language was still very similar. Quite different was the language of the Westerners, those of Attu and the Rat Islands.

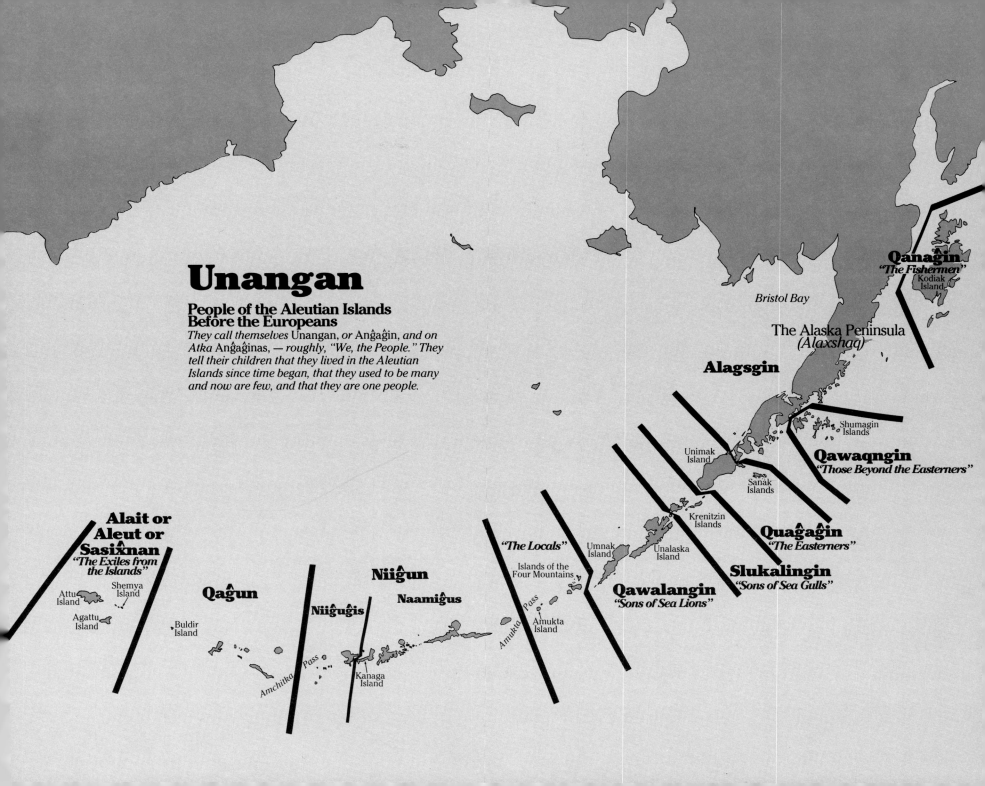

Unangan

People of the Aleutian Islands Before the Europeans

They call themselves Unangan, *or* Anĝaĝin, *and on* Atka Anĝaĝinas, — *roughly, "We, the People." They tell their children that they lived in the Aleutian Islands since time began, that they used to be many and now are few, and that they are one people.*

Qanaĝin
"The Fishermen"

Kodiak Island

Bristol Bay

The Alaska Peninsula
(Alaxshaq)

Alagsgin

Shumagin Islands

Qawaqngin
"Those Beyond the Easterners"

Unimak Island

Sanak Islands

Krenitzin Islands

Quaĝaĝin
"The Easterners"

Slukalingin
"Sons of Sea Gulls"

Umnak Island

Unalaska Island

"The Locals"

Islands of the Four Mountains

Qawalangin
"Sons of Sea Lions"

Alait or Aleut or Sasiẋnan
"The Exiles from the Islands"

Attu Island

Shemya Island

Agattu Island

Qaĝun

Buldir Island

Niiĝun

Niiĝuĝis

Naamiĝus

Amchitka Pass

Kanaga Island

Amukta Pass

Amukta Island

When sea and tides washed away portions of the beach on Hog Island in the summer of 1976, several skulls and assorted bones were exposed. Although it is impossible to determine even the approximate age without carbon-dating, it is the theory of qualified examiners that the skeletal remains predate the era of Russian occupation and are relics of internecine warfare among the islands.
(Bob Nelson)

The people differed in physical appearance; especially the Attuans were different. To this day many people believe that the Attuan women were taller and much more beautiful than women in other islands. Physical anthropologists know that among the prehistoric Aleuts there were people of at least two different types: large, heavy-boned ones, and small, delicate-boned ones. Some scholars call the heavy-boned ones Proto- or Pre-Aleut, believing that their skeletons represent a population that inhabited the islands before the ancestors of modern Aleuts came; others call them Paleo-Aleuts, meaning that the physical type changed over time, and both types of skeletons represent members of the same population. Some believe that the modern population represents the descendants of a single people, who lived in isolation in the islands since the time of the formation of the Bering Sea. Others think that the modern Aleut population represents an amalgam of many groups who came to the islands at different times.

The languages spoken by the historical Aleut people are related to the languages of the Eskimo, most closely to the dialect spoken by the Sirenik Eskimo of Siberia. The Attu language, the most divergent in phonology, grammar and vocabulary from other Aleut languages spoken in the Chain, remains to this day unanalyzed in comparative perspective and is almost extinct. It is quite possible that the Attuan language, when properly analyzed, will provide us with a key to the Aleut enigma.

The archeological record is uneven, but it indicates that for the last 3,000 years (and possibly for much longer), all Aleut groups have shared important aspects of material culture and all had a sophisticated technology adapted to efficient exploitation of a sole subsistence resource: the sea. The oldest archeological site in the Aleutians, Anangula, dated ca. 8000 B. P. (before present) shows that the earliest inhabitants, possibly survivors of Beringia, were, too, sea mammal hunters.

There is as yet little agreement on the origin, development, and cultural affinities of the modern and prehistoric populations of the Chain, except in the most general way, that there is a linkage to northern Japan and Siberian Pacific Rim.

Modern archeological investigations in the Aleutians are sketchy. Don Dumond was moved to write: "The research which has been carried out along the Alaska Peninsula and along the Eastern Fox Islands is not adequate enough for us to be able to give a firm picture of cultural relationships" (see D. E. Dumond, 1977: 70 and 77).

Veniaminov recorded in the 1820s in the Eastern Islands the legends about migration by sea from the West, about the ancient homeland in a country where there was no snow and fruits of the earth were plentiful; also about ancient abandoned village sites, with remains of large dwellings, which the Aleuts pointed out as habitations of people who lived there before their fathers came here.

On the other hand, in the 1780s the Russian skipper Zaikov, a veteran of 30 years' service in the Aleutian waters, one of the first to stay for several years on the Peninsula and to explore the Bristol Bay area, recorded the Aleut tradition current there that these Aleut groups moved to the Islands from the East, destroying and displacing local population. This, of course, agrees with the tradition, also recorded by Veniaminov, that some Eastern Aleut groups claimed a remote kinship, a common ancestry, with the Tlingit, a notion vehemently denied by the Tlingit when asked by Veniaminov, but for which support has been provided recently by Frederica de Laguna: she found that in the Yakutat area many Aleut place names are known even today and she recorded Tlingit traditions indicating that the area of their settlement once upon a time was an Aleut territory.

There is another Aleut legend, unnoticed or dismissed by scholars, but which caused many Russian skippers a lot of grief: the legend of a large island or group of islands far to the South. Many searched in vain, but the tradition was still repeated in the late 1800s.

In my opinion, the data could all be reconciled by assuming that the Aleutian Islands, as today, were a crossroads for different people and that, over a long span of time, there were periods of relative isolation and other times when strangers came from the East, and some, in lesser numbers, from the West and South.

II. THE WAY OF LIFE

By the end of the 17th century A. D. the major islands with a good fresh water supply were occupied or economically exploited by one or more Aleut groups. Numerous small islands and the active volcanic cones were not occupied, but many were used occasionally.

While a major cultural boundary ran along the Amchitka Pass, and there were significant cultural differences between the Atkans and the Eastern Aleuts, especially in matters of belief and ritual and social organization, the mode of subsistence provided a common denominator for all Aleut groups.

The technology everywhere was adapted to extensive and intensive utilization of marine resources. Regional differences in technology existed, but these were less significant than the similarities. From Attu to the Shumagins, the people hunted every available sea mammal species, fished for the deep-water fish, and relied wherever possible on the seasonal salmon runs. The hunting and deep-sea fishing were the domain of the men. Seaweed and driftwood were important resources. The first was widely used to make fishlines and snares for land bird hunting. Driftwood was the basic material used in building dwellings, boats and weapons. Only occasionally was driftwood "wasted" as fuel.

Aleut watercraft were a variation of skin boats used throughout the circumpolar region from Greenland to Siberia, but they were developed to a degree of excellence not found elsewhere. The large skin boat, the *baidara*, still used in the Pribilof Islands to transport heavy cargoes, was used for mass transport of people and goods: mostly, when a village shifted its habitation from the summer to winter village or vice versa, or when the village went visiting.

The craft in daily use was the *baidarka*—the sleek, long and narrow, elegant Aleut kayak.

Each man possessed at least one single-hatch *baidarka* and a village's strength was estimated in terms of the number of *baidarkas* it could muster. Important individuals had two- hatch *baidarkas*. These were also used to train young boys in navigation and hunting techniques. In the Near Islands, a three-hatch *baidarka* was developed, and the Russians brought it to the Eastern islands in the second half of the 18th century. A *baidarka* was usually built by a specialist, but all males had sufficient knowledge to construct one when needed.

An Aleut, trained from childhood to handle a kayak, is said to have been able to right a capsized one and to repair one that sprang a leak by supporting himself with the help of sealskin floats. Floats were used, too, to provide additional stability in rough seas and, in a very bad storm, several *baidarkas* could be lashed together as a very buoyant raft. The double-bladed paddle enabled the hunter to use his weapons while maintaining control of his craft.

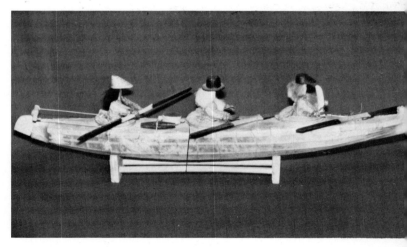

Top
Native of the Aleutian Islands.
(Watercolor and ink. University of Washington, Seattle, Edward W. Allen Collection)

Above
Many Aleuts excel at the art of wood carving. This model baidarka *was made by Sergie Sovoroff of Nikolski.*

Each *baidarka* carried a complement of sophisticated equipment. The hatch was secured against seepage with a waterproof "belt" made of sea mammal gut; the *baidarka* carried a bone or driftwood pump, which employed the Archimedes principle, for use in emergencies. On deck, within easy reach of the hunter, were his weapons, secured by baleen or sinew loops: harpoons, throwing boards, darts, lines and fishhooks. Below deck the hunter carried his food supplies, drinking water and ballast. Persons could be transported below decks also. Long-distance trips and hunting trips of many days were commonplace. An Aleut hunter reportedly could paddle from 12 to 18 hours and achieve speeds up to eight miles per hour.

The throwing board, the *atl-atl,* was the

This elaborate knife was found by the city crew at Unalaska during a post digging job. Its present whereabouts are unknown.
(Unalaska City School)

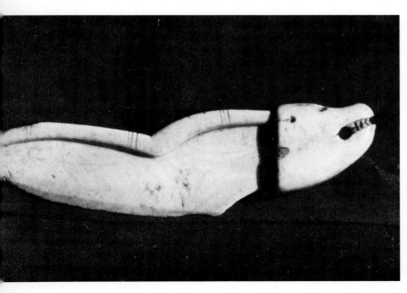

Aleut weapon by choice. Not only was it suited for use at sea, because it required one arm only; it also increased the hunter's range and power. Each man owned a number of *atl-atl* and a great quantity of darts, which were equipped with several types of points, each type suitable for a particular game. Darts used in hunting sea otters were gaily and colorfully decorated. Aleuts also used harpoons and spears thrown by hand.

Each man habitually carried a knife or a short dagger, which was used in a variety of ways. In war, the Aleuts preferred *atl-atl* and the knife. They had the sinew-backed bow and arrow, but this weapon was reserved exclusively for use against fellow men and then on land only.

Seals were hunted at sea by means of a dart or harpoon with a float attached or by a harpoon thrown from shore. At sea a decoy fashioned of sealskin and imaginatively decorated was sometimes employed. Seals were also taken on shore, where they were clubbed by special seal clubs. Sea lions and fur seals were, as a rule, hunted collectively by a group of hunters. Walrus were hunted on shore, by groups, and here heavy spears or lances were used as weapons.

Whales were hunted only in the eastern Aleutians. Whale hunters, men set apart by their choice of prey, were believed to die young or, escaping death, to become hopelessly insane. They hunted as individuals, even if several hunters pursued the same animal. The kill was attributed to a single hunter whose dart struck the beast closest to the rear fluke.

Men hunted a variety of birds at sea, using light small pointed bird darts, and on land with snares made of seaweed or sinew or baleen. It was said that daring young men took cormorants by hand during nighttime, when the birds were secure in their nests on high cliffs. Young men also collected eggs, and many lost their lives when they fell from the rocks.

Deep-sea fishing was the domain of men. The seasonal fish, salmon, were usually taken by women, assisted by children and a few of the old men. Fish were taken by spears, sinew bagnets, or trapped by stone weirs. The only method of preservation was air drying of filleted fish.

Women, assisted by children, gathered intertidal fauna, clams, mussels, occasional octopus, which in times of scarcity provided a margin of security. The tideflats were also the sustenance of widows and orphans. In season, women collected a variety of edible plants, mostly berries, used as condiment, and some edible roots and green plants like *petrushki.* Often, women waited for the ground squirrels to assemble a considerable supply of roots, and then raided the caches to save themselves the labor of digging. They ate their food raw, only occasionally boiling the fish or seal meat by stone boiling method. Men cooked their food when camping near hot springs.

Aleut clothing was similar throughout the Chain. Men wore ankle-length parkas of birdskins and women parkas of sealskins trimmed with sea otter fur, except in the Shumagins where men wore sealskin trousers and sea lion boots. Elsewhere, trousers were not used and footwear of any kind was rare. For parkas, puffin, cormorant and murre skins were preferred. The parkas had no front opening, but at the neck a stand-up collar completed the garment. On Attu, use of fishskin clothing was reported.

The old style waterproofs were made of sea mammal gut, with an attached hood, drawn tight around the neck, with sleeves, secured at the wrist by means of a drawstring, and reaching below the knee or to the ankles.

Many garments, especially women's festive ones and those worn by chiefs and important men, were elaborately decorated. Often the inside of the feather parka was colored with ochre red. The collar, the seams, the hem, the sleeves often sported strips of sea lion throat membrane, richly embroidered with hair or bead embroidery. Decorative fringes were used widely. These were made of fur strips, or the throats of sea lions, dyed in various colors.

Women wore necklaces, arm and leg bands, earrings, ear-, nose- and lip-plugs. Facial tattoos were widespread, in some areas used only by women who sometimes even tattooed upper torso, while elsewhere men used tattoos also.

Hats were unknown in everyday life, but men wore wooden hunting hats, normally a simple open-crowned one with a short visor. On ceremonial occasions and in sea otter or whale hunts the elaborate ritual hat, with long visor, decorated with ivory sculptures, sea lion whiskers, bright bird feathers, and painted in polychrome, was used by important men. Such a hat was worth three able-bodied slaves. Hats of special type were used in ritual. Hunting hats were made by men, usually by skilled masters or possibly ritual specialists. Ordinary clothing was made by women, who took a long time to complete a garment. Their skill in sewing and embroidery was so great that Captain Sarychev thought they could provide competition to the most refined European needlewomen. They used bone needles, with a slit at the end, and sinew thread which they prepared themselves.

The household chattels of an Aleut were few: stone lamps that burned seal or whale oil and provided light and warmth; a variety of baskets and mats, woven of dried beach rye grass or, lacking rye, of the stems of the wild pea. Here too, the Aleut love of color and the feeling for design were asserted, and the baskets and mats were prized not only for their excellent utilitarian properties, but also for their colorful and decorative designs.

Sea mammal skins, provided by the men, and a few skins obtained in trade from the mainland of bear, wolf, caribou and marmot, rounded out their wealth.

Some women became midwives, assisting

A young girl models a replica of an ancient Aleut hunting hat, made by Anatoly Lekanof.

young mothers in labor. Many native plants were used for medicinal purposes by "knowledgeable women" and also by those men who had become shamans—ritual specialists—who cured the sick, foretold the future, controlled the weather, and strove to avert any misfortune threatening their community. Many had extensive knowledge of local pharmacopeia, using plants for medicine and occasionally to induce a trance or as poison. It is not known with certainty if Aleuts used aconite and rannuculus poison in their hunting. If so, its use was restricted, known only in the Eastern Aleutians and then only to the select few—whale hunters.

Aleuts built their villages along the shore.

The interior was inhospitable and dangerous, and survival in the mountains for any length of time was impossible. In the mountains lived the mysterious Outside Men, human in appearance, who occasionally came to the villages to incite young men to join them, or (though rarely), to steal young maidens. From the mountains, too, came the very real danger of volcanic eruptions, avalanches, mudslides and ash falls. A village could be destroyed by a mountain, buried in debris, or its water supply and fish resources destroyed by ash and lava. Only the very brave ventured into the mountains, to get sulfur needed to make fire easily, or to get obsidian of which the best dart and spear points were made.

Permanent villages had to be so situated as to make possible successful defense against raiders and also to provide an alternate easy escape route by sea. Therefore, villages were often located either on promontories or spits or narrow necks so that *baidarkas* could be portaged. In the West, the villages were very small, sometimes numbering no more than 30. In the East, villages were larger, numbering somewhere up to between 200 to 300 persons. An average village size was about 60 persons.

Each village claimed a territory, which the inhabitants exploited. In each village were lookouts, manned constantly. The watch had a double function: to scan the shore for anything useful cast up by the sea (whale carcasses were joyfully announced) and to watch for enemy raiders.

Visitors had to obtain local permission to hunt, fish, or obtain and use other resources. Each group had a permanent, named winter and summer village; in addition, each family had summer fishing and hunting grounds, to which they dispersed during the appropriate season; there were also warrior assembly points or areas; and guest villages—a space where visitors, especially those who came by invitation to the seasonal feasts, built themselves temporary habitation.

In the East, each winter village had one to three or four large communal dwellings; summer villages tended to have smaller individualized dwellings, each housing a polygynous extended family. In the West, individual familial dwellings predominated.

Within each dwelling the space was divided between constituent familial units for sleeping and working places. Each "cubicle" was separated from others by grass mats and most had additional small spaces dug out in the back of the sleeping quarters. These were used mostly for storage, occasionally as an additional sleeping chamber, and, in times of a surprise attack, a hiding place. Children, hidden in such chambers, sometimes survived an enemy raid. The same chambers were sometimes used for burial of the dead.

Children were valued and were trained early by adults in the necessary skills: boys to hunt, to handle the kayaks, to be warriors. Girls learned from their mothers to sew, to work skins, to embroider, and to make baskets.

Aleuts liked to travel and visited kinsmen often, either singly or as a group. On such occasions they traveled in the large *baidaras* and sometimes stayed with their hosts many months.

Usually, a maternal uncle saw to it that his sister's son of proper age and aspiring to the warrior status, was included in a trading or war party. No Aleut was considered ready to assume his adult role in the society if he was a stay-at-home. Many were very daring and set out for far places.

A man desired many wives, but usually made do with just as many (or just as few) as he could support. A young boy, seeking his first wife, was expected to go and live for awhile in her father's village. The Aleuts preferred to marry patrilateral cross cousins—father's sister's daughter—which over time resulted in a systematic marriage pattern anthropologists call "sister exchange," and

Interior of a barabara *in Unalaska.*
(From engravings by John Webber, official artist for Capt. Cook's Third Journey, 1776-1780)

also in the development of an endogamous agnatic lineage, linked to a territory. Dispersed in many villages, these kinship groups controlled large territories through numerous ties of consanguinity and affinity.

War was a serious business, and long-distance raids were never undertaken without proper preparation. Usually, a well-known warrior, who had a solid reputation for wisdom, bravery and cunning, announced that he was ready to lead a war party. The war leadership was dual: a lieutenant was appointed whose job it was to take over should the leader be killed in battle. The object of any raid was loot and captives, unless it was a blood feud and killing for revenge was expected.

The village chief had the ultimate say in war and administered justice, punishment being meted out for a well-defined series of crimes, ranging from telling tales to treason. Free and slave were punished unequally. Aleut society was stratified on the basis of rank, but not wealth. There were chiefs, notables or nobles, commoners, and slaves. A free Aleut could be

put to death for a variety of crimes, but only a traitor or a slave would be subject to bodily mutilation before death, and only the slave to corporal punishment and mutilation during life. Captives formed the main body of slave population, but orphans, too, were enslaved. Slaves could be sold and could be killed at the funeral rites for chiefs and important notables.

In each region or territorial polity encompassing several allied villages there was a chief, *primus enter pares,* whose sole function, as far as we know, was to declare war and establish peace.

Within each political unit, the internal peace was also fragile. Fierce, independent and proud, men quarrelled over personal honor, avenged insults, abducted—or reclaimed previously abducted—women. Women had considerable sexual freedom, and while men were supposed to be tolerant of the womenfolk's dalliances, in real life tempers flared.

Personal conflicts escalated, involving kin, friends, allies; someone got killed, revenge was called for, and feuds continued from one generation to the next.

Boys learned early to be warriors. Old age was respected, but many an elderly man chose not to return from one last hunt, although suicide was acceptable among Aleuts only in exceptional circumstances, for example, to avoid capture by victorious enemies. Children inherited their father's status, but personal prestige counted for much and was earned through skill in hunt and leadership in battle. Whale hunters were both respected and feared. A breed apart, they had secret charms and potions they used on their weapons, potions concocted out of the substance of corpses. These charms had secret powers that in the end destroyed their owners. A whale hunter had to prepare himself through secret rituals and, upon return, to purify himself before it was safe for others to associate with him. Even in death the whale hunters retained their special status: they were buried in caves with elaborate ceremonies, and the next generation sought greater and special, though fleeting power through contact with their remains. Lesser men were buried in the ground, the bodies wrapped in mats and sometimes inserted in double coffin-like structures.

The Aleuts believed in a Creator, who was male and whose domain was the sky. His was the life-giving power, manifest in the sun and in the waters of the earth: Aleut men greeted the sunrise; pregnant women bared their bodies to the rays of the sun; water was the purifying and healing agent; men ritually immersed themselves in streams and the ocean; the wounded were immersed in the waters of the sea, and unruly children held in the cold water until they learned self-discipline.

Each man could establish a link with the Creator through a personal guardian "presence"—manifest as an animal, bird, or feature of the terrain—and each man carried an object symbolizing this presence with him at all times.

There was evil in this world and it emanated from the Evil Spirit. Specific places were associated with this evil principle and these were dangerous to visit. Good people avoided them altogether. It was evil that caused death, illness and misfortune.

Sea otters occupied a special place in Aleut world view: The first sea otters were an incestuous human pair, a brother and sister who, some said, committed suicide or, said some others, the man was murdered by his sister when she discovered the identity of her secret lover. She threw his body and then herself down into the sea from a high cliff, leaving the grieving parents to bewail the fate of their children. It was in response to parental grief that the Creator transformed the pair into the sea otters. It was for this reason that a sea otter hunter must dress himself in festive clothing and adorn his person with items used by men as well as women when he set out on a sea otter hunt.

Any enterprise, be it war, hunt, or major fishing expedition, required ritual preparation and appeal to the protective presence and Creator. Reverential silence was observed at the commencement of any enterprise, which led an early Russian skipper, Cherepanov, to remark, "They pray before an enterprise, just like us."

In December, communal feasts to give thanks for the bounty of the sea and to ensure future success and well-being were held. Ceremonial foods were served to assembled guests, ritual dances held, and individuals performed masked dances, recounting their exploits in hunt and war.

The Aleuts knew that beyond the islands the world was inhabited by other people who spoke different languages and had different customs. Once in a while—so seldom that generations would pass without the event repeating itself—the sea cast ashore a vessel of strange make, from which the Aleuts obtained metal and worked it over by hammering it cold into any shape they desired. Sometimes there would be castaways, or a vessel would enter a bay, but these strangers were few and easily handled. It is to be assumed, then, that when in the year 1741 the villagers of Adak and Shumagins reported two different vessels under sail, manned by strangers of unfamiliar appearance, who offered in trade metal knives for a few Aleut trinkets, no one was unduly alarmed nor had a premonition that the world as they knew it and as their forefathers knew it was about to change.

The kadargargh *was an image of the Deity, a very powerful amulet often hung from a rafter in the* barabara. *Made of ivory, bone or wood,* kadargarghs *were prayed to by men before they left on hunting trips. Amulets were also worn to symbolize the ever-present guardianship of the Creator. This carved image was discovered at Unalaska.*
(Unalaska City School)

Aleut Mummies

By William S. Laughlin

Dr. William S. Laughlin, chairman of the Laboratory of Biological Anthropology and professor of Biobehavioral Sciences, University of Connecticut, first came to the Aleutian Islands in the 1930s as a student of Aleš Hrdlička, American Museum of Natural History, and has been working in the Chain longer than any other scientist. His latest book, Aleuts: Survivors of the Bering Land Bridge, is published by Holt, Rinehart and Winston. Excerpts from it and from an abstract he presented at the 1979 Moscow-Leningrad IREX conference, follow.

One of the outstanding indigenous achievements of the Aleuts was the preparation and preservation of mummies. Many burial caves and log tombs have been reported from the eastern and central Aleutian Islands. The largest number of mummy burials was found on Kagamil Island, on the west side of Samalga Pass, some 40 versts west of Umnak Island. Approximately 200 mummies have been recovered from two caves on Kagamil Island.

These mummies represent a pre-Russian population of high density. They span the entire age range from newborn infants to aged adults of both sexes. Their age composition yields a high life expectancy, exceeding that of the Eskimo population.

The preparation of mummies rests upon a complex cultural development involving: 1) a sophisticated knowledge of human anatomy and medical practices; 2) a thematic belief in a manipulatable power that resides in the human body; and 3) concern for the continuation of the power inherent in the dead, preserved by mummification, rather than a fear of the dead. The practice of mummification is a product of a sophisticated culture in which low fertility and low infant mortality were combined with considerable longevity. The older persons served as mentors and technical experts. The demographic profile of the Aleuts rests upon a rich and diverse marine resource base. The Aleut mummies are splendid evidence of the intellectual achievements and of the demographic foundations of the Aleuts prior to foreign alteration.

The mortuary packages stored in caves or rock shelters often included kayaks and hunting equipment of the men, armor, shields, knives, drums, masks, and with the women various dishes of wood, knives, basketry, mats, and other utensils. All in all these mummy caves are actually museums showing much of the material culture of the people, and of the people themselves, for their skeletons and much of their bodies are preserved, and at the same time they reflect much of the religious beliefs.

The manufacture of mummies indicates as much technical skill as the manufacture of boats. Many items of the material culture, especially those made of perishable materials such as basketry, wood, and skins or sinew, could not be recovered from excavations in the village mounds because they had decayed in the earth. Only the mummy caves and the collections made by early European visitors show the range of things made by the people and the skill and artistry with which they made them.

Mummification was not an isolated achievement or bizarre trait but an understandable practice firmly rooted in a pragmatically oriented culture. The fact that the Aleuts studied comparative anatomy, using the sea otter as the form most similar to man, and that they conducted autopsies upon people who died are closely related. Their knowledge of human anatomy is amply demonstrated in their enormous vocabulary for anatomical terms. The basic objective was the preservation and use of the spiritual power that resided in the human body. This power could be preserved in the body, or let out of the body, but in all cases it had to be regulated and handled with expert care.

As recently as 1862 the advice of mummies was sought. The Russian Orthodox Priest Lavrenty Salamatov of Atka encountered the continuing belief in the power of mummies. He noted, in his travel journal, that during paganism the Aleuts made mummies which they called "Dry Ones" or *askhanas* (Dead), then paid the same homage to them as their idols. To learn about the success of a hunting ex-

Aleut burial in Cold Cave, Kagamil Island, has a radiocarbon date of circa 1,000 years ago. Burial matting of wild rye grass (Elymus mollis) is remarkably well preserved.
(Ted Bank II)

pedition a man would prepare himself by fasting, avoiding his wife, by washing in a stream and dressing in his best clothes. Cleansed, inside and out, he approached the mummy cave and called out in a loud voice, "I am coming to you to find out about so and so. Show me what it is to be." He then carried a gift into the cave and placed it before the mummy. The gift might be black paint or ochre and the wing or feather of a hawk. He then withdrew for a while. During the hunter's absence the "Dry One" displayed various objects which were then interpreted as a sign for the future.

THE MUMMIFICATION PROCESS

The body of a deceased person was kept inside the house where he died, sometimes for several months. Often, but not always, the viscera were removed. Most often an incision was made in the lower abdomen and the intestines were drawn out through it. Other organs might also be removed at the same time. Dried grass was then stuffed into the abdominal cavity. The body was carefully and frequently wiped and of course kept quite dry. Without exception the body was flexed, with the knees drawn up to the chin, the heels against the rump and the arms drawn or folded so that the hands were frequently covering the face. A common way of handling the body was to place it in a large cradle of the same sort used for infants. This cradle was made with a wood frame, round or rectangular with rounded corners and a leather basin deeper on one side than the other. It could be carried on a mother's back or suspended from a beam when inside the house. For the deceased the cradle was suspended from a roof beam over the same place that the person ordinarily slept. Finally, the relatives would dress the contracted body in its best garments and encase it in various layers of intestine, seal, seal lion or sea otter skins and perhaps a layer of mats or of basketry. The entire bundle was finally lashed with braided sinew cord; in at least one case a net had been used for the final lashing. It might then be set in a wooden dish or in a cradle for removal to a cave and its final position. It is likely that the mummy was ready for removal by the thirty-first day after death but, owing to wishes of surviving relatives, was sometimes kept in the house much longer.

MUMMY FROM SHIP ROCK OFF UMNAK— This mummy was discovered by Aleš Hrdlička, anthropologist who worked in the Aleutians in the 1920s and 1930s. His collection of artifacts and papers is at the Smithsonian, Washington, D.C.
(Smithsonian Institution)

If a somewhat secluded cave or rock overhang was nearby, within a few miles at least, the mummy might be carried there. The essential prerequisite was to keep the mummy dry though close to the ocean. These *asxaanas* (departed ones) carried on a full round of activities at night including hunting, eating and dancing, and therefore needed to be near the ocean.

Inside the cave the mummies were placed on hewn planks supported by scaffolding. The posts had to be driven into cracks in the stone or wedged tightly between top and bottom because there was not enough earth to set posts in the ground. On Carlisle Island, we found portions of mummies that had fallen to the shore some 70 feet below when the cave itself was destroyed by wave action cutting into the cliff. Remnants of the ends of posts were still wedged in place in the inner wall.

A number of mummies, over 35, had been placed in a rock shelter on Ship Rock, a small island in the pass between Umnak and Unalaska islands. Apparently they were placed on the ground (rocks) and planks laid over them with the upper ends of the planks resting against the cliff wall. They had been painted red and had some whalebone also used for facing. Still another type of burial was in a rectangular log tomb, divided into compartments.

More commonly, if no cave or rock shelter was available, a little wood and sod hut was constructed for the purpose. Timbers, roughly the size of fenceposts, were stacked against each other forming a little conical tent and over them sod was placed. The grass on the sod continued to grow and eventually the little house blended into the color of the countryside but could be distinguished by its shape.

Most mummies have been found in the eastern Aleutians, some in the central area, but none have been reported for Attu or other of the Near Island group in the west. According to one Aleut, the Attu people "did not believe in mummies," and it is likely that this custom was diffusing from east to west and had not yet reached the remote islands before the arrival of the Russians interfered. □

III. THE RUSSIANS

Russian domination of Alaska, though relatively short-lived, deeply influenced the subsequent cultural development in the area.

The conquest, accomplished in an amazingly short time, was the work of individuals whose overt, known motivation was mainly economic: to open and exploit a new source of fur bearing animals for the China market. The government exercised only minimal control. While St. Petersburg was concerned in exploration and security on its Eastern frontier, the political situation in Europe was such that the North Pacific often had *no* priority.

The Russian claim over the Aleutian Islands and part of the Pacific Coast rested on the discovery of these shores by the 2nd Kamchatka Expedition, commanded by Vitus Bering in 1741. This expedition consisted of two ships, the *Sv. Petr*, Bering's flagship, under the effective command of Sven Waxell, and the *Sv. Pavel*, commanded by Alexei Chirikov. The crews of these vessels were recruited in the main locally, in Siberian settlements near Okhotsk and Kamchatka, a frontier region. Here, among the cossacks of the garrisons and the dwellers of towns, stories had circulated for many years about a fabulous land beyond the "Eastern Sea." If not riches, then position, status, and honors from the Crown could become the lot of those who successfully established and maintained a hold on the new territory.

Both ships, sailing separately, reached the Northwest Coast, and both ships hove to in the Aleutians: the *Sv. Petr* in the Shumagins, the *Sv. Pavel* also in the Shumagins and later in the Andreanof Islands, presumably off Adak. Several major islands were sighted.

Those on board the *Sv. Petr* first came in contact with a group of Aleut men in the Shumagins. Waxell, who was out in a longboat to replenish the ship's water supply, tried to communicate with them. The Aleuts would not approach the longboat until Waxell ordered three men, a Chukchi and two Russians, to wade ashore. When the exchange was completed, the Aleuts attempted to detain the Chukchi. Waxell fired his musket into the air twice, and in the ensuing confusion the Chukchi escaped.

The crew of the *Sv. Pavel* encountered, several days later in the Shumagins, and then, once again, off Adak, a number of warriors in *baidarkas*. Captain Chirikov noted that the Aleuts disdained cloth and various trinkets offered in trade and clearly indicated by gestures that they wanted to obtain metal knives.

The story of the return voyage of the *Sv. Petr*, the beaching of the ship on what is now Bering Island, the terrible winter spent there, and then the return to Kamchatka in the following year, need not be recounted here. It is believed that the cargo of furs brought home by the survivors of the *Sv. Petr* provided the impetus for the organization of the first commercial expeditions to hunt fur bearing animals in the Aleutians. It should be noted, however, that by this time the Kurile Islands were within the purview of the Siberians and were known as excellent hunting grounds. In any case, the organizer of the first fur gathering expedition to the Aleutians, Emel'ian Basov, Sergeant of a Kamchatka garrison, had interest in the fur trade as early as 1733 and was not backward in utilizing the expertise of Bering's former crew members.

Initially, the merchant-financiers of large commercial centers such as Moscow participated only minimally in financing the ventures. The capital and labor were raised by shareholders, often local residents who staked their entire substance on a single venture and enlisted as ordinary crew members or hunters.

The crews were paid by shares in the catch. Between 30% and 50% of a crew were Siberian natives: prior to 1769, predominantly Kamchadal, later Kamchadal, Koryak, Yakut and Tungus.

The vessels were constructed by the men who sailed them of local materials and, in part, by local techniques. As metal of any kind, and especially iron, was very scarce, the vessels were constructed without nails, the joints and planking lashed together by thongs. The ships were small, with few amenities.

The belief that these ships were not seaworthy is fallacious and reflects the opinions of Imperial Navy personnel who sailed in British-built ships. Nor is it true that the early Russian fur trade vessels did not outlast a single voyage: several vessels are known to have made five or six voyages, each lasting from two to six years. Two or three voyages per vessel was the rule.

The men who sailed these vessels came from all parts of Russia and from all walks of life. They were tough men. They faced incredible hardships and often death. They did not spare themselves and were not likely to spare others. Few of them ever became rich; this was the lot of absentee financiers and those few who, after a successful voyage, pulled up stakes and returned to their homes.

Most of the men who conquered the Aleutians for Russia spent their lifetimes sailing the waters of the Bering Sea or hunting in the islands. In the end, they lived like Aleuts, married Aleut women, had Aleut children, and acted like Aleuts: a generation later they would arouse only contempt from gentlemen of the Imperial Navy and foreign adventurers who came along on the Imperial ships. In the lifetime that they had spent in the islands, they had learned the currents, winds, the vagaries of the weather and they could sail the Aleutian waters better than many a Navy man: when Captain Krenitsyn and Lieutenant Levashev sailed from Kamchatka to the American coast in 1768, many experienced fur hunters were aboard their ships.

Many were violent men and some were brutal. Though the skippers and foremen gave lip service to the instructions which dictated peaceful and lawful fair dealings, many circumvented the instructions; a few justified brutal violations by claiming self-defense. Thus the commander of the *Sv. Evdokim* accounted in 1747 for the first murders of that era—the killing of 15 Attu warriors who refused to surrender a metal part of non-Russian manufacture for examination.

In general, the Russian-Aleut conflict in the early period was local and sporadic; much depended on personalities involved and on the situation. While some skippers and foremen permitted kidnappings and rapings, others maintained tight discipline and managed to establish excellent relationships with local Aleuts. In Attu, Rodion Durnev, known to have been a leader in at least three voyages from 1754 through 1763, became very popular. In the summer of 1757, when Durnev was ready to depart from Attu, Aleuts gathered from many islands to give him a proper send-off. On Umnak, Glotov is known to have established good relations with the Aleuts of southwestern villages: the names of Glotov's shipmates are still in use as family names by several important families of the Nikolski village; Glotov himself gave his name to the nephew of the local chief.

Andreian Tolstyk, who entered the Aleutian trade in the 1740s was a frequent visitor in the Near Islands, the Rat Islands and Andreanofs, and wherever he went the contact was harmonious and mutually profitable. In 1750 he brought to Attu from the Bering Island a breeding pair of blue foxes, which by 1756 multiplied to several hundred. Apparently it was he who introduced the fox trap in the Near Islands and he also introduced the use of nets for sea otter hunt, a practice he borrowed from the Kamchadal.

By 1762 Russian skippers reached the mainland and the island of Kodiak. It is possible that

the Alaska Peninsula had been reached as early as the 1740s by Andrey Vsevidov, of whose extended voyage to unknown islands no record remains. It is almost certain that it was reached about 1754, when Petr Bashmakov, building a small vessel, *Sv. Petr and Sv. Pavel* on Adak out of the wreckage of his ship, sailed east. When he returned to Kamchatka in 1755, he carried a rich cargo, including 140 large walrus tusks.

Official notification of the Russian government about the large territory claimed for it to the east of the Andreanofs was made by the foreman and government representatives aboard Stepan Glotov's ship the *Sv. Julian*, which dropped anchor on the southwest side of Umnak, in the small bay at Cape Sagak facing Samalga, September 1, 1759. Glotov reported the existence of Unalaska, Unimak, Krenitzin islands and the Alaska Peninsula, which at that time he assumed to be, on the

basis of Aleut informants' statements, a large island.

The departure time of Russian fur hunters from Kamchatka as well as their return sailings were determined by the winds prevailing at certain seasons. Usually they spent the first winter on one of the Komandorskies, provisioning their vessels with sea mammal meat and at the same time hunting the fur bearing animals there. In the next sailing season, they moved east: in the early years Attu was a popular spot, but very early they began to expand into the Rat Islands, and then east of Amchitka Pass, into the Andreanof and Fox islands.

Once in the islands the Russians dragged the vessels on shore for the winter and established camps or settlements, building for themselves Aleut-style semisubterranean dwellings, storage houses, and—one item of luxury—the steam bath house.

Between 1789-91, Captain Sarychev mapped the Aleutian Chain from Amchitka Pass eastward. These drawings are from his voyages. Top, from left—Spirkin (Biorka), Akutan, and the tip of Unalaska Island. Center—Beaver Inlet, Unalaska Island, near Spirkin and Akutan. Bottom—Sarychev's Slava Rossiyi (Glory of Russia) towing a longboat near Beaver Inlet. Two Aleuts in single-hatch baidarkas paddle nearby.
(From Sarychev)

The crew was divided into hunting parties. One such party or *artel'* stayed with the main camp; others traveled in sea mammal skin boats — the *baidaras* — propelled by oars, through an extensive territory, often to other islands. Sometimes these hunting parties inflicted themselves as unwanted guests on Aleut villagers.

Aleuts visited and traded for skins. Very soon Aleuts began to hunt for the trade. To ensure safety for their scattered hunting parties, the Russians demanded hostages, a practice long standard in Siberia. They attempted to obtain as hostages young boys, close kin of chiefs and important Aleut notables, but Aleuts often delivered slaves and captives. Occasionally a hostage was a relative of a chief, sent to acquire education. In later years several of these men were utilized by the government as mediators between the government and native peoples. These young men traveled sometimes to Siberia and learned on such trips that the fur hunters were accountable to government representatives, and embassies were sometimes sent to ask for protection against the ever-increasing violence and arbitrariness of fur hunters.

The violence increased in direct proportion to the escalation of the fur trade. The decades between 1760 and 1780 saw the largest number of expeditions being sent out to the expanding territory. It was during this period that big money entered the fur trade and fortunes were made by absentee financiers. The pressures on the skippers and foremen to show profit must have grown enormously.

At the same time, Aleut resistance in the more populated eastern islands hardened. War erupted in 1763, when at least seven vessels were in the eastern Aleutian waters. Four of these, wintering 1763 on Umnak, Unalaska and Unimak, were destroyed and their crews killed. Of over 200 men, Russians and Kamchadal, only seven survived.

It is believed that the conflict was triggered

by birching of a small Aleut hostage, who happened to be a son of an important Aleut chief. This seems unlikely in view of the fact that neither the survivors who reported to the Port Commander, nor Glotov and Solov'iev who rescued the survivors, mention such an occurrence. All, however, stress that the hostility was general and organized, and that it represented an alliance of Umnak, Unalaska and Krenitzin islands and possibly Unimak Aleuts. The Krenitzin Island Aleuts were considered ringleaders by Solov'iev, while Umnak Aleuts claimed the honor for themselves. It is probable that Russian crews, notably Bechevin in *The Sv. Gavriil,* who left a trail of violence from Atka to the Alaska Peninsula, soured the Aleut attitude. Since they were a warrior society and invaders customarily received short shrift, the Aleuts organized for war in the Aleut manner: by ruse and surprise. At any rate, in 1762 Bechevin, either alone or in alliance with another Russian skipper or skippers (we know little of the situation), destroyed four villages on Unimak, waging a campaign of destruction until he was met by superior Aleut force at the village of Pogromnoye. It is more than likely that the situation on Unimak affected the events of 1762-1763 on Unalaska and Umnak.

Stepan Glotov, who arrived at the scene in

A view of Illiuliuk settlement on the island of Unalaska *shows the settlement at the foot of a bare mountain partly covered with snow. There is a good-sized church and a number of small company houses, and some Aleut* yurtas, *as the Russians called them, semi-dugout dwellings. Between the church and the nearest house is a flagpole, and between the village and the shore are several gardens and a vessel, probably a* baidar, *or large, open skin boat, lying bottom up.*
(I.G. Voznesenskii, reprinted from *The ALASKA JOURNAL®*)

June of 1764, took in the survivors, among them Ivan Korovin, who immediately set out to find and punish the guilty. At Kashega Bay he found anchored the *Sv. Petr and Sv. Pavel* commanded by Ivan Solov'iev, and here the decision was taken to establish the upper hand on Unalaska. Solov'iev proceeded systematically to gather information on Aleut village strength and then attacked village by village from Umnak to Akutan Pass.

Aleuts attempted to meet Solov'iev's detachments with arms, but he was vigilant and utilized to the utmost the available firearms. In several encounters, with minimal casualties to his own force, he reported about 200 warriors killed, a tremendous loss in able-bodied men. Solov'iev then proceeded to destroy any *baidarkas* found on premises, and to break throwing boards, darts, spears and bows and arrows. In short, he destroyed not people so much as their means of survival. It is by these means, and not by genocide, which is largely mythological,[1] that he broke Aleut resistance in Unalaska and entered Aleut folklore under the nickname *Solovey*.

This man, who in 1790 would be remembered by Aleut chiefs of Unalaska as the Destroyer, understood and respected the Aleuts. He apparently spoke Aleut—his rendering of place names can be matched with Aleut place names in use today—and he left us the best and earliest accounts of the way of life in the eastern Aleutians.[2]

He is credited with establishing the village of Iliuliuk on Unalaska as a permanent Russian settlement either at the end of the conflict 1765-1766, or on his next voyage in 1771-1776. The Russians called this village Dobroye Soglasiye—The Harbor of Good Accord.[3]

The atrocities attributed to Solov'iev in later literature were not committed in the year of Unalaska conquest. The Russian government, sensitive to such occurrences, would hardly have assigned him to serve as a pilot under Lieutenant Levashev in 1769, had this been the case. In the 1770s, on his next private voyage, his subordinates are known to have committed outrages in the Krenitzin Islands, and the government instituted a judicial proceeding against the skipper. He was recalled, and died destitute. The final disposition of the case will remain unknown until the Soviet researchers publish the archival material pertaining to this period.

The dispatch of the Levashev/Krenitsyn Expedition is a convenient bench mark for the next period in Aleutian history: consolidation of conquest and intensification of government involvement.

When Catherine the Great ascended the throne in 1762 she inherited a complex and difficult situation. However, the beginning of her reign was a period of peace and it is in this period that she established the governmental policy regarding Russia's American possessions. It is at this time that the "Secret Government Expedition," under Captain Krenitsyn and Lieutenant Levashev, was dispatched to the Aleutians.

This expedition formed the Kamchatka squadron of a much larger project: the search for a direct route to America via the polar region. The project was developed by the famous scholar Mikhail Lomonosov, who argued that in summer the Polar Sea above 80° N latitude should become ice free and thus could provide a fast, safe and economical route, permitting efficient, effective government control of the new territories.

Capt. V. Ya Chichagov, sailing from Archangel past Spitzbergen to the American shores (with Greenland as alternate destination) was ordered by the Admiralty to rendezvous in the Aleutians with Krenitsyn/Levashev, sailing from Kamchatka. The government was convinced of the plan's eventual success to the point of issuing detailed instructions to the commanders for mutual support and exchange of information, and of members of the crews, to familiarize the greatest possible number of seamen with both routes to America.

Denis Chicherin, then Governor of Siberia, by personal order of the Empress, gave the expedition his full support, assigning a number of experienced Aleutian seafarers, among them Stepan Glotov, Ivan Solov'iev, Ivan Ponomarev, Mikhail Nevodchikov and Alexei Druzhinin. He supplemented the admiralty instructions by ordering Krenitsyn and Levashev, while waiting for Chichagov, to explore, map and describe the Aleutian Islands, Kodiak and the American mainland shores. The Aleutian veterans were to serve as pilots and guides.

The squadron sailed from Kamchatka in summer 1768, and the two ships made Unalaska Bay on 20 and 22 August. Here their first encounter with Aleuts was friendly and they received news that a Russian vessel was operating at Umnak. This was *The Sv. Pavel*, commanded by Afanssiy Ocheredin, who arrived at Nikolski Bay in summer 1766, almost immediately after Glotov's and Solov'iev's departure.

Both navy vessels proceeded east and Krenitsyn chose to make camp in Issanotski Strait. Levashev returned to Unalaska and camped for the winter in the Inner Bay which today is called in his honor Captain's Bay. Here he received Aleut hostages from Afanssiy Ocheredin. Ocheredin reported that he had lost 15 men in the Krenitzin Islands, killed by hostile natives.

In the meantime, on August 30, 1768, the *Sv. Andrean and Natalia,* commanded by Luka Vtorushin, made port at Umnak, then proceeded to deploy hunting parties, in the main, in the Krenitzin Islands. Both skippers delivered to Levashev the *yasak* (tax in furs) they claimed they had collected from the natives. Aleut chiefs from the Krenitzins brought additional hostages to Levashev, apparently as security and a token of good will. The standard practice of taking hostages had been stopped by Catherine by decree, but unfortunately Levashev was not aware of it and this insidious practice continued for almost two decades, eventually deteriorating into impressment of Aleuts into the labor force.

Levashev, who did not like Aleuts personally but strictly enforced government policy of fair and equitable treatment of them, apparently stabilized, at least for a time, the situation in the Umnak-Unalaska-Krenitzins area.

While Levashev's stay at Unalaska was uneventful, the situation was far different at Unimak where Krenitsyn wintered. Aleuts in the area were hostile and well organized. In the end Krenitsyn hesitated to send out far-ranging exploring parties and would not permit dispersal of his men even in search of fresh provisions. Scurvy was rampant. During the winter 39 men died (some authorities claim 69 fatalities), among them Glotov and Druzhinin. Krenitsyn grew increasingly nervous as his crew diminished, so that on one occasion when a *baidarka* flotilla was passing through Issanotski Strait at night, he ordered cannon fired, luckily without hitting anyone.

By the end of May 1769, Krenitsyn refloated his ship, was joined by Levashev and they sailed for Kamchatka without mishap. However, Krenitsyn drowned on July 4 and Levashev proceeded alone to St. Petersburg to report to Catherine the Great in detail. His account of violations by fur hunters then present in the islands regarding interaction with the natives probably led the empress to re-emphasize in a new decree that the Aleuts were to be treated with kindness and fairness in all matters of trade, and collection of the *yasak* was to be abolished.

Very soon after Levashev's departure from Unalaska, the *Sv. Ioann Ustiuzhskiy* under Dmitriy Shoshin arrived in the Fox Islands, joining Ocheredin and Vtorushin in renewing their assault on the Krenitzin Islanders. Ocheredin, by force of arms, had established full control over Four Mountains Islands prior to Levashev's arrival.

No other ships arrived the next year, as Kamchatka ports were closed to all shipping in order to prevent the spread of smallpox, but in 1771 Ivan Solov'iev once again came to the Islands, arriving at Akun in August.

From here he proceeded to Sanak, which was allied with the Unimak and Peninsula Aleuts. Overt conflict erupted when the interpreter from Akutan, alone out on an errand in the Aleut village, was tortured and murdered in December. Solov'iev maintained himself by show of force and constant vigilance, but, if his report is to be believed, there were few casualties on either side.

The Sanak people blamed attacks on Solov'iev's hunting parties on Alaska Peninsula Aleuts who, according to Solov'iev, threatened total annihilation of all Russians and Aleuts who allied themselves with the Russians. Nevertheless, Solov'iev sent a large exploring party to the Peninsula in the spring 1772 which safely returned to Sanak.

In July Solov'iev returned to Unalaska, establishing himself in Unalaska Bay and dispatching parties to hunt in the Krenitzins. It was, according to Veniaminov, Solov'iev's lieutenant, Nastrubin, who at this time, "to teach a lesson," wantonly killed with no provocation a number of Aleuts, including women and children.

In Russia, Catherine was facing a war with Turkey (1768-1774) and the growing hostility of Austria. In 1773 the massive Pugachev Revolt erupted and was suppressed only with great difficulty. Elsewhere in Europe, the imminent separation of the American colonies from England raised Russian hopes of weakening her rival, but also increased possibilities of direct confrontation with England over the American Pacific shore.

By 1774 it was clear that England was actively seeking an alternate route to America, with the specific aim of establishing a firm hold on the North Pacific shores. That year, Captain C.J. Phipps sailed past Spitzbergen, like Chichagov, to seek the polar route, and, like Chichagov, was turned back by pack ice at 80° 48' N latitude. At the same time, news spread that the English government was readying a new expedition under the famous navigator James Cook, specifically charged with finding the passage from the Pacific north of Kamchatka to the Atlantic.

That year Chancellor von Staehlin, Secretary to the Imperial Academy of Sciences, published a work titled *An Account of the New Northern Archipelago, lately discovered by the Russians in the Seas of Kamchatka and Anadir,* which, it was claimed, was based on firsthand reports of Russian skippers with a map ascribed to Lieutenant Syndt, who had explored the Bering Sea in 1764.[4] Cook took the publication with him as the newest available information about unknown seas. The map proved to be grossly inaccurate and helped to create the myth of ignorance and total illiteracy of Russian navigators and merchants in the Aleutian trade, prompting a member of Catherine's government to publish anonymously a correct account.

Cook apparently suspected that the publication was a plant, intended to make difficulties for the expedition. However, he successfully reached the Northwest Coast and proceeded toward the Aleutians, encountering signs of Russian penetration but refusing to acknowledge Russian presence.

Cook's ships, the *Resolution* and the *Discovery* touched briefly at Unalaska Island in July 1778, and then proceeded north to explore the Bering Sea shore of Alaska. They returned October 3, 1778 to the same harbor, which today is called English Bay (Samagnudax) and spent there a total of 23 days. Here the English were visited by Gerasim Izmaylov, who gave Cook an accurate map, and by Yakov Sapozhnikov, a simple straightforward man who did not drink or engage in debauch, whom the navigator liked enormously. Cook also appreciated Russian cooking, remarking that they could make even whale meat palatable.

Cook himself went ashore but rarely, and then only in the vicinity of the ship to hunt. Several of his officers, however, visited a nearby Aleut village where they were entertained by ladies, and the expedition's artist, John Webber, sketched the Aleut dwelling (please see page 88) and the two now-famous portraits of a man and a woman (right).

Several enterprising officers visited the Russian settlement at Iliuliuk, going there via Beaver Inlet trail across the mountains, visiting en route an Aleut settlement at the mouth of Beaver Inlet. Ledyard, an American in English service, volunteering to investigate the Russian settlement for Cook, traveled there below deck in an Aleut *baidarka.* He was subjected to the traumatic experience of a sweat bath before the Russians would permit him into their house.

The English learned that the Russian hunting crew consisted of Russians, Kamchadals, and Aleuts, whom, so the English believed, the Russians enslaved and who were, in fact, hostages. The English also observed that many of the young Aleuts learned Russian, that the Russians and Aleuts nightly prayed together and shared the same large barracks, built in Aleut style, with a door added.

Failing to see bows and arrows, they surmised that the Russians disarmed the Aleuts. Yet, Cook's men obtained in trade a significant number of throwing darts, a weapon whose advantage over the bow and arrow in the Aleutian context the great navigator apparently underestimated.

The Russians exaggerated the numbers of settlements and of Russians present in the islands. Most of the information was conveyed by gesture; the Russians did not speak English, the English did not speak Russian. No one knew German, and none could understand Cook's French.

Cook's visit had enormous repercussions for it laid the basis for English claims on the North-west Coast, arousing the Spanish government which extended its claim along the California coast to Nootka Sound. Expedition reports of the fur wealth to be obtained on the American Pacific coast stimulated almost immediate entry of British and not long thereafter American merchantmen into China fur trade, and encouraged British and American expansion of the sealing industry into the North Pacific.

The reaction in Russia to this incursion in what the government considered Russian territory was immediate. Support for the private merchants was intensified and before long massive, direct government action was planned.

Alarmed by foreign intervention, Russian

Two Aleut Portraits.
(John Webber, official artist for Capt. Cook's Third Journey, 1776-1780)

97

officials mounted an expedition to circumnavigate the globe, remove any symbols of territorial possession erected along American coasts by foreigners and to establish defense. The commander, Captain Grigoriy Mulovskiy, had full governmental powers, including discretion to use the force of arms to prevent settlement by foreign nations in Russian territories.

Mulovskiy's expedition never sailed, however, for in 1787 war with Sweden erupted with renewed fury and his frigates were ordered into service against the Swedish navy. At the battle of Eland, in 1789, Mulovskiy was killed. It was left to the small two-vessel Kamchatka squadron under Captain Billings, formerly with Cook, to reassert government prerogatives in the Aleutians. Exploration, security of borders and territorial waters, establishment of law and order, were the tasks of Billings' and Sarychev's expedition (1785-1793). They were specifically charged to check the activities of Brig *Mercury*, an English vessel reportedly a privateer for Sweden, and the presence of Japanese vessels. In 1780 a Japanese vessel was wrecked off Rat Island, and the escaping rats gave the island its new name.

In the meantime, Grigoriy Shelekhov was laying the foundation for effective monopoly of the Aleutian fur trade. A dreamer, builder of an empire, totally ruthless in dealings with his family, friends, business partners—not to speak of the natives—Shelekhov planned no less than the settlement of Russian America for generations to come. He cheated and ruined his partners; married off his daughters to influential men in the capital to gain spokesmen for his plans. He pirated crews, managers and navigators from his competitors and former supporters.

By 1783, with his wife's capital and support, he had built and equipped three vessels: *Sv. Mikhail*, commanded by Olesov; *Sv. Semeon and Sv. Anna,* commanded by Dimitri Bocharov; and *The Three Hierarchs, St. Basil the Great, St. Gregory the Theologian and St. John Chrysostom;*[5] the latter he personally sailed with his wife.

By 1787 he had established a firm base at Kodiak, utilizing such brutality that a complaint was formally filed against him by paramedic Britiukov. Undaunted, he returned to Okhotsk, lobbying for a monopoly, equipping additional vessels and recruiting settlers to expand operations eastward of the Aleutians.

Gradually he squeezed out less well financed traders, often forcing pitched battles between independents and his own men. Like a spider at the center of his web, Shelekhov's Alaskan manager, Alexander Baranov, moved to spread the dominance of the company from one region to the next.

But these events were yet to come. In the meantime, in the years 1789-1791, the vessels *Slava Rossiyi* (Glory of Russia) and *Chernyi Orel* (Black Eagle), commanded by Captain Sarychev and Lieutenant Hall respectively, under the overall command of Commodore Billings, sailed the Aleutian waters twice, mapping the Chain from Amchitka Pass eastward. Sublieutenant Khudiakov, a surveyor, was dispatched in a *baidara* to map the Bering Sea shore of Unimak and the Peninsula. Hall and the expedition's physician Roebeck recorded the first known vocabulary of Aleut language in two dialects.

Sarychev himself mapped Unalaska, conducted a population census, made a record of Aleut settlements and place names, learned to maneuver the *baidarka*, attended Aleut ritual feasts and shamanistic seances, and passed his spare time playing chess with the Aleuts, who consistently won: their rules differed significantly from the Russian chess game.

In 1791, Sarychev, Billings and Hall, while at Unalaska, conducted an investigation of charges of misconduct by Russian skippers and took testimony from local Aleut chiefs who lodged stringent complaints against Polutov, Ocheredin, Lukanin, and others, all now in Shelekhov's service, for their forcible and involuntary abduction of Aleuts of both sexes. For the first time the complaint was voiced that Aleuts were robbed of their food stores and other provisions, such as sealskins *(lavtaks),* and that payments were withheld for the furs they delivered to the company. They compared the depredations visited upon them by these men to Solov'iev's vengeance a generation before. At the same time, they exonerated skipper Cherepanov, whom they judged as fair, and had praise for the skippers of the rival Panov company, for whom they liked to work and hunt. In short, at this time the Aleuts were still able to maneuver, playing off one company against the other, but this freedom of action was coming to a close.

Shelekhov's dominance in the area was constantly growing. Baranov arrived in the fall of 1790, putting in at Unalaska in Kashega Bay on September 28 en route to Kodiak. Here, during a storm, the ship was wrecked and Baranov forced to winter. He utilized the time by taking stock of the island resources. By 1792, he took over at Kodiak from the relatively easygoing Evstrat Delarov, but his authority at this time did not extend to the Chain, though the Shumagins and the Peninsula came within his orbit by 1793.

But neither Shelekhov, nor after his death in 1795, his heirs, were about to let the Aleutians slip through their fingers. In 1796, one of the shareholders in Shelekhov's company, Emelian Larionov, was dispatched to establish a permanent settlement on Unalaska. Larionov had in the eastern Aleutians the same authority that Baranov wielded at Kodiak and later at Sitka. Larionov brought the Pribilofs under the aegis of his office and added these islands to Shelekhov's company "territory," by the beginning of the 1800s. Prior to that time, the Pribilofs were exploited, on behalf of Shelekhov's company, out of

Sarychev's captions on this photo place the scene at Captain's Harbor,
Unalaska Island, with these notations: #1 observatory tent; #2 where lies
the body of Okhotsk navigator; #3 Aleut yurtas (dwellings);
#4 Promyshlennyie kazarmy *(Promyshlenniki [Russian trader-hunters]*
barracks). Sarychev's ship, Slava Rossiyi (Glory of Russia), *is at lower left.*
(From Sarychev)

Atka. There, Ivan Ladygin, skipper of the vessel *Dobroye Predpriyatiye Sv. Aleksandry,* with 41 Russians, arrived in 1795, and sailed from there to the Pribilofs, establishing a base on Saint George in 1798.

In the meantime, in 1796 the first Orthodox missionary arrived at Unalaska, but his stay there was short-lived. Hieromonk Makariy was a member of the Kodiak Mission, which came to Alaska in 1794. Assigned by his superior, Archimandrite Ioasaf, to the Chain,

he traveled in *baidarka* from Kodiak via Unga, the Peninsula and Unimak. At Unalaska, he soon went into action against Shelekhov's men, especially the then resident foreman Kochutin, who was in charge prior to Larionov's arrival. Makariy assembled a delegation of prominent Aleuts, six in all, and, aided by one of the last independents, Merchant Kiselev, sailed for Russia. The delegation made their way to St. Petersburg and lodged their complaints before the highest

civil and ecclesiastical authorities. However, Catherine the Great was dead. Her son Paul was lending his ear to the proponents of the monopoly. Napoleon was on the march through Europe. If Shelekhov's company was willing to hold the American territory for the crown, Paul would support it and grant it privileges. Under the circumstances, the Aleut complaint was noted, but no effective relief from the oppression given. Makariy was sent back to Alaska, and drowned, together with other members of the Mission, on the return voyage aboard the *Phoenix* off Unimak. In 1799, Emperor Paul granted the monopoly to Shelekhov's company.

The Russian government realized the importance of the change and, in one last gesture in the spirit of Catherine, dispatched an official letter to Sergey Pan'kov, Chief of Atka, charging him to explain the new order to the Aleuts and promising good treatment.

But under the monopoly, and Baranov's autocratic mode of management, the last vestiges of Aleut freedom in the eastern Aleutians were rapidly diminishing: impressment into the labor force, forced resettlement to Kodiak, Sitka, the Mainland, and, above all, to the Pribilofs, reached its peak ca. 1806-1810. Larionov, at Unalaska, was focusing on the fur seal as the main crop animal and intensified the exploitation of the Seal Islands. By 1802, he shipped such a large quantity of furs that the price at Kiakhta fell, and the company directors ordered Baranov to take over the Unalaska operation. Baranov assumed the overall jurisdiction over Unalaska District, including the Pribilofs, by 1804. He ordered that all natives and Russian settlers sign a written statement that they would deliver furs only to the company at prices set by the company. As labor was needed at Kodiak, as the Koniag population diminished, Larionov began to implement Baranov's order to ship men: Russians and Aleuts were transferred from Unalaska and the Pribilofs to Kodiak; the first party, under foreman Sukhanov, of men with families, comprising 14 persons, in 1804; the next, comprising 60 hunters, in 1807. At various other times additional small parties were shipped to Kodiak, for a total of about 150 persons equipped with 90 *baidarkas,* and an additional 200 persons were dispatched to the Pribilofs.

In 1806 Unalaska was visited by Rezanov, Shelekhov's son-in-law and an intimate of Emperor Paul, and now head of the Russian American Company. He was accompanied by the young former Navy officers, Lieutenants Khvostov and Davydov, and his German confidant, Dr. Langsdorff. Rezanov was liberal with distribution of medals, praised Larionov's management, and ordered establishment of an institution for destitute girls. Also, he had a

Russian whipped publicly. On his orders a new census was conducted, according to which in 1806 there were 1,898 persons, of all stations, Russians and Aleut, resident in Unalaska District.

Larionov died soon thereafter, and was replaced by Fedor Burenin. During his tenure, in the winter of 1806-1807, Unalaska was stricken by an epidemic which manifested itself in chest congestion. Burenin reported that the disease killed about 350 people.

By 1812, Burenin's place was taken by Ivan Kriukov, formerly a crew chief in the Shumagins. Kriukov eventually settled at Nikolski, married an Aleut woman and founded the influential Kriukov family. He built in 1806 the first Orthodox chapel in the eastern Aleutians at Nikolski, and in 1808 the chapel at Unalaska was built. It was Kriukov, who on a visit to Irkutsk, persuaded the young priest Ioann Popov Veniaminov to come to the Aleutians.

In the western Aleutians, under the jurisdiction of the Okhotsk Office of the Russian American Company, all was quiet. Communication with the Siberian mainland or with Sitka became nonexistent: ships called at Atka, Attu or the Komandorskies at intervals as great as five years. Very few Russians remained in the Islands. In 1808, the ship *Sv. Petr i Sv. Pavel,* under skipper Pyshenkov, called at Atka. Excited by the news of the vessel's arrival, people assembled from far and wide in Korovin Bay, including Rat Islanders who were brought to Atka by Lazarev from Amchitka about 1790-1800 in order to "rest" Amchitka sea otter grounds. The ship brought to Atka the epidemic which caused the large death toll at Unalaska the previous year. So many died that it was impossible to bury the dead properly.

Ivan Ladygin, nominally in charge of what remained of the Company's "Atka Detachment," aging and sick, left with Pyshenkov. Ordinary hunters assumed the management—

whatever was left of it—of Company affairs. By 1811, there were seven Russians in residence in Atka and vicinity and two on Attu. The Aleut population reverted to almost purely subsistence hunting. Trade was minimal, supply of Russian goods practically nonexistent. The Russians lived like Aleuts, some of them became polygynous and fought over women. During these years, twice an Aleut chief, and once the chief's representative, made his way to Okhotsk and there complained that some Russians were too free with Aleut women. Many of these unions became lifelong marriages. The people were all baptized by laymen and considered themselves Christians, but the shamans continued to practice their arts and old beliefs were still vital.

Communal feasts to give thanks for the bounty of the sea and to ensure future success and well-being were celebrated. Ceremonial foods were served to assembled guests, ritual dances were held, and individuals performed masked dances, recounting their exploits in hunting and war. This drawing of an Atka Aleut ritual dance, identified as "The Faith of the Americans: Celebration in their own Manner" (bottom line), is a detail from a map, dated ca. late 1750s-early 1760s. The Russian text identifies the men at the upper left as "Americans," the figures on the right as "their wives." Inscriptions associated with the structure in the center are "American yurta [house] of earth [earthen]," with the notation "entry by ladder" in the center. The two naked men in front are each holding a buben—a tambourine, or drum. The naked hatted man, dancing in the center, holds a puzyr, customarily translated as bladder, but actually meaning balloon or bubble. It was made of various animal stomachs. The lady standing to the right of the house is holding a nerpichiy puzyr, a seal bladder.
(Detail from an early 1770's map, courtesy of Svetlana G. Fedorova and Dr. Richard A. Pierce, Limestone Press, Kingston, Ontario.)

амбракащовъ брта звлбнам

ро лесицъ

ерпа плтзбровъ

пу16рб

бубенъ

бубенъ

амеряпсанцовъ фера птляспа поахъ манеру веселятпся

A number of Atkans, led by a Russian, Solomein, in three *baidaras*, settled on Attu, building a village at Chichagof Harbor, separate from the native Attuans. Solomein opened Buldir Island as a new hunting ground for his people.

The Russian leadership at Atka was assumed about 1814 by Ivan Vasil'yevich Mershenin, who negotiated a contract with Okhotsk Office on a shareholding basis. One of the shareholders was the Atkan chief. Many Aleut villages continued their independent existence under the Aleut leadership, most populous on Adak, and, above all, on Amlia. Rat Islanders returned to Amchitka in 1812 where they settled in a place called Novaya

Finlandia, in honor of the vessel which carried them home. About this time, ca. 1814-1816, a group of Aleuts from Attu, most of them settlers from Atka, joined the Russian colony in the Komandorskies established in 1805.

At this time the Rat and the Andreanof islands served as a refuge to Aleuts fleeing from the increased economic oppression in the eastern Aleutians. The diminishing profits offered by the Atka District caused concern in the Company's main office and by 1823 a reorganization was ordered: the western Aleutians were put under the jurisdiction of the Governor General of the Russian America.

By 1826, under Governor Petr Chistiakov, Atka District was organized on the model im-

plemented earlier in the eastern Aleutians. The first manager of the new breed, Ivan Sizykh, arrived and the old village of sod houses, sod house chapel, and the two log cabins built in 1811 by Vasil'yev and his crew when they wintered there were destroyed. Incidentally, Vasil'yev constructed the first oven of bricks made of local clay and baked the first loaf of bread. He also rebuilt and repaired the forge, built under Mershenin, which was operated by means of coal mined locally. Now a settlement was constructed according to Chistiakov's plan on a spit at the entry to the eastern arm of Korovin Bay.

By this time the government and the Company had renegotiated the monopoly charter,

This wood carving of a dove watches over the altar gate in the chapel of Saint Innocent of Irkutsk in the church at Unalaska. It was carved by an unknown Aleut at an unknown date, probably about 1826-1828. It was allegedly part of the altar screen (iconostasis) of Veniaminov's original church. Veniaminov tells us that all interior woodwork and specifically the artistic decorative carving was done by Aleuts. The dove is reminiscent of the seabirds in ivory that Aleuts attached to sea otter hunting and ceremonial hunting hats.
(Lydia Black)

This photograph shows a rubbing made of the plaque now at the Unalaska Historical Society commemorating the consecration of the chapel of the Dormition of Our Lady on the island Akun, 1848. The plaque, of lead, incised probably by knife blade, states that the chapel was built by Chief Ivan Pan'kov with his comrades and was consecrated by Priest Grigoriy Golovin in the presence of the entire community and visiting dignitaries, including the chief of the Unalaska office of the Russian American Company.
(Lydia Black)

and under the new governance the Company was obliged to establish schools, hospitals and support the Church. Both at Unalaska and Atka, hospitals were constructed with an apprentice physician in charge. Smallpox vaccination, first introduced in Russian America in 1822, became mandatory, with the clergy assisting in vaccinating the population, in the wake of the smallpox epidemic of 1838. This epidemic hit Unalaska hard, especially outlying villages where the old traditionalist chiefs and the shamans argued against vaccination. This epidemic did not spread to the western Aleutians, however.

In 1825 the first resident Orthodox priest arrived in the eastern Aleutians: the famous Father Ioann Veniaminov. In 1828, Yakov Netsvetov, a son of an Old Voyager,[6] who served in the Aleutians since the 1790s and was at one time crew chief on Saint George, and of his Atka Aleut wife, was en route to his home island. Schools, previously established by the local Company offices under the governmental mandate, were placed under the jurisdiction of these exceptional men. Soon the instruction in the schools was conducted in Aleut as well as in Russian and schools were established in outlying villages. On Amlia, the chief's son, Fedor Dediukhin, taught in the local school. By the end of the 1820s life in the Aleutians stabilized: the Aleuts in Company employ received salaries; independent villages were paid for their furs in accordance with an established schedule of payments; social advancement was possible; Aleuts and Creoles—that is persons who could claim at least one Russian ancestor—occupied managerial, decision-making positions. Ustyugov of Unalaska and Anton Netsvetov of Atka commanded Company ships and explored the Bering Sea and Alaska; Osip Netsvetov, at the shipyard in Sitka, built the Company's ships. Soon the clergy numbered several Aleuts in its ranks, priests who served in their own communities, like Lavrentiy Salamatov on Atka, or became missionaries on the mainland. On the Pribilofs, the man in charge of Saint Paul and Saint George was an Unalaskan, Kasian Shayashnikov, whose two sons, Innokentiy and Paul, later served Unalaska and Saint Paul as priests. In the 1840s Kasian Shayashnikov and his Aleuts repelled an attempt by a group of American whalers to occupy Saint Paul by force: they stood them off with firearms. Grigoriy Terent'yev, a Creole, married to Elena Netsvetov and for long in charge as Clerk and Supercargo in the Sitka Office, eventually assumed the management of the Atka District (in 1833). Several Aleuts became paramedics or assistant physicians. An Aleut, Vassiliy Kriukov, painted the icons for the

The manuscript of
the Gospel of
Saint Matthew, in
richly decorated
silver binding, is
one of the treasures
of the Aleut people.
The Gospel was
translated into
Fox Aleut by
Saint Innocent
of the Aleutians
(Father Veniaminov)
and *Ivan Pan'kov,*
Chief of Tigalda.
(Lydia Black)

newly constructed Church of the Holy Ascension of Christ in Unalaska. Aleut carvers decorated the Unalaska Church with beautiful carvings, some of which survive to this day. At Atka, the Church of St. Nicholas, begun in 1828, was completed in 1830.

Veniaminov, with the active assistance of Tigal'da chief Ivan Pan'kov and Stepan Kriukov of Nikolski, devised an alphabet suitable to transcribe Aleut phonemes and began translating Church literature and creating new works of spiritual content in Eastern dialect. Netsvetov adapted the alphabet and Veniaminov's translations to the Atkan dialect. He was assisted in his work by Amlia chief Nikolay Dediukhin. These men studied the Aleut language, compiled dictionaries, and wrote ethnographic descriptions of Aleut culture.

There were disasters. In 1813, a snow avalanche on Atka overwhelmed a large communal dwelling; 18 persons were buried under the snow, of whom only five were dug out alive. In 1826, for a reason we do not now know, a famine struck Adak. Many able-bodied adults died of starvation and the survivors moved to Atka. Adak became abandoned. A village on Umnak was buried under rock and rubble when Tulik Volcano (Okmok) exploded in 1817, but the people, on the Pribilof Islands at that time, escaped. Pogromnaya village on Umnak ceased to exist when the majority of the population, traveling in a large *baidara* on a visit to another village, was lost at sea. In 1862, Amlia lost 13 able-bodied men in a single disaster at Ilak. The village was abandoned, survivors moving to Nazan Bay on Atka. Soon thereafter, after an earthquake, the people of the Korovin Bay settlement on Atka began to transfer their village to Nazan Bay also.

A new village was established on Wosnesenski, predominantly by Fox Island Creoles.

The people of Sanak were resettled on the Peninsula, establishing Belkofsky in 1823, to provide more effective conservation for the sea otter banks on Sanak.

The old ways persisted in tradition and folklore, in music and dance, in artifacts and skills, in hunting and conservation practices widely adopted by the Russian management. These blended with the new: bread, pancakes, pastry, salt and tea became necessities. Women used silk thread to embroider their baskets. Metal utensils and tools were in wide use, and the musket and the rifle became as familiar to men as the throwing board. Sails were added to the *baidarkas*. The use of Russian musical instruments became widespread. Men sang in church choirs. Slowly, an Aleut intellectual tradition, based in pride in their literacy, began to emerge. Church music with a distinct Aleut character developed.

Representatives of the Imperial Government defended the civil rights of the Aleut population before the highest councils of the land, urging better economic conditions, more medical services, broader education.

The population stabilized. In spite of introduction of new diseases like tuberculosis, there was now a small, steady population increase and Aleuts began to believe in the future.

But international politics was to deal them yet another blow. The United States was expanding her boundaries. English, Canadian and American whalers, pelagic sealers and sea otter hunters, claimed freedom of the seas. A three-mile limit was about to be established by the International Arbitration Tribunal.

In Saint Petersburg it was decided that the effort of maintaining control over the American territories, impossible to effectively defend, was, in the long run, unprofitable in terms of international diplomacy. Russia was too extended, too weak, to effectively prevent foreign encroachment. And so the decision was made to sell Russian America to the United States.

An effort was made to protect the rights of the population: by terms of the Treaty, all "civilized" inhabitants were to receive United States citizenship with full rights, duties and privileges. The Orthodox Church was to be assured full freedom, including freedom to maintain schools. The Russian flags were hauled down and the Stars and Stripes raised, and the Aleuts found themselves classified as Indians, the wards of the State. For another 100 years they lost the power to control their lives.

NOTES

1. As Dr. Christy G. Turner III demonstrated, the Russians lacked the weaponry to effect the mass murder attributed to them in popular literature. Examination of early primary sources reveals that the reported numbers of victims were increased by various authors, as time passed.
2. Solov'iev's accounts are the only ones giving information on religious rituals. Only one account, that pertaining to the 1764 voyage, has been published by Andreyev in 1948. The second account, available in the archives in the USSR, pertaining to his 1774 voyage to Sanak, Unimak and the Peninsula, is known only in a synopsis, published by Oglobin in 1892 and by Pallas, 1781-1783.
3. Designation of this congenial name may have originated for the same reason that motivated much of the writing of history of the 19th century: to paint the Russian-American Company in the most positive way and the independent hunters in the worst.
4. See Lydia T. Black, *The Question of Maps*, Proceedings of the Conference of the Sea in Alaska's Past, held in Anchorage, 1979. Staehlin's publication was a deliberate plant intended to mislead the English.
5. This vessel is known in popular literature as *The Three Saints*.
6. "Old Voyager" was the name, like "Pilgrims" or "Pioneers," applied in the 19th century to those who sailed in the days of independent companies, prior to the establishment of the monopoly and creation of the Russian American Company.

*. . . bring what preserved you against
slaughter and invasion . . .*

12
Early American Years

After repeated prompting by American whalers and traders, the United States Navy made a reconnaissance of the North Pacific Ocean with an expedition of five ships from 1852-1863 and, taking advantage of the fact that Russia was engaged in losing the Crimean War, quietly scouted her possessions in the Aleutians as well.

Lt. William Gibson, who directed the Aleutian effort, jubilantly wrote his commanding officer, Lt. John Rogers, in October of 1855:

"We have made reconnaissance of the Aleutian Islands with a degree of completeness which in that region of prevailing tempests and fog has exceeded my most sanguine hopes. We have determined the latitude and corrected on a chain of chronometric differences all the principal islands except one, Agattu not seen, and most of the smaller islets and rocks of that archipelago. The passages between the islands have been carefully examined and headlands measured, numerous points triangulated and shorelines traced and several harbours surveyed."

His surreptitious work was about the sum total of American knowledge of the Aleutians at the time of the purchase of Alaska from Russia in 1867 and, indeed, Gibson's charts would serve into World War II, for there was little government interest in the territory in the years that ensued.

"To this new domain flocked men of all conditions of life—speculators, politicians, office-hunters, tradesmen, even laborers. Nor were there wanting for loafers, harlots, gamblers and divers(e) other classes of free white Europeans not seen in these parts before; for of such is our superior civilization," noted historian Hubert Howe Bancroft, but government emphasis was on Southeastern, the capital seat at Sitka and at Fort Wrangell, to which the bulk of military troops were sent. The Aleutians were only briefly occupied, 1869-1870, and with disastrous results.

"The vandalism displayed by them in the destruction of old Russian property left behind was worthy of those old Vandals who were such famous destroyers as to have left us, for so many ages, their name as a synonym of all the acts of wanton destruction and pillage," observed Isabel Shepard, wife of the commander of the steamer *Rush* which followed in the wake of the troops.

After that Aleutian Islanders were somewhat relieved to make do with only an occasional visit from a revenue cutter and one customs agent whose lot must have been frustrating indeed. Bereft of regular mail service until 1891, it was often 13 to 22 months between paydays, and collection of duties on foreign imports was often less productive.

"There is probably no better opportunity for smuggling in any part of the world than amidst the tortuous channels of the Alexander Archipelago and among the Aleutian Islands," historian Bancroft observed. And appointment of a deputy marshal to the area in 1884, "to perform the duties of a constable under the laws of Oregon" did little to help.

In 1871-1872 W.H. Dall surveyed the Aleutians for the U.S. Hydrographic Office, justifying the number of Aleuts in his crew to the Treasury Department with the happy note that "the wages of such sailors would be lower than the usual standard," and that "if the crew were comprised of Aleuts, the fatigue and pri-

*A photographer on the Revenue Cutter
Albatross took this remarkable picture of
Attu residents in the early 1890s. Residents of
this village were progressive in dress and
thought. Their village had been headquarters
for regional Russian rule before sale to the
United States.*
(National Archives)

Attu Village.
(As seen by Henry Wood Elliott,
Our Arctic Province, 1886)

vations of the service would be much more cheerfully borne."

Results of their labors appeared in the first *Pacific Coast Pilot* in 1879 and Dall expanded it in a series of charts on subsequent expeditions, although the first lighthouse was not established until 1902.

Luckily Dall was a scientist with broad interests and, in addition to his duties for the Hydrographic Office, he avidly catalogued flora, fauna, native artifacts and even mummies for the Smithsonian Institution (then the

National Museum) and preserved much of what we know about the Aleut people of old.

"We were obliged to follow the general usage in applying the name Aleut to the tribes inhabiting the region west of the Kaniagmuts (Eskimos) although it is a word foreign to their language and of uncertain origin," he wrote in *Cave Relics of the Aleutian Islands.* "Their own name for themselves is Unangan."

"Aleut differs markedly from the Eskimo language in that it is much richer and they can count from one to one hundred thousand by a decimal system while the Kaniagmuts reach their limit of numbers at one or two hundred," Dall noted, adding, "they are not uncleanly compared with other tribes," and "their form

of Shamanism was in many respects peculiar and their rites more complicated and mysterious than those practiced by other tribes . . .

"It is a matter of constant regret that in their propagandism, the early missionaries took every means, secular as well as spiritual, of destroying all vestiges of native beliefs and the rites which were practiced in connection with them."

In 1870 Dall estimated there were 1,384 Aleuts plus 270 Creoles (mixed Aleut-Russian blood) with 405 more Aleuts and 95 Creoles doing duty in the Pribilofs for a total of 2,154.

Ten years later naturalist John Muir, cruising on the *Corwin,* set the count at 2,369, the highest population figure ever recorded by a contemporary observer, but he noted deaths had exceeded births in nearly every Aleut village and predicted "it is only a question of time when they will vanish from the earth."

According to a report from a revenue cutter commander of that era, "Tuberculosis is the main scourge. . . . The second great cause of death is scrofulous disease, taking the form of malignant ulcers . . . causes of subacute rheumatism . . . and pains and aches of a few days' duration are very frequent. . . . Pulmonary phthisis is not uncommon . . . there are diseases of the eye . . . malnutrition . . . substandard housing . . . alcohol abuse."

So bleak were the prospects for Aleut survival that Peter Trimble Rowe, first Episcopal Bishop of Alaska, testifying at a hearing before the U.S. Congressional Committee on Territories on the subject of financing education, said: "What is the use of appropriating $200,000 for the educating of the Indian

This charming picture of Unalaska Harbor in 1879 is not signed, but the style and date lead authorities to believe it may be the work of Henry Wood Elliott, customs agent who frequented the Chain during this period.
(Charles Bunnell Collection, University of Alaska Archives)

While other villages went modern, Attu retained traditional charm well after the turn of the century. Wooden walls are something new, but the grass roof testifies to the people's Aleut heritage.
(Charles Bunnell Collection,
University of Alaska Archives)

children of Alaska if it is impossible on account of their diseased condition and other things for them to avail themselves of it? And then again you are only spending money to educate a child that probably will die in two or three years."

Malnutrition was perhaps the key, for game was running out, not only fur-bearing animals which Aleuts hunted for a wage but also those on which they depended for food, clothing and transport.

"To hunt or fish, in fact to live, the Aleut is totally dependent on his skin canoe," Dall pointed out in 1874. "To make this canoe he must have hair seal or sea lion skins. From various causes the sea lions are not now to be found, as formerly, within reach of the large

settlements, except in the Pribilof Islands. This made no difference under Russian rule, as the sea lion skins were taken under the company's direction at the Pribilof Islands, and were given to the Aleuts gratis. Now, on the contrary, they are obliged to buy them and to buy them of the company who holds the lease on the Pribilof Islands, except in very rare cases. As the company's agents in the natural course of business will sell these materials only to those natives who are known to bring all their furs to the company's store for sale, it follows that the lease of fur seal islands carries with it a practical monopoly of all the fur trade of the Aleutian nation, that is to say, the sea otter as well as the seal trade."

Russians had instituted conservation practices but the American government, which was enjoying rental plus $2.62½ per skin from the Pribilof fur seal islands, allowed an enormous kill by its lessee, Alaska Commercial Company, and issuance of a regulation prohibiting anyone except Alaska Natives from taking fur bearing animals failed as a conservation measure.

After the United States' takeover, the sea otter kill more than doubled, and in the first 23 years the American fur catch topped Russia's total shipments for a period of 125 years, leading an observer (Samuel Applegate) to conclude: ". . . the only deduction to be drawn from such figures is that under the the the American regime the fur industry of Alaska has been conducted with criminal carelessness and wastefulness, which must end with its annihilation in the near future."

In 1870 Congress limited killing of seals to the Alaska Commercial Company in the Pribilofs, making it unlawful to kill females and seals under one year old, and tried to curb pelagic sealing (the taking of animals at sea where sex and age cannot be determined and chances of recovery are poor if animals are killed by gunfire rather than traditional harpoon).

There was only occasional enforcement, however, and Isabel Shepard, touring the area in 1889, reported "forty or more sealers in Sand Point (Pirate Cove) of whom a number were British . . . sealing as they pleased."

In 1880 there were 16 pelagic sealing boats, by 1892 some 122; and Alaska Commercial, frantic because skins taken by off-island competitors were driving their prices down on the London fur market, successfully lobbied Congress to enforce closure of the Bering Sea.

In 1892 the U.S. Navy was dispatched to assist the Revenue Service in policing the area; the eight warships embarked under command of Robley D. "Fighting Bob" Evans in his 1,200-ton cruiser *Yorktown*.

Many of the sealers were Canadians, backed by the Vancouver Sealing Association, and Evans decided, according to his memoirs, if he could confiscate their supply ship, "legally if I could, illegally if I must," he could break the organization once and for all.

The supply ship of the fleet, with about $600,000 worth of pelts, was ultimately confiscated for violating customs regulations and released on $60,000 bond, while the skins were returned to their owners because the international court upheld foreigners' rights to hunt outside the three mile limit in the Bering. Americans had no recourse in this court, however, and policing did put many independents out of business.

There persists from this era the tale of buried gold—more than a million dollars' worth—slated to pay off the ill-fated sealing fleet when Fighting Bob made his capture. According to the story, Gregory Dwargstof, a British Columbian Indian said to be the craftiest of the seal pirates, rescued this treasure from the fleet's supply ship and buried it on Adak, only to be shipwrecked thereafter and die as the result of exposure, leaving a treasure map.

Cans of gold coin are said to have been recovered by GIs on Adak, but no record of Dwargstof or his ship, the *Hitslop,* has been found.

Also legend are stories of Japanese seal poachers who warred with the cod fishing fleet and are reputed to have invaded remote Aleut villages, raping the women and terrorizing the general population.

Upper right
In 1892 the crew of the Revenue Cutter Albatross *found Atka with several modern buildings, but traditional* baidarkas *can be seen on racks above the beach, and some residents apparently still occupied sod houses.*
(National Archives)

Right
Industrious Aleuts at the village of Chernofski are shown in front of their sod, grass-thatched house with a large catch of salmon drying for winter use in 1890. This village was a viable settlement until about 1928 when an epidemic decimated the population. Survivors moved to Kashega and Unalaska.
(National Archives)

However, in 1911 the United States and Russia (the only two nations in the northern hemisphere with fur seal rookeries) negotiated a treaty with Japan and Canada (two nations without sealing grounds but in whose waters the animals swim), offering each 15% of the pelts taken ashore in exchange for abstention from pelagic sealing, and pirating finally came to a halt.

Action to protect the sea otter was also added to the 1911 treaty, and none too soon. Henry Swanson of Unalaska, who participated in the last sea otter hunt in 1910 as a boy of 14, recalls his stepfather, captain of a steamer which carried a 12-*baidarka* crew, cruised all summer from Sanak to Kodiak with only 14 otter pelts to show for his efforts.

"They were almost extinct," he recalls. "We got $2,000 each for them on the London market. The demand was there but not the otters."

In 1913, prompted by the Secretary of Agriculture and the Department of Commerce and Labor, President William H. Taft declared the Aleutian Islands Reservation as "a preserve and breeding ground for native birds, for the propagation of reindeer and fur bearing animals, and for the encouragement and development of the fisheries."

Coe and Chuck Whittern were reared at the Jesse Lee Home (though it was not in operation as a home at the time) from 1949 to 1957 when their parents were stationed in Unalaska as missionaries. Coe went Outside to get a teaching degree after the death of his father, but determined to return and buy the place he had loved during childhood. Returning to Unalaska to teach in 1969, he realized his dream. The old house is still in use, but will soon need restoration of its foundations.

The islands of Akun, Akutan, Sanak, Tigalda, Umnak, Unalaska, Sedanka, and most of Amaknak were later excluded from the Refuge, which extends from Attu on the west to Unimak and Amak Islands and Sealion Rocks on the east.

The only arrest later documented in USF&WS archives correspondence seems to be that of Unalaska resident Rodney Hearn, who, in 1931, pleaded guilty to "shooting a songbird," was fined $25 and forfeited his shotgun to the court.

Nor were the Aleuts given many options to hunting and fishing. Many, well educated in Russian schools and literate in both Russian and Aleut, found both languages outlawed under the American regime. Although legally allowed to operate after the purchase, many Russian schools were forced to close down or cut back for want of funding, and after the Russian Revolution even Orthodox priests were without backing.

The Woman's Home Missionary Society of the Methodist Episcopal Church in 1885 dispatched the Reverend and Mrs. John H. Carr to open the first American school and church in the Aleutians, at Unga, where, happily, gold had just been discovered. Mrs. Carr died the next year at the age of 22 and her husband returned to the states, although the school was continued through private funding.

Undaunted, the Methodist women in 1890 opened the Jesse Lee Home, a school and orphanage named in honor of one of their earliest missionaries. Later they secured a 160 acre site at Unalaska for the home.

The Reverend Sheldon Jackson, general education agent, followed up by establishing a reindeer herd on Unalaska Island to bolster Native economy. Although herds later thrived elsewhere, Unalaska's was the very first Siberian import and for some reason did not survive. However, the orphanage—staffed by able nurse Agnes Sowle, whose marriage to a much-needed medical man, Albert Newhall, certainly aided the cause—was soon getting rave reviews.

According to the report of the Treasury Department in 1893, six orphan girls sent to the mission in 1890 from among "the poorest, lowest, dirtiest and most ignorant . . . who could not speak a word of English, in two years learned to write English as well as the average white school child of similar age."

But there was a darker side to the missionaries' mercies, for they initially believed the main goal for Native children was adoption by white families, and so many children were shipped outside the territory that Aleuts finally petitioned against the home.

The cause was taken up by Joseph Brown,

Right

Four young gardeners from the Jesse Lee Home in Unalaska are laden with the harvest of their extremely productive fields in the summer of 1910. Second from the right is Simeon Oliver, later to become a talented musician, lecturer and writer (Son of the Smoky Sea). An Eskimo born at Chignik, Oliver spent most of his younger years at the home, and returned to Unalaska in 1979 to give the commencement address at the high school—his first visit home since World War II. At the far right is Gordon Gould, who at the age of six was sent by his mother from his Unga home to the Jesse Lee Home to get an education. He became the first native-born Alaskan to be ordained a Methodist minister.

teacher at the newly-established Unalaska Public School, who in 1910 charged that children were often adopted out over protest of next of kin.

Later appointment of the Newhalls to head the home seems to have brought more friendly relations, perhaps because Newhall had second thoughts on earlier church policy. In 1913 he wrote a letter of protest to officials charging that instructors at Chemawa Indian School in Oregon, aided by the superintendent of education, were forcibly taking indentured children destined for his mission.

"Jesse Lee Home has in times past sent many children to the states, some to Carlisle (Indian School)," he conceded, but he concluded that the youngsters usually wanted to come home.

In addition, Newhall and his wife selflessly provided medical help to the isolated areas, saving many lives. Their home served for children of visiting sea captains and traders as well as local Aleuts and they were "mother" and "father" to many youngsters who never knew parents of their own.

It helped, too, that Dr. Newhall greatly respected Alexei Yatchmenoff, known as chief

Simeon Oliver (far left) *returned to Alaska in 1979 after an absence of more than 15 years and renewed long acquaintance with numerous Anchorage friends before going on to an emotional homecoming at Unalaska.*

In 1959, after years of planning and promotional work, Dr. P. Gordon Gould (left) *saw one of his great dreams become a reality, when Alaska Methodist (now Alaska Pacific) University was dedicated in Anchorage.*

115

The Unalaska ferry is a long-standing institution. Here it is in action about 1910, using manpower rather than an engine.
(Photo by P.S. Hunt, Talmadge Collection, Archives, University of Alaska, Fairbanks)

of all chiefs from Kodiak to Attu, was his friend and traded language lessons with him.

The loss of the family (Mrs. Newhall died in 1917 and Dr. Newhall transferred in 1924) and the mission itself—moved to Seward in 1925—was strongly felt.

Unalaska, sheltered by Amaknak Island, provided a superb anchorage known as Dutch Harbor and earlier as Lincoln Harbor. This harbor long served as spring headquarters for the Bering fleet and a supply base for gold stampeders headed to Saint Michael and Nome. By 1910 the area was surprisingly cosmopolitan, with several bars, a dance hall, hotels; even a tennis court and fine private homes like the ornate Victorian "Bird Cage" of trader Sam Applegate, and "Garfield House" (later referred to as "Dolly Madison House") which is said to have been built by President James Garfield for a niece whom the family wanted to get out of the country because she was pregnant and unwed.

No visit from any member of the Garfield family is recorded, but it's certain the house served as a lodging for travelers. Jack London is thought to have stayed here, to have dreamed up a novel, *The Sea Wolf,* before the hotel's great fieldstone fireplace and, although his journals do not record an Unalaska visit, this port was a routine supply stop for ships returning from the Klondike.

London is also supposed to have named nearby Mount Ballyhoo and to have placed a metal box at the top with a logbook where fellow climbers could sign in. Early coast-guardsmen claimed this honor too, but, since

Above
The crew of the power schooner Union Jack *dress cod on the deck. The cod fish fleet consisted of large mother ships from which men fished in small, double-ended dories. Base for the operation was Popof Island, where a customs house and numerous stores were established. Neighboring Unga also had many shore-based cod fishing operations.*
(Photo from John N. Cobb Collection,
University of Washington Library)

Upper right
Unalaska youths display their catch for photographer Noah Davenport who served as local commissioner for Unalaska from 1910 to 1912. The fish are salmon, still in good supply here.
(Boaz Collection, Archives,
University of Alaska, Fairbanks)

the book was stolen, the mystery remains unsolved.

No question, however, but what Unalaska often swarmed with visitors. The 1910-1912 diary of Noah and Clara Davenport, resident teacher and judge of that era, records a steady stream of visiting ships, lively social evenings and engagements with the "Unalaska Royal Brass Band" and "Russian Symphony Orchestra."

Clara Davenport was quick to note the Aleut women kept up with the latest fashions, observing wryly, "It must be humiliating to our stylish white ladies, tho', to find their brown sisters just as keen on fashion as they. Even some of our schoolgirls wear 'set-snug' dresses."

The area surrounding the Chain was also coming alive. In 1876 the first American cod salting station was built on Popof Island and

was followed by dozens of other successful (though not wildly lucrative) ventures for packing both cod and herring. Salmon canneries were established at Squaw Harbor, Sand Point and Ikatan Bay, and in 1925 P.E. Harris and Company managed to wrest from the Federal government nearly 40 acres at False Pass for a salmon cannery.

A gold strike made in Unga in 1886 ultimately became the Apollo Mine which produced $3 million for Alaska Commercial. A town built near the mine was designed by a top San Francisco architect and boasted a school, hospital, U.S. Commissioner, courthouse, jail, several stores, a railroad and two churches.

In 1908 the main vein of the Apollo was lost at the face of a fault and the mine closed. A cyanide plant was built in 1915 in an attempt to rework the tailings, but the operations,

which required 200 men, were interrupted by World War I and never reestablished.

Hopes flared briefly in 1916 when prospector George Cushing announced he had found the lost Apollo vein. Apparently nothing came of it except perhaps a stock offering.

Longtime Apollo manager Frank "Unga" Brown managed to hold out with a one-man mining operation until the late 1930s. The mine was eventually sold and resold, but never operated again.

Villagers gamely turned the big cyanide tank into a dance hall and Unga continued to prosper as long as fishing was good. By 1925 it

was producing 71% of the dry salt cod in Alaska, a year later 91%, and it continued to thrive until larger fishing boats became the most lucrative, making its shallow rock-strewn harbors unattractive.

A fair gold strike was made by Louis Hermand at Popof in 1904 and it employed some 40 to 50 miners for several years. Klondike and Nome stampeders, stopping to resupply, had modest success prospecting off Unalaska beaches, and another strike was reported there on Pyramid Peak in 1900. Stock was sold in a company to produce this gold, but high values promised in early assays

This Russian plane landed at Dutch Harbor in the 1920s.
(Collection of Lillie McGarvey)

never were realized and legend has it the whole venture was a scam.

A commercial mining operation for sulfur was started at Akun in 1919, but due to bad weather which constantly damaged facilities, and the wreck of the *Dora* en route to supply the plant, the company folded after a few seasons.

There was also a large coal find at Unga, but

it proved to be too poor a quality to be valuable, even for local heating.

A modern, shore-based whaling station, financed by Norwegians at Akutan in 1907, did well despite the fact the company's chartered bark, *Hadyn Brown*, was lost with several hands the first season.

The Russians introduced sheep raising in 1835 to provide meat. In 1918 Andrew C. Smith, with William MacIntosh of Oregon, decided to try ranching on a large scale, introducing 500 ewes to Dutch Harbor, Unalaska. Over half the stock died the first winter, and the following year MacIntosh and Smith split the survivors, sending half to Chernofski and the other half to Nikolski, and then separated their operations as well into the Western Pacific Livestock Company (Unalaska) and the Aleutian Livestock Company (Umnak).

In 1926 an additional $60,000 worth of stock was shipped to Umnak with Seattle newspaper headlines which declared western Alaska was destined to become one of the greatest sheep raising centers in the world, but by 1932 both operators were in receivership and subsequent managers only broke even at best, due to problems of rough terrain, hard weather and remote markets.

In the only grazing effort west of Umnak, Harold E. Bowman experimented with karakul sheep at Kanaga, mainly because the man who sold them to him had hoped to sell them in the states and was not allowed to land them there or in Panama and was desperate to be rid of them. Some reports say the exotic sheep did not survive while Bowman's goats thrived. According to another account, the government, from whom Bowman leased Kanaga, asked him to remove the animals. In any case it was not a money-making venture.

Cattle, too, were tried with about the same degree of success, although some breeds do very well surviving in the wild here.

At Popof an imaginative breeder tried to cross cattle with buffalo, but only the buffalo

Whaling

Although Aleuts successfully hunted whales before the coming of the white man, their Russian conquerors were slow to capitalize on this vast Aleutian resource. A shore-based Russian enterprise, using Aleuts and primitive hunting methods, was reported at Kodiak in the early 1800s, but the meat and oil realized was apparently for local Russian consumption.

In 1835 the American whaling fleet discovered the waters of the Gulf of Alaska, hunting first on Kodiak grounds south of the Aleutians, then, about 1840, on into the Bering Sea. In 1852 more than 200 ships headed for Bering Strait through Unimak and Seguam passes and the waters near the Komandorskies.

Russians considered these activities a trespass. It wasn't until 1849 that they themselves entered the industry, the Russian-American Company becoming a partner in the Russian-Finland Whaling Company. This venture was a failure due mainly to the Crimean War

The Akutan whaling station was the scene of great activity as three baleen whales were butchered. Oil, pet food and fertilizer were the main products of this station.
(Photo by Harold Heath, from collection of Victor B. Scheffer)

Henry Wood Elliott, who served as treasury agent and traveled the Aleutian Chain in the 1870s, drew this picture of whale hunting at Akun for an early report. Unlike Eskimos, who followed the whale to its death, Aleuts shot the animal with a poisoned harpoon, then waited for the carcass to float to shore. (From *Our Arctic Province*, 1886)

which blocked Russian ports and also because they entered the competitive field too late in the game.

The Russians did profit in that Unalaska early became a supply base where the whaling fleets stopped in the spring and at the end of the season to take on coal and provisions. The village's position as a port of call was so well established that, much later, business was further increased with the gold rush—stampeders usually stopped there to pasture sea-weary horses and enjoy the area's fine hotels—and as a base for the U.S. fleet of revenue cutters.

However, it was not until the great whaling fleets met their end—some lost in the crushing ice of the Arctic pack, others made obsolete by their inability to utilize the whole carcass of their catch as whale stocks became severely depleted—that the Aleutians became a true base for the whaling industry of Alaska.

In 1907 Norwegians financed a small whaling venture at Akutan and with an infusion of American capital incorporated as Alaska Whaling Company about 1912. The price of baleen had been steadily dropping and the market for oil began to give way because of the increasing popularity of petroleum products, but Alaska Whaling prospered because its shore-based operation efficiently rendered entire carcasses into dog food and fertilizer products.

A substantial modern plant, huge oil storage drums and a dock were built on the excellent harbor just a few miles from Akutan village. Local labor was utilized whenever possible, and the company store also proved a boon to the community, which stabilized with the new industry. And, as a side benefit amused neighbors noted, Akutan Natives learned to swear in Norwegian with a versatility lacking in Aleut.

Apparently worried about competition, backers of the Akutan firm introduced legislation into Congress in 1915 which would have prevented any rival from building within 75 miles of their base. Congress saw through the move because passage would have given Alaska Whaling a virtual monopoly over both major ocean passes of

The Akutan whaling station was abandoned shortly after the start of World War II. Here Bill Tcheripanoff explains to Jacqueline Turner how the old meat cookers worked. (Christy Turner)

the Chain. But no matter. Their competition, based in Southeastern Alaska and Kodiak, could ill afford expansion. The last rival called it quits in the early 1920s, moving its gear to New Zealand.

Stubbornly the whalers of Akutan hung on taking 100 or so big whales a year until the beginnings of World War II sent them back to their native Norway.

The last whaling season at Akutan was in 1939. Shortly thereafter the base was leased to the U.S. Navy, which rebuilt the wobbly dock and used it for refueling Russian freighters. At the war's end the property was returned to its owners, but the processing plant—outdated and rusty—burned to the ground. □

survived without care. A few of them can occasionally be spotted today, but they are shy of humans.

There are also a number of wonderfully strong wild horses in the eastern Chain, descended from the days when horses were necessary transport, but again, the terrain makes roundup impractical.

Herds of reindeer, imported at government expense in the early 1900s, did well at Atka and Umnak, but in the wild, and to this day the animals defy any attempt at domestication.

About the only really profitable experiment of this era was fox farming. Early Russian explorers found blue fox on the Komandorskies. Trader Andreian Tolstykh brought a breeding pair of blue foxes to Attu. Other breeding pairs were "planted" on a number of islands.

Traditionally, Aleuts had little use for fox, which is inedible and has delicate fur, but equipped with Russian trapping technology and a market they began to profit from the trade. Generally, of course, sea otter and fur seal pelts were more in demand, and while these animals were plentiful the value of fox remained low.

About 1880 Capt. Otto Carlson, former agent of the Alaska Commercial Company at Unga, built pens at Sand Point and began what is believed to have been the first American attempt to domesticate foxes in the area. He was unsuccessful with silvers, but his blue fox paid off so handsomely that other men—Neil Pete,

Trader Harold Bowman, shown here on his boat with a child believed to be his daughter Patsy, bought furs and transported fox trappers and supplies to many islands during the lucrative fox years of the 1920s. His Kanaga Ranching Company allied with Atka residents in the building of a modern store, just one of his many successful ventures.
(Photo by Charles Henry Hope Sr., from collection of Lillie McGarvey)

Andrew Gronholdt Sr., John Hubelys and Russian Charlie—all began similar experiments.

In the Fox Islands, Sam Applegate correctly assessed a bleak future for the sea otter trade, although he'd made considerable wealth in it, and in 1897 he planted blues on Samalga. He'd come to the Chain as a meteorologist in the U.S. Signal Corps at Unalaska and mapped the geologic features of coastal Alaska as captain of the schooner *Nellie Juan*. He picked his fox island well, allowing the animals to run free but hiring a watchman to feed them in the winter, and fur buyers were impressed with the results.

From 1901 to 1912 the price Applegate commanded per pelt rose from $22.48 to $72.18 and he harvested a total of 570 animals from the four by one-half mile island of Samalga.

As the market improved, Applegate, who had long supplied isolated villages with his trading vessels, began to involve the Aleuts in

The officers and crew of the Coast Guard Cutter Haida posed for this picture at Unalaska about the early 1920s.
(Collection of Lillie McGarvey)

Kathryn Diakanoff Seller was born of a good Unalaska family. She was left temporarily in the care of the Jesse Lee Home where her quick mind came to the attention of Sheldon Jackson. Under the patronage of that educator, she attended Carlisle Indian School where she was a contemporary of famous athlete Jim Thorpe. Later she went on to get her teaching degree, married Harry Seller, an amiable Englishman, and came home to teach with Harry. She pioneered the school at Atka, incurred the wrath of local trader Sam Applegate by starting a Native store to break *his stranglehold on that community, survived his attempts to get her fired, and took a second teaching job at Unalaska. She and her husband had six children, one of whom— Harry Jr.—was killed on navy duty near Dutch Harbor, and another died near Atka. Mrs. Seller survived to teach in bush communities throughout Alaska and is now in a rest home in northern California. This photo was taken at Unalaska about 1912.*
(Barret Willoughby Collection, Archives, University of Alaska, Fairbanks)

fur farming and, according to some, took advantage of them.

In 1911 at Atka, according to the account of the newly-installed government school teacher, Kathryn Seller, there were only two Natives who could speak English; all were dependent on the trader for supplies and many in debt to him. She also charged he paid far too little for their furs.

Being Aleut herself—one who had been lucky enough to have attended Carlisle Indian School in Pennsylvania and go on to college for a teaching degree in the states— Mrs. Seller's sympathy lay with the Atkans, and she and husband Harry publicly took on the trader, writing letters of protest and helping Atkans organize their own cooperative store and fur trading business.

Applegate protested that, on the contrary, he had done a great deal to help the people of Atka and that the Bureau of Education had no right to compete with free enterprise. He also tried to get Mrs. Seller fired, but her superintendent, who had suggested the co-op initially, stuck by her. Shortly thereafter, when the hunting of fur seals and otters was banned, Applegate became an absentee landlord, keeping the lease and trapping on Samalga until 1920, but retiring comfortably to California.

Under government guidelines the islands were leased at $25 per year but trapping permits were free to Natives, making them suddenly sought-after partners for white entrepreneurs.

N.E. Bolshanin, deputy collector of customs at Unalaska, advised Aleuts to make application for 19 islands under this provision in 1916 and helped them in staking and stocking other islands over the next three years, but he appears to have done best for himself, making $14,300 in one season and an additional $49,000 on a three year lease on Kavalga, which qualified him as the most successful lessee in the early years of fur farming in the Aleutians.

Fox Trapping in the Aleutians

By Henry Swanson and Raymond Hudson

During the 1920s and 1930s *Henry Swanson* (below) traveled among the fox farming islands of the Chain as a trader in his boats, *Kanaga Native* and *Alasco-IV.* During World War II he was an outpost tender for the military around Unalaska and Adak and piloted tugs for the Navy. Today, at 85, he is a revered partriarch of the Aleutians.

The Fox Islands, those eastern Aleutians that include Akutan, Unalaska, Umnak, and the Islands of Four Mountains, were not the only Aleutian Islands where fox lived. When Glotov returned from the first Russian hunting expedition into the Fox Islands, he had over 2,500 fox skins. Of less value than the exquisite sea otter skins, fox skins nevertheless became an important fur resource during the period of Russian exploration and ownership of Alaska. The Russians introduced at least two types of wooden fox traps among the Aleut hunters.

The most frequently used trap was constructed from a section of a log. A slot was carved halfway through the log and a hole was drilled through the core. A twisted loop of whale sinew stretched through this hole and was secured at each end with wooden pegs. Fastened into this sinew at the center of the log and rotating through the slot was a hardwood plank into which spikes were fastened. The entire

A curious blue fox gets what is probably its first look at human beings at remote East Holtz Bay, Attu. With sharp barks it ordered its family to the safety of the den, then boldly shadowed hikers, barking insults.

Right
In the early 1900s Atka Natives formed a cooperative store to get out of the clutches of a white trader, and soon were making money in the fox trade. This photo was taken by Mr. and Mrs. Harry Seller who taught there from 1912-1914 and helped the people form the co-op.
(From collection of John Seller)

123

apparatus when set was sprung by a trip wire that the hunter stretched across a fox trail. When released, the spiked plank hurled into the fox and pinned the animal to the ground.

The second type of trap, also constructed from wood, resembled the letter H with a bow attached to its top. This trap was placed in front of a fox den and released when the fox accidentally tripped a stick. The stick held an arrangement of wooden legs which kept the bow drawn tight. When released, the bow shot down a vertical shaft to which was attached a horizontal bar which pinned the fox to the bottom of the trap.

Fox trapping remained a secondary source of income for Aleut people throughout the Russian period and until the overhunted sea otter population declined near the end of the 19th century. The Aleutian Islands then became the home of a new industry: blue fox farming. There were no farms as such, but rather complete islands were transformed into breeding locations for the blue phase of the Arctic fox.

Prior to the introduction of the blue fox industry, fox populations occurred erratically in the Chain with various islands inhabited by concentrations of a single type or phase of fox. Beginning at the east, red fox were found on Unimak, Tigalda, Akun, Akutan, Unalaska, Umnak, and one of the Islands of Four Mountains, Chuginadak. The next islands had no fox until Amlia which had silver fox, probably planted by the Russians. Atka had blue fox, now believed to have been introduced by the Russians.

Great Sitkin had an unusual breed of monstrous red fox. These animals, the size of wolves, were eliminated one winter by Henry Swanson. The island was subsequently stocked with blues.

Adak had silvers while Kanaga was populated by a variety of red fox. The Atka people said that these red fox with their soft, beautifully red fur had been brought from Siberia by the Russians.

There were no fox on Tanaga, Kiska, Amchitka—indeed none occurred until Attu, which was populated by blue fox.

Samuel Applegate was the first person who actively planted blue fox on the Aleutians. In 1898 (about the time he introduced the now prolific ground squirrel to Unalaska Island) he leased Samalga Island for two years. He stocked the island with seven pairs of fox and by 1900 he had about 150 fox. The winter of 1900 he trapped 55. By 1900 several islands had been leased, but it was not until after 1910, when the sea otter hunting was curtailed, that blue fox trapping caught hold.

A person could lease an island—large or small—for $25 a year from the federal government. The best islands were those with good beach fronts that provided the fox with regular food. The steeper, more rugged islands were less desirable, but bird populations on these islands would support a good sized fox population for a few years. The birds, previously unmolested by predators, nested in the

Far left
USF&WS biologist Kent Hall baits a fox trap for what is believed to be the last fox on Agattu.

Left
Bad news fox tracks cross those made by man. USF&WS biologists, attempting to transplant endangered Aleutian Canada geese to new locations, systemically undertook a program of fox eradication on Agattu. In the fall of 1978 a single set of tracks turned up on Agattu beaches. Biologists set out poison baits and believe the island is fox free today.

grass and on the beaches. The appearance of young pups corresponded with the disappearance of newly laid eggs. Before long the birds began nesting on cliffs and isolated rocks.

If feed was plentiful the fox trapper did not have to wait long to harvest on the island. The pups, born around May, matured and reproduced early. Two or three pairs, on a good island, could result in a trapper's recovering 100 or more pelts in two or three years. Henry Swanson stocked Little Tanaga with a pair of blue fox. Three years later he took off 140 pelts and left a healthy breeding stock to continue.

Once an island had been leased it had to be cleared of any fox populations that might drive off the smaller blue fox. A trapper would spend a winter on the island trapping and shooting. Winters were utilized to make a profit from the recovered fox pelts. The next fall the island would be stocked with a few pairs of blue fox. After two or three years the trapper would return to the island in October. This was a little early to begin trapping, but the small boats and uncertain winter storms dictated getting to the islands early. The trapping season would last until January, but occasionally, if the boat was late, trappers would be stuck on their islands until May or June.

Islands were leased by individuals, partnerships, and by entire villages. Unalaska village leased Carlisle; Nikolski leased Tanaga, west of Adak; Atka village leased Amchitka; Attu village had Agattu. Frequently individual people in the village also had their own islands.

Stocking the islands with blue fox became big business. By 1932 53 Aleutian Islands were leased for blue fox. Eventually all the islands were stocked except for Buldir and a few islets.

The money poured in. Henry Swanson recalls one season at Atka when there were three buyers to purchase skins from the local people. There was so much money in town that nobody had any small bills with which to make change or purchase goods. Henry remembers a trapper asked him for a loan of a few dollars. Henry examined his pockets and said, "I can't do that, but if you need money here's a couple of hundred dollar bills."

"Naw," the trapper replied, "I've got a lot of those, but I need a couple of dollars to buy something!"

By the mid-1930s the price for blue fox fur had dropped 50%.

By 1941 it was down to nothing.

After World War II a few men supplemented their family incomes by trapping, but the era of the blue fox islands was over. □

Still the big money had yet to be made when Harold Bowman the empire builder arrived on the scene with the backing of the First National Bank of Seattle in the early 1920s.

Quickly establishing the Kanaga Ranching Company, Bowman then allied himself with Atka Natives by going in with them 50/50 on the building of an ultramodern village store. He ingratiated himself with the village of Nikolski as well, and by 1929 2,200 of the 3,000 pelts taken in the Aleutians were through Bowman's interests.

Again, a schoolteacher, Ernest P. Stowell, sounded the alarm, complaining in 1930 that Atka Natives were being mistreated, that their interests were neglected in their store partnership with Bowman and in their leasing of several islands, and that their chief, Makary Zaochney, who worked for Bowman on salary, was in league with the trader. The departments of Agriculture and Interior, which dutifully undertook a two-year investigation, reported it appeared that Bowman had indeed used Zaochney to gain control of the store, where he succeeded in indebting the Natives unnecessarily and had further burdened them with the unsolicited sale of two boats he happened to want to be rid of.

However, investigators found no actual evidence of criminal activity, hinting that if anything illegal was afoot, Bowman was smart enough to cover it up. And so the matter stood.

By all accounts, the store Bowman built for them was a fine one. Perhaps they indebted themselves, but in 1931 the village of less than 100 people grossed $65,000 by combined trapping efforts, and by some accounts they topped that in other seasons.

The boat Bowman sold them for $50,000, the 60-foot *Iskum,* may have been overpriced, but they needed it and were devastated when it sank on an uncharted rock about 24 hours after delivery, with Bowman's skipper at the helm.

For the most part, Atkans remember this trading period with some satisfaction, for it was the first time since the coming of the Russians that Aleuts had ever managed to get ahead. There were good trapping years when the Atkans were able to refurbish their homes and improve the looks of the village by dragging in white beach rock for ornamental walkways, and to start a band which traveled to other villages to compete with other Aleut bands and to play for dances that lasted all night.

Neighboring Nikolski also made economic gains under Kanaga Ranching, although Bowman profited heavily, according to the recollection of one old-timer, by removing a new engine and installing an old, neglected motor when he sold them the trading vessel, *Umnak Native,* in 1929.

Three years later in a severe storm the engine collapsed and, unable to hold anchor, the vessel wrecked, taking nine lives and many valuable furs. Still the *Umnak Native* had served three years and it seemed to be the consensus that poor navigation of the captain—the only white man aboard with the exception of Russian Bishop Antonin Pokrofsky—caused her doom as much as the failed engine.

And other villages, dealing with other traders, fared worse. The standard of living was less lush at Attu, for example, perhaps

Left

In the 1920s and 1930s Native bands were very popular in the Aleutians and traveled from village to village providing music for a wonderful round of social evenings. This photo of the Unalaska band was taken by Kathryn and Harry Seller.
(Collection of John A. Seller)

Below

This picture of Attu's gentlemanly chief Mike Hodikoff was taken by a USF&WS agent in 1931. The setting appears to be Attu, with old Russian cannons visible beside this great Aleut leader. Once hearing Chief Alexei Yatchmenoff referred to as the "Chief of the Aleuts," Hodikoff corrected the speaker politely but firmly: "Him Unalaska Chief. I Attu Chief." When his village was captured by the Japanese in World War II, Hodikoff was taken to Japan where he died in captivity. He was deeply respected by villagers and outsiders alike.
(National Archives, USF&WS file)

Below

Russian Bishop Antonin Pokrofsky was traveling from Unalaska to Nikolski in 1932 aboard the Umnak Native *when, in a severe storm, the engine collapsed and the vessel wrecked, claiming nine lives and many valuable furs. Bishop Antonin spent 11 days on Umnak before rescue. His survival was due in part to a crate of oranges which provided nourishment during this period of shock and exposure.*
(Collection of Lillie McGarvey)

Above

This photo was in the file of anthropologist Aleš Hrdlička and is believed to have been taken at Attu about 1936. Hrdlička much enjoyed the village, especially Chief Mike Hodikoff and his famous aunt, Maggie Prokopeuff, nicknamed "Rock of Ages." Chief Hodikoff is smiling in front row at left (with young child); Maggie Prokopeuff is behind him, slightly to his left, in black coat. Among the others pictured are: Marie, Anesia and Alfred Prokopeuff, Ann and Anesia Hodikoff, Stepan, Fekla, Laverenty and Meteraphen Golodoff, Jenny Krukoff, Alec Persoff, John Artemenoff, and Chief Hodikoff's brother in front row center.
(Smithsonian Institution, Anthropological Archives)

Above
An army plane touched down at the Dutch Harbor dock in 1924 in the course of a round the world flight.
(Collection of Lillie McGarvey)

Right
Anfin Rod owned and operated a herring saltery at Unalaska during the 1930s. The fish were shipped via Alaska Steamship. This harbor scene was one of many photos of those times which were made into postcards.
(Photo by Charles Henry Hope Sr. from collection of Lillie McGarvey)

Chief Makary Zaochney of Amchitka posed for USF&WS agent Frank Dufresne in the early 1930s with ingenious sealskin-covered skis of Aleut design. The hairs of the fur helped to brake the skier when he climbed uphill and to speed the downhill slide.
(National Archives)

because their trader was underfunded and could not keep their store well supplied, but he did help them make the transition from sod *barabaras* to modern homes.

Bowman himself appeared to be doing fabulously well, chartering Alaska Steamship to deliver building materials for a full-fledged mansion at Kanaga which he staffed with a maid and a Japanese cook, and building an enormous dock and warehouses.

It was his dream to build a "Fur Rendezvous" to which trappers from throughout the Chain could come, sell, buy supplies and simply get together socially. The project was well underway in 1928 when he sold his fox furs for $105,025 and in 1929 when he grossed $231,125. That was, however, the peak year and after that the price of furs fell rapidly with the Depression. The lucrative fox years had come to an end.

It was destined to happen, even without the Depression, old-timers maintain. "I doubt that the Aleutian blue could have held up like the Norwegian blue," speculates Henry Wheaton who trapped for Bowman and later managed the Atka store for him. "It just wasn't that good a quality."

With the loss of market, the economic benefit of maintaining fox farming as a priority on the refuge needed a second look. The Bureau of Biological Survey sponsored a three-year study of the Aleutians to gather information on the status of its wildlife.

Olaus Murie led the expeditions in the summers of 1936 and 1937, looking especially at fox-bird relationships while cataloging bird and mammal populations for each island.

All along the Chain the biologists heard the Aleuts tell of vast numbers of birds that were present before the foxes came. Often Murie and his team would find only a remnant population or none at all.

"It soon became apparent that the most important problem confronting us was the con-

The U.S. Coast Guard cutter Shoshone *was typical of those stationed at Unalaska to patrol the Bering Sea against poachers. Prior to World War II there were usually two or three of them in the area, all named for various Indian tribes.*
(Collection of Lillie McGarvey)

flict between fox farming and the preservation of the Aleutian avi-fauna," the researchers concluded. Even the sea otter, still precariously low, seemed to be deterred from expansion by fox farming activities.

Murie's group drew up a list of islands best suited for fox propagation and a list of islands that they recommended be reserved for wildlife.

In 1939 H. Douglas Gray, Aleutian refuge manager and member of Murie's expedition, formalized the proposal for reducing the number of fox farming islands but World War II interrupted the program.

. . . you were swept
down the dark aorta into the furious sun.

13
World War II

In 1943 the Navy informally assigned an officer to prepare an official war diary of Dutch Harbor but, according to the records, the order was canceled in less than a month. The project was reinstated in 1944 but the security man found it tough going. Having been among the first to reach Dutch Harbor after the Japanese attack, he was interested from the beginning in events of this period, but "strangely enough—even three short months after the bombing—he was unable to get a clear account or understanding of what actually happened during those fateful days. Already many of the men then stationed at Dutch Harbor had been reassigned and those that remained either would not talk or told utterly divergent stories."

"Why this should have been the case is not understandable, for the defenders of Dutch Harbor had nothing to conceal," the Navy historian puzzled. "They did a splendid job from start to finish, and the truth needed no embellishment."

By all accounts the defenders of Dutch, though green to combat and ill-equipped, acquitted themselves well, but elsewhere the bloody Aleutian campaign was dogged by serious blunders. The Japanese invasion was initially kept secret for morale and security reasons, and despite subsequent public information, heavy censorship served handily to cover embarrassment of military leaders, so that the Aleutian campaign is often entirely omitted from accounts of World War II.

Yet at one point the outcome of the war hinged on Aleutian action and the bitter experiences there played a large part in the planning of successful invasions elsewhere.

The reports and records of different military branches are as divergent as accounts of the Dutch Harbor bombing, however, and we may never fully know the true cost of the Aleutian war.

In 1904 the government withdrew Kiska as a naval reserve and 12 years later began a small base there, but abandoned the project after only a few dock pilings were driven.

Land was set aside for a wireless station at Dutch Harbor in 1912, but no military installation. A 1921 report on government coaling stations observed that the Chain was practically without defense and warned any stores there "would be subject to captivity by enemy raids." But the dust of World War I had scarcely settled, the nation was enjoying a feeling of well-being, and Aleutian installations went unguarded.

In 1934 and 1935 the Navy, working with the Hydrographic office, established a sun station on Kiska and surveyed some of the Chain by air. In the process Japanese ships were observed making soundings and charting passes and harbors. Atka Natives also reported being visited by Japanese map makers, and Navy suggested to the State Department that if

Young Naval artist Lt. William Draper was green to combat when he hit the Aleutians in 1943 and saw his first combat at Amchitka. Later he served in the jungles of Bougainville, the Marianas and covered major conflicts in the South Pacific. Today he is a well-known portrait artist in New York city and his list of sitters reads like "Who's Who" but he still travels in pursuit of landscapes far afield and remembers his Aleutian experiences with nostalgia. The paintings by William Draper on page 131, 134, 143 and 144 are part of the Combat Art Collection, Navy Archives, U.S. Navy Yard, Washington, D.C.
Right
Main Street. *Artist Draper stayed at Dutch Harbor about a month and did nine paintings of the rapidly expanding military facilities. Here is the main street, with the Alaska Commercial Company at right and a few marines and sailors around the dock at left.*

This photo of the U.S. Navy wireless station at Dutch Harbor, taken about 1916, shows the towers blown down, victims of high winds. Service was restored within 24 hours by erection of a new pole.
(Collection of Lillie McGarvey)

foreigners were going to continue to scout these waters in the name of fish and wildlife research, an observer be placed aboard. This was not acceptable to the Japanese and so the State Department let the matter lie, dismissing Navy concerns as paranoia.

That same year Brig. Gen. Billy Mitchell warned the House Military Affairs Committee that Alaska was the "key point of the whole Pacific . . . He who holds Alaska holds the world. It is the jumping-off place to smash Japan. If we wait to fight her in the Philippines, it will take us five years to defeat Japan."

Under the Treaty of Limitation of Naval Armament with Japan the United States was bound not to install any defense posts in the Aleutians until expiration date, 1936, and in the same year Anthony Dimond, Alaska dele-

gate to Congress, wrote Claude Swanson, Secretary of Navy, that it was not too early to consider defense.

"It seems sufficiently evident that if serious difficulty arises between any other nation and the United States, the Pacific not the Atlantic Ocean will probably be the scene of conflict," he reasoned, pointing out that the Great Circle Route touched on the southern shores of the Aleutian Chain.

But Dimond was a voteless delegate, and when he introduced a bill for $10 million to build air bases in Alaska, Congress wrote off his plea as "pork barrel."

"Why should anyone want Alaska?" asked one incredulous congressman.

When Hitler invaded Europe in 1939, the Joint Chiefs of Staff decided to bone up America's western outposts under "Plan Orange," prepared in 1928 and later revised in 1937. This plan recognized Alaska, Hawaii and Panama as a strategic triangle, and gave Lt. Gen. John DeWitt the job of preparing the West Coast and Alaska for possible attack. DeWitt dispatched Col. Simon Bolivar Buckner

Jr. to assume command of the Alaska Defense Force with some 800 men of the 4th Infantry Regiment and practically no funding.

Some $50 million was spent on installations in Hawaii but the best Alaska could wrest from Congress was $4 million for a cold weather testing lab until the spring of 1940 when it was learned Soviets were building bases on Siberian coasts. Although Russia would become our ally, the Hitler-Stalin pact produced a red scare and Congress belatedly approved $350 million for Alaska defense.

Buckner quickly assessed the importance of the Aleutians which stood only 650 miles from Japanese military bases, and insisted Capt. Ralph Parker, his Navy counterpart, set up a tour of the Chain for him. During this survey, made a year before Pearl Harbor and 18 months before the Aleutians were attacked, Buckner chose runway sites from which he would later defend: Umnak, Adak, Amchitka, Kiska, Shemya, Attu, Unalaska, Cold Bay and Port Heiden.

The Japanese, meanwhile, boldly continued their survey work. Atka Aleuts reported

Japanese floatplanes landing near their fishing boats in 1940, and they spotted them again at the south end of their island after Pearl Harbor.

Working without Congressional appropriations, Buckner began to build a major base at Cold Bay. He put down the beginnings of $12,700,000 Fort Mears near Dutch Harbor and established an air base to supply and defend it and $11,200,000 Fort Glenn on nearby Umnak.

These installations were kept top secret, built in the name of Blair Fish Packing Co., Saxton & Co. and Consolidated Packing, and the ruse was so successful that Japanese believed there were no defensive air stations within 1,000 miles of Dutch, until the second day of the attack against Dutch Harbor.

The Navy held back from establishing in Alaska, however. On the day Pearl Harbor was attacked, Army forces in Alaska numbered 22,000 and Air Force 2,200, while Navy had only about 500 men, 67 of them at Dutch Harbor.

Shortly after Pearl Harbor a $75 million Navy base was under construction at Unalaska and weather stations were established at Kiska and Kanaga. Construction began on a Marine barracks at Dutch Harbor, nurses moved in, the town of 50 whites and 250 Aleuts boomed with 450 construction workers, and duly recorded in the official naval record is the existence of a whorehouse at nearby Expedition Island.

Ferry service to the island was a mere 10 cents, the historian noted, "but the return fare was $2 and what additional expense incurred from negotiations with the madam and her five beautiful girls was the individual's own problem.

"This trading post continued to have a monopoly on Expedition Island until mass evacuation of civilians occurred on September 4, 1941, and since that time there has been no similar establishment at this base."

The naval station at Dutch was commissioned September 1, 1941, with a flagpole presented from the civilian workers and 1,000 in attendance. By April of the next year a submarine port was in operation, although it left much to be desired.

"It is interesting to note the perplexed facial expressions of the submarine captains being shown the Dutch Harbor submarine base," the historian observed. "It consists of two nests of dolphins and a catwalk approach."

In January 1942, Japanese subs were spotted in the area, three of which fired and dived on contact, and in April the first Aleutian plane crash was recorded (from ice on the wing) with three officers and one enlisted man dead and four crawling to safety.

Meanwhile Japan debated on military strategy. Adm. Isoroku Yamamoto, commander in chief of the combined fleet, was an early proponent of air power and he was plagued by the fact that five first-class U.S. carriers had escaped the attack on Pearl Harbor. If he could lure the carriers to the Aleutians where his bombers would have short range and easy advantage over them, he'd have a good chance at Midway, his next important target. This would also cut the supply line between the United States and Russia.

Others of the Japanese command wanted to focus on Australia, but on April 18, 1942, Lt. Col. James Doolittle made a daring raid on Tokyo and other heartland cities, settling the question. No one knew from whence Doolittle had made his strike (actually from the carrier *Hornet* in the central Pacific), but since he had been raised in Alaska that was the guess, and Japanese leaders decided they could not afford to leave their homeland unguarded. They would attack Dutch Harbor as a diversion to draw U.S. naval forces away from the Midway area. They intended to occupy islands in the western Aleutians where they could establish flying boat patrol bases. This foothold in the Aleutians would be within easy range of the American mainland, 12 hours' bombing distance from Seattle's Boeing plant and the Bremerton Navy Yard, and within pointblank range of the Soviet Union. Their overall plan was to establish a line of defense from the Aleutians through Midway to New Guinea, behind which they could negotiate a peace. Fully aware of their own limitations for a protracted war, they also were worried that the Americans would use the Aleutians as an invasion route.

The man chosen to direct their daring offensive was Rear Adm. Kakuji Kakuta, and under him Lt. Comdr. Masatake Okumiya, rated one of Japan's best air technicians and a crack pilot

On June 4, 1942, 10 Japanese fighter planes, 11 dive bombers and 8 low-level bombers attacked in a second and more deadly raid on Dutch Harbor, first bombed a day earlier. One of the casualties of the second raid, in addition to fuel tanks, a beached ship, the air station dock, a half-built hangar, and a gun emplacement, was this hospital building.
(William H. Hall Collection)

Ships and Shapes. *Artist William Draper portrays an intelligence class in ship identification at the air base at Umnak. Silhouettes of American and enemy planes paper the walls in the cramped quarters of a Yakutat hut.*

until he was seriously injured as a test pilot shortly before Pearl Harbor.

The attack was set for the first week in June, and on May 20 naval intelligence got wind of it, although they weren't sure whether the target was Los Angeles, San Francisco or Alaska.

Unbeknownst to the enemy, American cryptanalysts had broken Japan's top secret "Purple Code" and, though constantly plagued

with radio static, were able to follow enemy communications through the early stages of the Aleutian campaign.

On May 30 Dutch was ordered to full alert and on June 2 the directive was issued that "men in exposed stations wear steel helmets" (World War I issue) in event of air raid. Japanese carrier planes were indicated in an area not over 400 miles south of Kiska.

As a precautionary measure PBYs and crews were dispatched to nearby coves and lakes, and at 6:45 A.M. June 3, Unalaska wired COMALSEC (Kodiak) for 10 additional 20 MM guns and ammunition.

One hundred and eighty miles to the southwest, the Japanese launched 10 "Kate" attack bombers, 12 "Val" dive bombers and 12

Zeroes. Shortly after dawn the seaplane tender *Gillis*, anchored in Dutch Harbor, picked up a squadron of blips on its radar screen about 10 miles off and signaled the captain of the naval station who called a red alert and ordered *Gillis* and five other ships in the harbor to start their engines for evacuation. They had five minutes to go.

High in the hills above, a young photographer, Dean Freiday, manning a battle station selected for its vantage point, was blissfully out of radio contact. He'd amused himself earlier by picking wild flowers, then curled up for a short nap on a large sign that read "Fox Farm, No Trespassing" which had fallen near his trench.

"About an hour later I was awakened by the drone of planes," he recounted. "Soldiers all over the hill (I was the only Navy man) were watching a formation of planes come over the far end of Unalaska Valley. The planes flew along near Pyramid Peak toward the far end of Captain's Bay.

"Just as everyone had assumed that they were a patrol from Otter Point, the first plane peeled off toward Fort Mears. Unalaska opened fire; bugles sounded up and down Unalaska Valley, and men scurried into trenches and foxholes. I jumped into the trench and got my camera ready for action. Bombs started dropping and the rhythm of the AA guns became fierce, with the slower ka-poom, ka-poom of the larger guns underlying the tat-tat-tat-tat-tat of the machine guns and the ping of the rifles.

"After the first few explosions shook the ground and my number didn't come up, the peculiar sensation of my visceral regions calmed down. The strength that carries you shaking afterwards, took hold of me. I photographed what action was in my field of view."

Below, Lt. Jack Litsey struggled to get his Catalina airborne for the mail run to Kodiak but was stopped by tracers from two Zeroes. His two passengers were killed, but Litsey maneuvered his burning wreck to a crash stop and scrambled to safety on the beach.

More successful was Ens. James T. Hildebrand who took his PBY off from a nearby cove and flew the south coast of Unalaska, where he engaged two Zeroes at Cape Aiak. Somehow Hildebrand managed to fly his slow floatplane under the belly of the Zero which he downed with his waist guns aided by ground fire. Then he wheeled up a valley where the fast-paced Japanese planes could not follow and headed for the nearest cloud cover.

The Japanese force, which encountered far more ground fire than expected, bombed Fort Mears only 20 minutes, then headed home.

Fort Glenn, unaware of the battle because of radio failure, was overflown shortly thereafter by four Japanese floatplanes which had gone off course and missed the main event. Pvt. George Stanley, washing linen outside the hospital tent, reported the enemy and went back to his task while 21 Warhawks scrambled. One Japanese plane was downed in flames and another crippled so badly that it crashed en route to its carrier. None of the survivors had any idea where the attack had come from and the location of the strategic base remained a secret.

But so did the whereabouts of the Japanese fleet. Ens. Marshal C. Freerk's PBY picked up a radar contact on the morning of June 4, investigated and found the Japanese carrier force southwest of Umnak. In another PBY, Lt. Charles E. Perkins, shadowing Freerk's contact with the carriers until a bomber strike could be made, attacked in a valiant effort that earned him the Navy Cross, but the Japanese fleet remained intact.

During the bombing of Fort Mears, Lt. William H. Gibbs located a Japanese carrier south of Amaknak and remained over it, radioing for bombers that never came, then flew home on his last cupful of gas. His efforts earned him the Distinguished Flying Cross, but his effort is not mentioned in most reports, nor is there any indication as to why there was no bomber follow-up.

An Umnak-based PBY piloted by Lt. Jean Cusick was attacked by a Japanese air patrol about 200 miles south of Dutch at 10 A.M. that day and shot down at a cost of five lives. Surviving copilot Lt. Wylie M. Hunt and two crewmen were picked up two days later by the

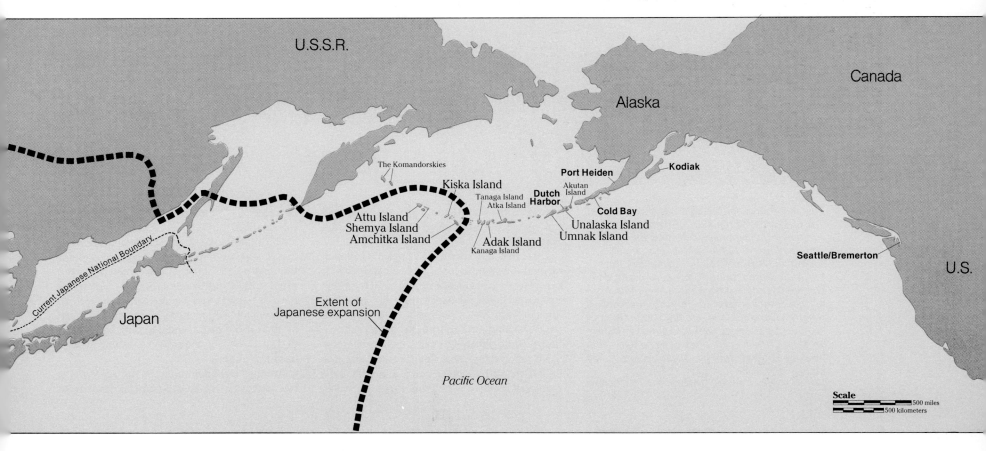

This is the Zero that helped Americans win World War II. At the start of the Aleutian campaign the Japanese Zero was the fastest and deadliest of fighter planes, for which Americans had no match. During an attack on Unalaska the pilot of this Zero made an emergency landing on Akutan, breaking his neck but leaving his plane intact. Americans repaired it and shipped it to the States where engineers learned its secrets and modified their air tactics to cope with these agile fighters. This photo was taken July 20, 1942, just after the plane's discovery.
(Hanna Collection, Archives, University of Alaska, Fairbanks)

Japanese; the first Aleutian prisoners, they did not reveal the location of the air base from whence they'd come.

Late that afternoon Lt. Lucius Campbell located a Japanese force of two carriers with escorting cruisers and destroyers and overflew for two hours broadcasting its location. Finally, with his rudder shot away and fuel tanks leaking, he retired to ditch halfway home. Unfortunately static had garbled his radio reports; his Coast Guard rescue ship was bound by radio silence, and it wasn't until Campbell reached Sand Point three days later

that he was allowed to file his strategic information.

Once the smoke cleared at Dutch, American losses appeared surprisingly light except for the deaths of 35 men. Major targets were the radio station and wooden oil tanks which had been at Unalaska for many years. Japanese attackers had been working under the handicap of 30-year-old maps, updated only by a photo of Dutch Harbor taken by a fishing boat a decade earlier.

Another disappointment to the enemy was late discovery of five American destroyers anchored at Makushin Bay on the far side of Unalaska. Admiral Kakuta ordered all available aircraft to attack but weather closed in.

The Japanese had lost one Zero with pilot and a floatplane with crew; a bomber on the initial launch and a second seaplane through enemy fire at Umnak, both without loss of life.

On June 4 the Japanese dispatched 10 fighters, 11 dive bombers and 8 low-level bombers for a second, more deadly raid; scoring hits on fuel tanks, the USS *Northwestern*, a beached ship which served as barracks and power plant, the air station dock, an uncompleted hangar and gun emplacement and the Dutch Harbor hospital.

Japanese planes also discovered the Umnak air base, engaging in a dogfight that cost two American P-40s of the 11th Fighter Squadron (the Aleutian Tigers), one Japanese fighter, two Japanese bombers and damaged three more bombers so badly that they crashed en route to their carrier. And at last Americans located the Japanese convoy, but left it unscathed due to repeated bomb failures and near misses.

American casualties at Dutch Harbor were 43 dead, including PBY ace Hildebrand and his crew who, after shooting down the first Zero of the campaign, disappeared on night patrol. Ten aircraft were shot down, six of which were PBYs.

Enemy losses were probably not more than half a dozen men, a couple of bombers and three additional Zeroes, but the last Zero felled proved costly.

Winged by Ens. Albert Mitchell's Catalina, Zero pilot Tadayoshi Koga lingered to down his assailant and machine gun the waist gunner, W.H. Rawls, who had survived the plane crash. Then Koga noticed his oil gauge showed loss of pressure and made the mistake of landing on soft tundra at Akutan, where his wheels stuck, flipping the craft and breaking Koga's neck but leaving the plane intact.

At that point in the war the Zero was the fastest and deadliest of fighters. Koga's craft, salvaged and tested, allowed U.S. test pilots to evaluate its weaknesses, and as a result the Americans modified their air tactics to cope with the more agile fighters.

Meanwhile the battle of Midway further sealed Japan's fate. On June 5 Admiral Yamamoto was forced to abandon that objective, stopped by the stunning loss of more than 3,500 men, 332 planes and several ships. Had he augmented his invasion force with the flotilla deployed to the Aleutians, strategists speculate he might have won the battle, but as it was Japan suffered her first major naval defeat in almost a century.

The Aleutian campaign, though by no means a clear victory, served to save face with the Japanese public, which was not to learn about Midway losses until the war's end; and Admiral Kakuta dispatched to invade the western islands.

On June 6 weather observers at Kiska's 10-man station radioed "unidentified ships entering harbor" and were not heard from again. Early that morning, 1,250 Japanese soldiers invaded Kiska and began splintering the small outpost with machine gun fire. Navy Aerographer's Mate William House ordered his men to run for it while he and J.L. Turner burned vital records, then headed for the hills themselves.

The U.S.S. Northwestern, *which served as barracks and power plant, was destroyed by a direct hit by Japanese fighter planes on June 4, 1942. Its rusting hulk still rears from the waters at Dutch Harbor.*
(Bob Nelson)

The enemy quickly rounded up all Americans except House, who managed to hide out 50 days before surrendering, 100 pounds less than his normal weight.

On June 9 Dutch Harbor reported Attu had not been heard from for two days although six-hour schedules were normally maintained. The government had feared for the small Native community and had long debated evacuation, but at a meeting called by Acting Governor E.L. Bartlett it was decided to leave the Aleuts on home ground unless actually under enemy attack.

"It is felt these people could never adjust themselves to life outside their present environment, whereas they could 'take to the hills' in case of danger and be practically self-sufficient for a considerable period," Bartlett's report explained.

Near the end of May the Navy had sent a ship to Attu to discuss the possibility of moving people off. Unfortunately bad weather kept the ship at bay and it finally steamed off, leaving Attu unguarded.

These are the men of the American weather station crew at Kiska, photographed just two weeks before they were captured by the Japanese when they invaded the island June 10, 1942. The men are identified as; standing from left: J.L. Turner, R.L. Coffield, William C. House, Lt. Mulla, H.E. Eckle, L. Yaconelli, M.L. Courtenay. Kneeling from left: J.C. McCandless, R.M. Christensen, W.M. Winfrey, M.G. Palmer, W.I. Gaffey. William House hid out on the island 50 days before surrendering. These men returned safely from Japanese prison camps at war's end, and the dog Explosion survived the Japanese occupation to meet Americans when they retook the island 14 months later. House returned to the Aleutians in 1979 to give the graduation address at Adak High School.
(Office of Naval Records and Library)

"On Sunday morning [June 7] a little after 11 we were all coming out of church when we saw them [the Japanese] coming out of the hills. So many of them . . ." Attu Native Innokenty Golodoff recounted in "The Last Days of Attu" (*ALASKA SPORTSMAN*®, December 1966). "Twenty came down. We had no knives, no guns, no nothing. The first batch had no boss. They were young and they shot up the village. They hit Anna Hoodikoff in the leg. Then a second bunch came and told them to stop. I saw one of their own men dead by the school house. They must have shot him."

Etta Jones, wife of the Attu schoolteacher, recalls seeing a ship enter the harbor but thought it was the long-awaited evacuation vessel. It was a Native who gave the alarm. Shortly thereafter gunshots echoed in the Chichagof valley, followed by unintelligible shouting.

According to Mrs. Jones's account, her husband Charles calmly sat at his radio transmitter reporting the attack to Dutch Harbor, then walked outside and gave himself up. Shortly thereafter a Japanese officer entered her cabin, confronting her with a bayonet and demanding, "How many have you here?"

"Two," she replied. "How many are you?"

"Two thousand," was his answer.

A day later the Japanese reported Jones had taken his own life. Subsequent examination of the body, recovered after the war, conclusively ruled out suicide, but except for Jones's execution the Attu prisoners were apparently treated fairly well. For three months they were allowed to remain in their own homes, then evacuated first to Kiska and then to Japan. With them they took personal possessions and furniture. "Everything except our homes," according to Golodoff's account.

"We tell them we didn't want to go but they tell us we must go to Japan and promise us they will take us home again when the war is over," Golodoff remembers. "None of us were scared when they took us on the ship—no women cried."

The Japanese at Kiska were discovered by an LB-30 from the 36th Bomber Squadron on June 8. The Americans had anticipated problems because of the loss of communications on June 6 with Kiska and Attu.

Innokenty "Popeye" Golodoff survived captivity by the Japanese from his village of Attu and moved with his remaining people to Atka to start a new life at the war's end. USF&WS scientists have high regard for Golodoff's knowledge of the Chain.

Once confirmed, there was considerable debate among military strategists as to whether or not the islands were worth fighting for. Authorities tried to temper public outrage by claiming the isolated Chain had little or no military value, but the War Department was embarrassed by the loss and wanted to recapture American soil.

On June 11 the directive was issued to Navy Lt. Comdr. Paul Foley to "coordinate all-out bombing Japs out of Kiska. Keep going until enemy is utterly destroyed or no Catalinas left to fly."

And bomb they did, losing half the PBY fleet to enemy fire and weather within 72 hours. Air Force Col. William Eareckson augmented their efforts with long-range runs from Umnak with little better success, for the Japanese were firmly entrenched.

The Navy, too remote from its targets at Dutch Harbor, based its PBYs at Atka, and on June 12 the Japanese retaliated, bombing that village. Damage was negligible, but as a precaution the Aleuts were ordered to disperse to their summer fish camps which were spread all along the coast.

"That night we saw a glow in the sky and wondered what it was," recalls Vera Nevzoroff, then a girl. "We found the Navy had burned our villages to the ground [to give the Japanese no quarter]. We had taken nothing with us. Nothing except what you take camping. They evacuated us first to Nikolski and then Southeastern. Saint Paul people were on our ship. I remember they had been allowed to pack. Some of them even had their washing machines!"

Akutan Natives were also evacuated along with Aleuts from Nikolski and Unalaska, leaving the Chain without women and bereft of two-thirds of its Aleut population.

There followed a series of sea skirmishes. Prospects brightened when the seaplane tender *Casco* at her station at Atka survived a direct hit from an enemy sub and two PBYs sank the marauder, delivering five prisoners, the first Japanese taken.

At the beginning of 1943 the Navy replaced Rear Adm. Robert Theobald with Rear Adm. Thomas Kincaid as commander of destroyers of the Pacific Fleet, a change that marked a new era of aggressiveness for the Americans.

Left with the seemingly hopeless striking force of two cruisers and four destroyers, Kincaid boldly blockaded Japanese shipping lanes, and under his command the major sea battle of the campaign was fought.

On March 26, 1943, the U.S. naval force commanded by Rear Adm. Charles H. McMorris engaged the Japanese fleet off the Komandorskies. The battle, led by the heavy cruiser *Salt Lake City*, (known as "Old Swayback Maru") lasted three and a half hours, the longest continuous gunnery duel in modern naval history. It dealt decisive blows to Japanese naval strength in the North Pacific.

In the fall of 1942 Americans began to move west. The Air Force selected Tanaga as a base but the harbor was poor, and Navy successfully held out for Adak, which had a fine port. Two transports of troops and an engineering force led by Alaska Scouts made an unopposed landing there August 28, 1942, and began building the major base for the Aleutians.

One of the Scouts, who had trapped on Adak, told the Army engineers there was a natural airfield — Sweeper Creek Lagoon, which at low tide was bare and smooth as a table top. Col. Carlin H. Whitsell and his men bulldozed a dike to divert the creek around the field, and installed a tide gate at the seaward end, open at low tide and closed at high tide. Eleven days after the first troops went ashore, an airfield was ready to launch a 43-plane raid on Kiska September 13.

Quarters were built for 15,000, and by late March 1943, Army, Navy and Air Force had all moved command headquarters to Adak where 96,000 men would be based at the height of the conflict.

Next stop was Amchitka, closer yet to enemy strongholds. Scouting parties under the command of Army Engineer Col. Benjamin Talley found signs the Japanese were surveying for an airstrip on this island, but the major obstacle to American invasion on January 11, 1943, was the weather. Extraordinary Aleutian currents dumped the destroyer *Whorden* on a pinnacle rock and an 80-knot wind and high seas quickly took her to the bottom with 14 men, but 2,100 men made it ashore, entrenched, fended off Japanese air attacks, and managed to have an air base operational by February.

Kiska's mountain peaks can be seen from observation posts at the north end of Amchitka, and U.S. forces made good use of this close proximity, bombarding the enemy daily, sometimes hourly.

Japanese reciprocated to the point that American ground crews became so nervous they once mistook a V of geese for an enemy squadron until an alert spotter reasoned, "They may be Japs but I never seen planes flap their wings before."

Left
This photo taken in December 1942 shows Adak well established as a port. Miles of submarine nets were set out and ultimately helped stymie Japanese efforts to supply Aleutian strongholds.
(National Archives)

Right
Adak Harbor. *A Liberty ship rests at the Adak dock while P-38s and P-40s practice maneuvers in the air above. When this painting was done, in early 1943, Lieutenant Draper was hoping to go with a task force to shell Attu, which was still held by the Japanese. But orders came down transferring Draper to the South Pacific, where he experienced and painted more combat scenes.*

Tired Tigers. *After a long day in the air, the Army's Flying Tigers under Lt. Col. John S. Chennault, son of Major Gen. Claire Chennault, line the field at Umnak. The planes of the Aleutian command had a definite tiger's head with black spots and white teeth, while those used by Chennault in China had the face of the tiger shark. In the background of Draper's 1942 scene is snowy Mount Tulik.*

Arctic Vigil. *A 37mm gun emplacement and tents of the gun crew are pictured against the background of Mount Tulik. Draper stayed at the naval air facility here on Umnak with a group of 300 men. He described the island as "unbelievably beautiful."*

"green" troops were chosen for the Aleutian campaign. It should be remembered that Alaska-based troops could not be used because they were widely scattered in various garrisons. The only large formation was the 4th Infantry Regiment which was too small to undertake an amphibious operation. The 7th Infantry did receive extensive training and was able to make several practice amphibious landings. However, some of the troops' equipment, such as their footgear, was totally inadequate for the semifrozen muskeg. Proper winterization had not been carried out on crafts or guns. Harbor charts were woefully inadequate, the communications system was sometimes worse than none at all, and to make matters worse, security was broken.

A week before the scheduled invasion, May 11, radio newscaster Walter Winchell broadcast the news: "To Mr. and Mrs. America and all the ships at sea . . . Keep your eyes on the Aleutian Islands," and the Japanese dug in in earnest.

The Alaska Scouts left Kodiak for the Aleutians with a weird flotilla of tugs, barges and fishing vessels. Joe Kelly, one of their number from Anchorage, sailed off to battle on a luxury yacht, the *Cavena*, a leisurely trip in which troops sauntered from the "Blue Room" to the "Gold Room" to their staterooms.

The Scouts themselves were equally unorthodox from a military point of view, "volunteers who didn't like the regular infantry," Kelly explains. "They tried to pick someone from every part of Alaska: miners, prospectors, trappers, Natives . . ." all masters at living off the land, crack shots and proven survivors. Their leader, the boyish-looking Col. Lawrence V. Castner, spoke their language and provided them with deadly commando training on which the Aleutian campaign would ultimately hinge.

"Castner's Cutthroats," as the Scouts were called, were green to combat but they were ready. By sad contrast the 10,000 men of the

Japanese bombs did little damage, however. Only two Amchitka casualties were reported before raids ceased entirely in February due to loss of enemy planes.

The Western Defense Command had planned to push next to Kiska, but Admiral Kincaid wrongly estimated enemy strength there at 9,600 (actually 6,000) men, and since the bulk of American sea power was deployed to Guadalcanal and North Africa, it was decided to make Attu the target on the assumption that it was less well fortified.

The charge has often been made that

7th Army Division and its reinforcements were dressed in short-sleeved fatigues, trained for Africa, briefed on tropical diseases (to keep their destination secret) and packed into five overcrowded transports.

At their head was Maj. Gen. Albert E. Brown, distinguished on World War I fronts but with no Aleutian experience. Lt. Gen. John DeWitt of the Western Defense Command had protested Brown's assignment because Brown was openly pessimistic over DeWitt's airy promise to the War Department that Attu could be taken in three days. DeWitt, unfortunately, had been sold on Kincaid's estimate that there were only from 500 to 1,600 Japanese at Attu, while over 2,350 lay in wait for the invaders.

Just after midnight on May 11, 1943, submarines successfully landed Castner's raiders with a crack scout team led by Capt. William Willoughby and 32nd Infantry Regiment on two remote beaches on the north side of Attu. Unnoticed by the enemy, they began pushing their way through snow and murderous terrain toward Japanese headquarters at Holtz Bay and Chichagof Harbor on the northeast end of the island.

By 7:40 that morning the main force of the Attu invasion stood ready to make Army's amphibious landing at Massacre Bay on the south side of the island, but their move was postponed due to fog.

No enemy was seen when they finally hit the beach at 4:20 P.M. but many early casualties were recorded.

"Failure to appreciate the weather conditions to be encountered resulted in seriously embarrassing the landing forces during early phases of the operation," headquarters conceded in a secret report on battle experiences. "Frostbite casualties exceeded battle casualties two to one."

In addition, Americans managed to lose 90 of their landing craft, some with crew, the victims of uncharted reefs, surf, williwaw, life jacket and equipment malfunction. By nightfall the southern forces were stalled; unneeded supplies piled up haphazardly on the beaches while necessary food and equipment were hopelessly delayed offshore and tanks and heavy equipment mired in tundra.

High above, the Japanese watched, snugly entrenched along cloud-shrouded mountain ridges that guarded Jarmin Pass, Brown's chosen route to the enemy stronghold to the north. Next morning the guns of American battleships blasted away at them, but the Japanese stalled the U.S. southern force until the eighth day of battle when our troops to the north began pressing defenders in a classic pincers movement.

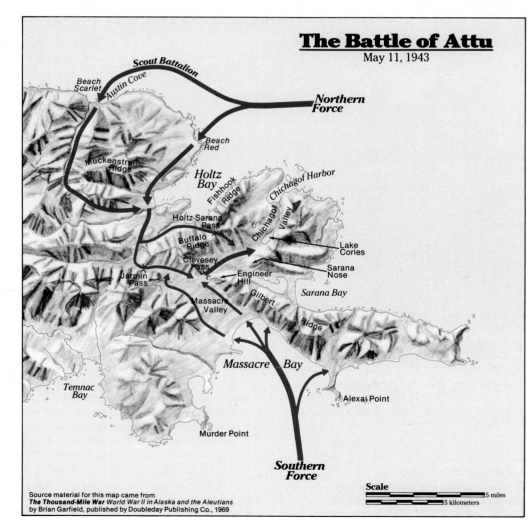

The Battle of Attu
May 11, 1943

Scout Battalion

Beach Scarlet

Austin Cove

Northern Force

Beach Red

Muckenstrum Ridge

Holtz Bay

Fishhook Ridge

Holtz-Sarana Pass

Chichagof Valley

Chichagof Harbor

Buffalo Ridge

Lake Cories

Clevesey Pass

Sarana Nose

Jarmin Pass

Engineer Hill

Sarana Bay

Massacre Valley

Gilbert Ridge

Temnac Bay

Massacre Bay

Alexai Point

Murder Point

Southern Force

Scale

5 miles

5 kilometers

Source material for this map came from
The Thousand-Mile War *World War II in Alaska and the Aleutians*
by Brian Garfield, published by Doubleday Publishing Co., 1969

yet get through to rescue them, but Americans managed to blockade, and with the arrival of Buckner's 4th Infantry, swelling the American ground force to 16,000, the enemy was hopelessly outnumbered.

Japanese bombers succeeded only twice in getting through. During one attack on May 23, six twin engine bombers were shot down by P-38 pilots from the 54th Fighter Group. The American air attacks ate away at Yamasaki's entrenchment. There were reports that Americans were using poison gas—later denied, although poison gas was listed as cargo in at least one Navy report. Stores were getting low and the only hope of the Japanese was to capture the American supply depot and turn American weapons against their foes.

At 3:35 on the morning of May 29, with the bloodcurdling cry of "Banzai," Yamasaki and his men stormed American front lines at Engineer Hill south of Chichagof Valley.

Later Americans were to understand the Japanese "Kamikazi philosophy" that it is

Major General Brown apparently acquitted himself well—the Chief of Staff subsequently cleared his record—but communications with headquarters failed entirely and, unaware of his battle plan, the high command relieved him of duty, replacing him with Gen. Eugene Landrum. At this point in the stalemate there were 12,500 Americans on the island with 1,100 listed as casualties.

As the Scouts and the 32nd Infantry moved into Holtz Bay and the Japanese command headquarters at Chichagof, the foe withdrew,

killing all their men who were too wounded to fight.

"The bodies were still warm when we got there," Joe Kelly remembers grimly. But he brightens as he recounts finding Japanese supply depots filled with tangerines, gin and sake; a welcome respite for the Scouts had been equipped with only one day's food supply.

Col. Yasuya Yamasaki, Attu's able defender, evacuated his remaining men [about 2,000] to the wild heights of Fishhook Ridge to the northeast, holding out hope that ships would

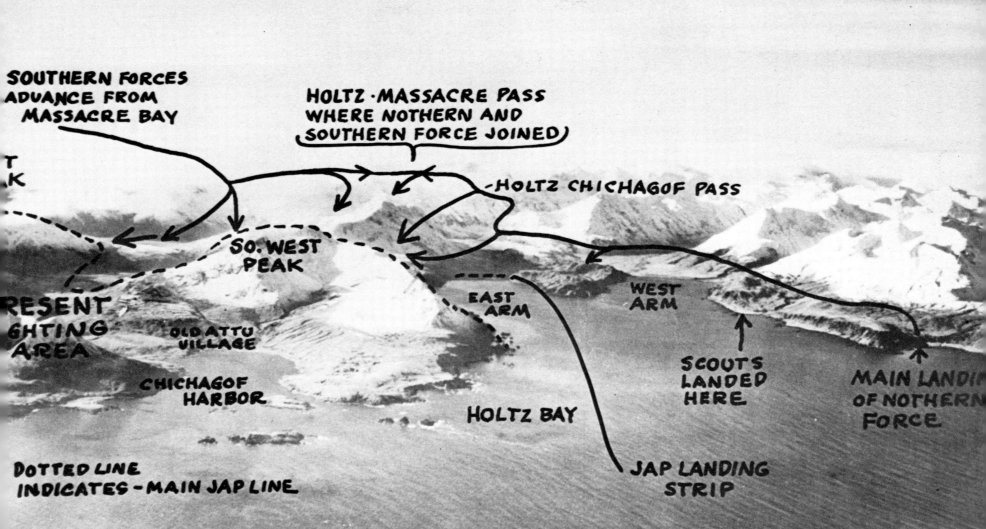

SOUTHERN FORCES
ADVANCE FROM
MASSACRE BAY

HOLTZ · MASSACRE PASS
WHERE NOTHERN AND
SOUTHERN FORCE JOINED

HOLTZ CHICHAGOF PASS

T
K

RESENT
GHTING
AREA

SO. WEST
PEAK

EAST ARM

WEST ARM

OLD ATTU
VILLAGE

SCOUTS
LANDED
HERE

MAIN LANDI
OF NOTHERN
FORCE

CHICHAGOF
HARBOR

HOLTZ BAY

DOTTED LINE
INDICATES - MAIN JAP LINE

JAP LANDING
STRIP

Some formidable and well-equipped Japanese officers as they appeared during the Aleutian campaign, 1942-1943.
(U.S. Navy Photo Lab - Adak, Courtesy of Ernest D. Leet, Lt. Comdr. (Ret.), former O-in-C)

better to die in battle than to surrender, but the concept was new to the green troops at Attu and they fled before Yamasaki's charge. Only the quick thinking of their leaders, Brig. Gen. Archibald Arnold and Col. James Bush, saved the situation. Mustering engineers, medics, some frostbitten infantry men, staffers and the cooks who had been preparing to serve them all breakfast, they defended the brow of the hill and turned the Japanese back.

The enemy regrouped, charged again and again, until there were none left to charge and Colonel Yamasaki had fallen, sword in hand. After 19 days of fighting all that remained was to ferret out remnants of Japanese troops in the mountains. A small number may have escaped by enemy sub but most died by their own hand, with only 28 or 29 prisoners taken. Burial crews counted 2,351 bodies.

Reports vary, but American dead numbered about 550, with 1,135 to 1,150 wounded and another 600 or so put out of action by disease, psychiatric breakdowns and accidents.

In the final days of battle a detachment from the 4th Infantry was moved to establish an air base at Shemya, and by late June American forces geared to invade Kiska. Estimate of enemy strength ranged from 4,000 to 7,000, and Kincaid mustered a landing force of 34,426 men, of which 9,000 were expected to become casualties.

D-Day was set for August 15, and meanwhile Kincaid threw every ship and plane he had into a blockade and bombardment of enemy installations.

Originally the Japanese had planned to evacuate Kiska by sub, but when the blockade made that impossible they boldly dispatched 12 destroyers, newly equipped with radar and counter-radar equipment.

After an aborted attempt in early July, the Japanese fleet returned to Aleutian waters July 24 and played a game of cat and mouse with the American fleet until thick fog served as a cover July 29. Nervously they twice launched torpedoes at suspected enemy targets which turned out to be Little Kiska Island. The Americans were off refueling and re-placing artillery spent earlier in an all-out attack on radar blips that have never been explained.

Two Japanese ships collided, putting one out of action and greatly limiting space for evacuees, but in 30 minutes over 5,000 Japanese soldiers managed to clamber aboard, the fleet upended anchor and made a dash for home.

"We left and went ahead at a speed of 30 knots. The first transport unit spotted a periscope northeast of Kiska, but the submarine immediately disappeared beneath the waves and thereafter wasn't seen again," a Japanese ensign recorded in his diary, captured later.

"At 0600 on the 31st the mist had completely cleared and at 1530 we entered Paramushiro Harbor. It seemed that heaven were celebrating our success . . ."

And, he gloated, it appeared the enemy had not discovered their evacuation.

"Thereafter, for day after day, they bombed and bombarded Kiska and on August 15, the landing of American and Canadian troops on that island was announced. Truly the height of the ridiculous."

Shortly after the evacuation, John Hakla of Seldovia, running a Kiska bombing mission from Umnak, noticed no enemy fire and observed nothing much had changed since his last raid. He mentioned the fact to his commanding officer but was told to forget it. Next mission he made a low reconnaissance and was still unable to raise fire, and he was sure the enemy had fled.

"But nobody wanted to hear about it," he recounts. "I was told the invasion was already planned and it was just too late to cancel. And when I still insisted, they transferred me out."

Americans' chiefs of staff were sure their blockade was tight and argued "evacuation was considered unlikely due to Japanese

Burial crews counted 2,351 Japanese bodies after the battle of Attu. Many died by their own hand (holding hand grenades to their chests) in the best of Japanese tradition which considers surrender to be unthinkable humiliation. This photo was made on the tundra flats between Massacre Bay and Chichagof Harbor and ran in Life *magazine on April 13, 1944, almost a year after the fact, in keeping with a general blackout on news from the Chain.*
(Hanna Collection, Archives, University of Alaska, Fairbanks)

This Navy aerial of Kiska Harbor shows the strength of the Japanese build-up at the time the Americans retook the island. Evacuating Japanese destroyed as much as they could and managed to escape the island without detection.
(National Archives)

policy and psychology and the determined defense of Attu."

Although recon photos didn't show it, the enemy might have entrenched farther inland, they worried. Besides, if they had evacuated, the landing would be "good training, a super dress rehearsal, excellent for training purposes," Kincaid reasoned.

Although the island proved deserted, the "exercise" cost the lives of 24 Americans and one Canadian shot by nervous comrades in the fog, with 31 wounded; and 71 dead, 34 wounded when the destroyer *Abner Read* hit a Japanese mine in Kiska Harbor.

Survivors, who had their troubles with frostbite, trench foot and rough terrain, were greeted by signs reading, "It's all yours, Yank!" plus graffiti maligning Roosevelt and a fantastic number of booby traps and mines.

A small dog, "Explosion," given by Ens. William Jones to the Kiska weather crew before their capture, welcomed occupation forces on the beach and was elated to find his old master among the ranks.

After Kiska, Americans continued to build up their defenses, using the Aleutians as a base from which to bomb the Kuriles, but for most of the tens of thousands of men stationed there, Chain duty proved a long wait under excruciating circumstances for a war that never came.

There was little troop rotation. Some went mad with isolation and boredom. Some succumbed to the elements, because even when bases were built with amenities such as electricity living was still hard. There survives at Adak a poem written on an outhouse wall:

It takes guts to serve your country
As a sailor or Marine
But a man must be a hero
When he visits our latrine.

Entertainers were sent: Olivia DeHaviland, Frances Langford, Joe E. Brown. Bob Hope claimed that the Aleutians were the only place on earth where a man could "walk in mud up to his knees bucking a snowstorm that blew sand in his face, while being pelted in the rear on a sunny day."

Roosevelt came, went fishing, and forgot his dog when he left, and a destroyer was dispatched to Seattle with the pooch. But despite occasional visits from big names, the men felt forgotten. A number, including one of America's most famous contemporary writers, later blamed their homosexuality on their Aleutian experience.

"A woman behind every tree," Bob Hope had quipped, and of course the tundra was treeless.

The only comforting thought was that punishment for minor military infractions would be light. "So what can they do? Send me to the Aleutians?" became the watchword.

After D-Day, pull-out was swift and unceremonious. Food-filled plates were left standing on the tables of remote outposts. At Tanaga men lined up all the base vehicles on the runway, drained the oil and left them running to freeze up. Few cared to stay and only a few ever returned.

Most of the Japanese captives from the Aleutians survived and were released at the war's end. Wylie Hunt and crewmen of his downed PBY came home along with the 10-man weather crew from Kiska. Comdr. William House returned to Adak in 1979 to give the graduation address.

Etta Jones, widow of the Attu teacher, was found to have weathered the war in fair shape, imprisoned much of the time in the Yokohama Athletic and Rowing Club. But from Attu village only 25 of the original 43 captives returned, some having died of tuberculosis complicated by malnutrition and perhaps maltreatment; and a couple (it's rumored) may have elected to remain in Japan.

One Attu child was found to have scars from beatings at the hands of her captors and an unhealed wound on her leg as the result of a stone thrown at her by a guard because she stopped working. However, the Japanese apparently treated the Aleuts better than most American captives, referring to them as "captive guests." The Natives were put to work digging and drying clay to make bricks and, amazingly, were paid a small wage for their labor. Toward the end of the war they were forced to survive on two-thirds of a cup of rice a day, but they ate as well as the guards assigned to them.

And ironically, Aleuts evacuated to Southeastern Alaska fared little better, suffering from lack of good food, housing, medical care and just plain broken hearts. Here, too, only about 50% returned.

Some, who were moved outside the state and forced to adjust to a whole new environment, elected not to return to the Chain, and many who did wished they had not, for little if anything was left of the life they'd known before the war.

American troops on Attu after the U.S. takeover commemorate a portion of the victory.
(William H. Hall Collection)

Aftermath

By Lt. Comdr. (Ret.) Frederick A. Messing
Extracted from his forthcoming book about the Aleutian campaign.

Frederick A. Messing, Lt. Comdr. (Ret.), was a platoon leader in the 50th Engineer Regiment (C). The hill on which the Kamikazi charge was stopped by the Engineers was subsequently named Engineer Hill in their honor.

The toll in dead and wounded wasn't great in our regiment. In fact, considering the heavy losses some of the infantry regiments had suffered, our 50th Engineer Regiment (C) had come out lightly. Nevertheless, losses in battle, no matter how light, are always taken hard by some or all of a unit.

I remember that a young, personable, stalwart lieutenant from Headquarters Company had been killed and everyone mourned his loss. In our company we had an outstanding buck sergeant and several other fine young men killed and a number wounded—and with the exception of all but two companies, every other unit of the regiment had losses in killed or wounded.

Our 2nd Battalion had suffered its heaviest toll when the Japanese, in a desperate Kamikazi charge, had broken through the infantry and run through our encampment in the wee hours of the morning while we were sleeping. (Some of our men were bayoneted in their sleeping bags.)

After running through our encampment, they had formed in a group on a hill and the cleanup, by members of the 2nd Battalion that followed, had also taken its toll before the Japanese were completely eliminated.

Company A, of the 1st Battalion, situated by itself on top of a hill, building a road to the front line, had also been overrun by a Japanese force and had been run out of its encampment but had regrouped a few hours later and in turn had eliminated the intruders. When I passed the A Company area a few days later, the burnt remnants of the mess and supply tents were still standing. Some of the Japanese who had seized the mess tent were slumped over the mess stoves and had probably been killed while eating American S.O.S. or whatever was on the menu the morning of the 29th of May, 1943, on the island of Attu in the Aleutians.

A friend of mine from Company F visited me after the battle. He told me that the young first sergeant of the company had been killed leading a part of the counteroffensive against the Japanese. He was only 21 but had been an outstanding topkick. When I had first joined the 50th Engineer Regiment (C), I had initially been assigned to Company F and during the trials and tribulations of putting our newly-formed company through basic training, the first sergeant and I had become fast friends.

He was basically a real gentleman and an outstanding soldier even at the tender age of 21. He had two loves, his family and the U.S. Army and he died in defense of both.

When my friend told me that the "Top" had died, my eyes watered and I turned away. I didn't cry but I wish I had. I believe that if I had, some of the seething turmoil that was in my mind at the time would have been released and I would have been a better man for it.

Attu backpackers hike a peaceful trail west of the area that in 1943 echoed with frenzied cries of "Banzai!" as Japanese troops swarmed out of the fog in a Kamikazi attack on Engineer Hill (inset). The 50th Engineer Regiment withstood the charge, turning the assault into an American victory.
(Inset photo by Alan Dudley)

WORLD WAR II FORGOTTEN

Congress is considering a proposal to clear World War II debris from the Aleutians, a service the United States government performed for the Japanese and Germans but failed to offer the Aleuts.

Price tag for a thorough job is a staggering $117,246,107 (1976 dollars) and a partial cleanup would cost $22,423,180 by conservative estimates. However, deterioration over the last few years has made old installations extremely hazardous near populated areas.

Also long overdue for consideration is official designation of Attu and Kiska battlefields as national monuments. The National Park Service has undertaken preservation of South Pacific battlefields, but the Aleutians were not even nominated for consideration until 1977 and the initial proposal has been returned for more information.

While little remains of Attu's fierce fight except bomb-pocked hills, Japanese fortifications are still in place on Kiska. Souvenir hunters have ripped off smaller items, but antiaircraft guns are still aimed at American approach routes, a rusting mini-sub stands in its dock, and bombed-out Japanese ships litter the magnificent harbor.

In 1978 relatives of the Japanese dead journeyed to both Kiska and Attu to pay homage and erect markers, but the only American token is a small brass marker in honor of the Aleuts of Attu village and a second plaque for the Japanese general who led the charge against American troops on that island.

The recently formed Alaska Historical Aircraft Society made its first reconnaissance of the Chain in 1978 and reported a good number of unique craft, but formidable red tape is involved in restoration and funding is also a problem.

Grant Hale, Air Force historian, reports with disappointment that the *Time-Life* series on World War II wrongly states Guam was the first American soil retaken from Japanese forces, with no mention of the Aleutian campaign.

"How quickly people forget," he observes. Except for families of the dead and the Aleut people for whom the past is too painfully close to ignore.

Above
The original Japanese shrine erected on Kiska in 1942 was left umolested by Americans when they recaptured the territory. In 1978 a party of Japanese survivors of Kiska and relatives of Japanese soldiers who died in the Chain traveled to this island and established new markers in memory of their lost comrades and relatives.
(Charles A. Simenstad, reprinted from *ALASKA*® magazine)
Right
Late winter's snow cannot disguise the stark ruins of World War II on the hillside above the cemetery at Unalaska.
(Stephen Bingham)

Left
Dutch Harbor and Unalaska are viewed through the rusting skeleton of a World War II Quonset hut.
(Tim Thompson, reprinted from *ALASKA*® magazine)

Above
The SeaBees have been busy burying massive dumps established on Adak during World War II. They have successfully covered and reseeded three of them, but this one remains to illustrate the scope of the job they tackled. Mind-boggling as it looks, it is heaven for collectors of old airplane parts.

Left
Quonset hut art on Amchitka, with Sad Sack on right.
(Charles A. Simenstad)

Above
Old military housing at Dutch Harbor is a snowy ghost town.
(Bob Nelson)

Left
Japanese guns still guard Kiska Harbor, one of the finest harbors in the Chain. Dozens of guns on Kiska and neighboring Little Kiska wait expectantly for American attackers. One still has a live shell jammed in its firing mechanism.

Right
Detail of Japanese antiaircraft gun at Kiska Harbor. This one is aimed at the Kiska volcano over which American flyers homed in on foggy days, flying blind over the Japanese installations.

Left
A Japanese mini-sub rusts quietly on its drydock at Kiska. The two-man craft was powered by batteries which can still be seen through a gash in the sub's side.

Above
Dangerous ammunition, unstable after nearly 40 years of rough Aleutian weather, litters Kiska.

Left
An abandoned church marks one of the bloodiest battlefields of the Aleutian campaign at Massacre Valley, Attu, where American troops were stalled for days by the enemy holed up on the hills above them. The building has deteriorated almost beyond repair, but trees planted around it by American soldiers have flourished.

Above
World War II pinups at Casco Cove Quonset hut, Attu.
(Charles A. Simenstad)

Right
A U.S. gun emplacement overlooks the Japanese airport area at East Holtz Bay, Attu. Americans fought bitterly to take this ground from the invaders who held it for almost a year. The Japanese airstrip, never completed, is in the distance near the edge of the bay.

A blaze of fireweed relieves the bleak stare of deserted barracks at Dutch Harbor (above), *where World War II's hollow relics waste away in row after desolate row* (right).☐
(Both by David W. Shapiro)

. . . It is a new day
The door of your room is closing.

14
Post War

At the outbreak of World War II there were only about 100 houses in the Aleutians, excluding the traditional *barabaras,* and no docks beyond Dutch Harbor and Kanaga. During the military campaign over 100,000 were housed here and when they pulled out the ghost towns they abandoned were off-limits to returning Aleuts, regardless of their needs.

Magnificent docks had been built throughout the Chain, augmented by a network of airfields, but at the war's end there was no provision for maintenance and these assets were eaten away by the wild Aleutian weather—roughly $100 million in construction costs shot to the winds.

More appalling, the most traditional Aleut villages had been destroyed in the conflict and those left standing were in shambles. Attu, described by a visiting botanist in the 1930s as a "little Eden," had been bombed flat by American forces in an attempt to retake the island from the enemy, and when Aleuts returned to California from Japanese prisons they were informed they would not be allowed to resettle, or even to move back to the Chain.

Desperately homesick, in most cases physically ill, the Attuans protested until they were sent to Seattle, and continued to protest until at last they were allowed to go back to the Aleutians. The government would not let them move to Attu because authorities argued they could not properly look after wards in such a remote location, but instead they sponsored resettlement at Atka, stronghold of Attu's traditional enemies.

With the exception of two private homes, Atka had also been destroyed. Now the government rebuilt, using surplus lumber from Aleutian bases. Homes went back on original lots, complete with plumbing except in the case of Attu people, who were excluded by virtue of being latecomers.

The handsome church at Nazan Bay was rebuilt in exact replica, but gone were the valuable icons which had graced it and gone, too, was the smaller church the village had built at their trapping base, Amchitka.

Even more severe was loss of leadership. Attu's bright, gentlemanly chief, Mike Hodikoff, died in Japan, and most Atka elders perished in Southeast Alaska. Survivors were hard put to pass on even basic survival skills—trapping, weaving and sewing—to a generation of uprooted youngsters.

Elsewhere, Aleut homecomings were almost as painful.

"Those of us who survived to return to Unalaska almost wished we had been among the dead," one refugee recalls. "Our houses were standing but there was nothing left. Soldiers had even shot through the walls just to entertain themselves. And we just lost heart."

A recently declassified Navy report dismisses the ruin of Native villages as no great loss, insisting most of the homes were in bad repair and dirty at the time of occupation; noting scornfully that there were no locks on the doors, ignoring any implication of trust that a lockless community might show.

A reporter for the Army magazine *Yank* saw things differently though:

"Before the war [the Aleuts] had lived in surprisingly fine homes considering their complete isolation. They often had linoleum and modern stoves and chrome ash trays and running water and gas illumination. On Attu the homes averaged about five rooms apiece. Their church was electrically lighted. Amer-

Some of the old World War II barracks at Dutch Harbor have been converted to rental duplexes, a boon to a community where housing is scarce.
(David W. Shapiro)

ican traders, looking for fox furs, had brought these tokens of civilization," he wrote.

"But Aleutian weather and three years of neglect had taken its toll, while GI moonlight requisitions and souvenir hunters did the rest . . . During the rough days of 1942 and 1943 plywood was very precious in the Aleutians. GIs discovered that Native houses were lined with plywood and they requisitioned it to line their foxholes. Glass windows and frames appeared in observation foxholes on temporary duty from abandoned Aleut homes. Souvenir hunters grabbed other choice items."

Many from smaller, more remote villages were encouraged to move "temporarily" to larger settlements, and although a fair number tried to resettle Biorka, Kashega, Makushin and other strongholds of the past, they were eventually discouraged.

The government attempted to make restitution for possessions destroyed under military occupation, but confusion reigned. The first Bureau of Indian Affairs (BIA) resettlement officer was "too lost in his assignment to accomplish this or administer the resettlement of the Aleutians properly," his superior confessed in a letter to the home office. A second man foisted off the job on Verne Robinson, then serving as marshal of Unalaska.

"There was a shipping bill for all kinds of stuff to be distributed: boats, victrolas, fishing gear . . . but just a part of it showed up," Robin-

Top
Sergie Golley opened his store at Atka during the trapping era and is still in business in the same shop. His house was one of two spared when the Navy burned Atka village.

Above
Atka berry pickers head back to the village as a storm descends. Destroyed by the Navy in 1942 to deny facilities to the invading Japanese, Atka was rebuilt after the war by Atkans and villagers from Attu.

Below
A modest celebration was held May 6, 1945, for Aleuts returning to Unalaska, but it didn't cushion the shock of discovering their homes were all but destroyed. From left: Gregory Shapsnikoff, Leonty Merculief, Carl Moller, Benjamin Golodoff and Nick Chagin.
(National Archives)

Right
The Russian Orthodox Church of the Holy Ascension of Christ and the Bishop's house are shown on a calm day at Unalaska.
(Lee Goodman)

son recalls. "Some of them got a lot, some didn't get anything."*

Results of settlement requested for Attu prisoners of war remain equally fuzzy and, as of 1951, no one had figured out how to cash the Japanese paychecks issued survivors for their work at the prison camps, although the Japanese government was apparently willing to honor them.

Even health care was neglected. Teachers sent to "rehabilitate" Natives on Atka in 1946 found them crowded together in partially built houses or living in tents and unusually susceptible to tuberculosis and other diseases.

The national death rate was 40.1 per 100,000; the Alaskan rate 359 per 100,000, and the rate for Alaska Natives was 765 per 100,000, with Aleuts in the upper percentile. Yet the government hospital at Unalaska was never rebuilt, leaving the Aleut region the only one in the state without a Native health facility.

And economically, returning Aleuts were handed additional defeats. When the government contacted Harold Bowman and other fur dealers to see if they wished to renew their fox farm permits in 1946, they declined, leaving remote villagers without traders or an income to trade.

The large number of military land withdrawals on the Chain stymied USF&WS, but there was little the refuge could do about it during the war and early postwar period.

"When you have an elephant by the leg, it is better to go along with him," refuge manager H. Douglas Gray reasoned upon returning to the islands at the close of the war. Eventually a compromise was worked out for joint military and USF&WS jurisdiction over areas required for military use.

---

*Note: The U.S. Senate just passed legislation to create a commission to study these inequities and as we go to press it is being considered by the House of Representatives.

Atka community requested permission to trap on its own island, Amlia, Adak, Kagalaska and Amchitka, but was told it must obtain permission from the military; this started a maze of paper problems. In 1947 Atkans trapped on Amchitka but lack of market discouraged further efforts.

The Attuans were granted permission to trap at their former homeland, Agattu and Semichi, provided they secured permission from the military, but transportation was nonexistent even if permission came through. Unalaska people were given a permit on Carlisle for one year only; Nikolski was offered Tanaga, Yunaska and Chuginadak; they trapped Tanaga in 1947, but few of these islands were prime trapping ground and the fur market sank as Natives wrestled with red tape.

Fishing was also poor. Military builders had filled in rich herring spawning lagoons of Unalaska, and codfish were fast disappearing. Oil spillage from military vessels had taken a heavy toll.

Marines return from patrol, July 1978, at Adak. Shagak Bay is in the background.
(Ed Reynolds)

During the war many Aleuts had done well at mainland jobs.

"They were industrious and steady," *Yank* Magazine reported. "They were anxious to avoid government help, to make their own living, and many got jobs with Alaska defense industries and at shipbuilding, mining and carpentry work. The evacuated natives soon managed to be self-supporting."

Almost no jobs were available on the Chain, however. Aleuts sometimes traveled great distances to find seasonal work, but at home the only option seemed to be living off the land.

The only continuous military presence in the Chain after Japanese surrender was Adak, reduced to housekeeping status by the Army, turned over to the Air Force in 1948 and then the Navy in 1950. Base population had dwindled to 1,500 when military planners took

Left
The latest in U.S. listening hardware crowns an American ship slipping quietly into Adak Harbor.

Lower left
There is a great deal of new housing and other construction at the naval base at Adak. In terms of population, this is the largest settlement on the Chain, though non-Aleut; and the station farthest west in the United States where military dependents are allowed to reside.

Below
The Coast Guard buoy tender Ironwood *has a permanent dock at Adak as a base for its work throughout the Chain. With its round hull this ship rolls even in the calm water of the harbor.*
(Michael Gordon)

Left
Coastguardsmen muster for early morning inspection at the tiny Coast Guard installation on Attu. The site was long held by invading Japanese and was rewon by American troops only after a long and bloody battle. Reflections in the photo represent rain on the camera lens.

Below
A Coast Guard plane lands at Attu on a rare clear day. Formidable mountains make landing impossible if the weather is thick. The Coast Guard LORAN Station still utilizes a World War II runway which is in bad shape and will require repairs in the neighborhood of $1 million to bring it up to safe standards.

a second look at the island's strategic importance and, in 1971, transferred Fleet Air Alaska Command there from Kodiak, closing out all other bases in the state. Wildlife refuge headquarters moved from Cold Bay to Adak in 1972. A number of World War II facilities, including airstrip and warehouses, were rejuvenated, modern housing added and an average population of 5,000 now makes this the largest settlement on the Chain, though non-Aleut.

Kiska had been abandoned almost immediately. Atka was under caretaker status in 1944. Troops moved out of Amchitka for good in 1950. After serving as a fueling stop for transports on the Great Circle Route, Shemya was abandoned in 1951, then taken over by Northwest Airlines as a refueling stop. In 1958 during the Cold War, the Air Force reclaimed the island, turning it into a top secret installation, which it remains today.

Distant Early Warning (DEW Line) stations were established at Scotch Cap and Nikolski, but phased out in the late 1970s.

The huge installations Americans built at Attu were evacuated in 1949 and eventually turned over to the Coast Guard, which now maintains a 30-man Loran station there. The isolated outpost has no vessel, but recruits gamely promise to feed any shipwreck victim who can swim ashore, and, since most of the lighted nav aids in the Chain were recently discontinued, their electronic beacons are very important.

Another Aleutian Coast Guard station, long maintained at Scotch Cap, closed in 1979, but the USF&WS has established an outpost there along with a station at Amchitka and field camp at Attu.

The Navy was unsuccessful in interesting Coast Guard in its Dutch Harbor facilities, so the land was put up for bid as surplus. Some of it was sold before Alaskans learned about the listing and protests from Unalaska residents eventually blocked sale of the rest.

Left
Shemya is one of the few World War II Aleutian sites still maintained. Today it is a top-secret installation where outsiders are not permitted to land without clearance.

Above
Shemya personnel participate in survival suit training in the chill waters of Alcan Harbor.
(William Henry)

169

One look at a navigation chart of Adak waters shows a "Chemical Munitions Dump Area" blanketing a large offshore area. Then along came the Department of Defense, working on a volatile project "vital to national security."

Initially it seemed a mission of peace, the testing of a "small" 80-kiloton hydrogen bomb (four times more powerful than we dropped on Japan) to gather important data for monitoring worldwide seismic detection systems. The detonation, code name "Long Shot," occurred October 18, 1965, and was declared a success although it produced a continuing tritium leak.

From the mid-1960s on, it was explained that the Atomic Energy Commission had decided weapons tests of larger magnitude must be moved away from Nevada, "where they may have adverse effects on Las Vegas." Amchitka, more than 1,000 miles from a population center, was the choice because "no realistic alternative is believed to exist anywhere else on American soil," according to an AEC public relations spokesman.

The second shot, "Milrow," October 2, 1969, was a 1.2-megaton "calibration test" to see if the island could stand the shock of a larger explosion. It worried conservatives who predicted the next test might be as much as two megatons, but they were wrong. What AEC had in mind was "Cannikin," a 5-megaton explosion—250 times more powerful than Hiroshima.

Governor William Egan, who with many other Alaskans feared the blast, invited AEC head James Schlesinger to bring his family if he thought the test would be safe and Schlesinger arrived at the scene with his wife and two of his eight children. They encamped in a specially built bomb shelter at the farthest end of the island. The test of the Spartan missile warhead was absolutely necessary to get the weapon into production, the AEC head explained.

In vain, Alaskans and anti-nuclear groups

protested. "STOP CANNIKIN, BOMB LAS VEGAS NOT AMCHITKA" signs blossomed—Reeve still has one on the airport wall at Adak. But by a narrow margin the U.S. Supreme Court rejected a plea to halt the test.

The nuclear device, buried 5,875 feet below the ground surface, went off November 6, 1971, registering 7 on the Richter scale and unexpectedly creating a large lake by draining five small ones. Sea cliffs fell, the intertidal bench rose on the Bering side.

No escaped radiation was detected and Schlesinger pronounced the event a success on the spot.

Scientists hired by AEC to follow up did note "the effects of Cannikin on geomorphic fea-

A simple plaque marks the site of the Atomic Energy Commission's "Cannikin" testing at Amchitka. One of the surprises of the testing was the creation of a large lake where there had been five small ones. Scientists who monitor the site annually report no dangerous radiation in the area where the controversial blast was detonated in 1971.

tures were considerably greater than predicted," and that counts showed "evidence of a real decline in sea otter population on both coasts adjacent to Cannikin" after the test. But no increase in background radiation levels attributable to Cannikin have been reported.

Whether the estimated $325 million the government spent on blasting Amchitka was worth it remains to be seen, and more puzzling is the terse announcement that "no further tests are planned for the Aleutians."

Although AEC drilled four additional blast holes at the time of Cannikin, the agency pulled out, at least temporarily. AEC monitors Amchitka yearly, but the possibility of leakage is considered so remote that the USF&WS has returned the site to peaceful pursuits: recovery of the endangered Aleutian Canada goose.

In the era of quiet that followed this period, there began a subtle renaissance. Aleuts, at first denied eligibility in the statewide Native land claims suit against Congress because of their high percentage of Russian blood, fought for and won the right to participate, and suddenly there was new pride in being Aleut.

Their soft musical language, long forbidden in public schools, could now be taught. Cultural heritage projects became popular.

Finally the fully chartered Aleut Corporation evolved with 38.2 million acres of land and about $12 million from the congressional claims settlement. Corporation management featured, on the cover of its first stockholders' report, a large map of the Aleutians with a tiny inset of the state of Alaska.

This was one of the smallest of the Native regional corporations and failure was predicted. Leadership was thin because so many Aleuts had left Alaska for want of job opportunities. Problems of transportation and communication were worse than those which faced other Native corporations in the state. But guided by a tradition of 8,000 years, the Aleuts invested in the sea, in fishing and supply boats, and—despite bloody corporate infighting reminiscent of Aleut wars of old—the corporation has managed to survive and to show great promise.

The nonprofit Aleut League, devoted to development and delivery of social services to the Aleut people, merged in 1977 with the

Right
Paul Slevert keeps a steady eye on the Coast Guard LORAN system at the base at Attu.

Lower right
During the 1976 king crab season at Unalaska, one of the first—and longest—strikes hit the industry. In an act of animosity toward the crew of the Royal Atlantic, *a boat which effectively broke the strike, other fishermen did a paint job which stated their feelings loud and clear.*
(Richard Eggemeyer)

Below
Aleuts have long been disturbed by the fact that map makers reduce their islands in size and append them as an inset on most Alaska maps. For the first cover of their annual stockholders' report after the land claims settlement, they reversed the process, giving the Chain the advantage.

The Aleut Corporation
1972 ANNUAL REPORT

Aleutian Planning Commission to form the Aleutian/Pribilof Islands Association, Inc.

Unalaska's village corporation, which fell heir to military installations including a fine dock and airfield which could be leased for high stakes, became the first in Alaska to pay a dividend to stockholders. Other villages in remote areas lack Unalaska's economic leverage, but most have been conservative in handling their windfalls. And some of the poorer villages are at last attracting federal grants, which have long flooded other areas of the state, for much-needed housing and economic development projects.

More important, perhaps, are two recent federal government actions affecting foreign fishing off the Aleutians. Changes in the International North Pacific Fishery Convention regulating the foreign harvest of salmon on the high seas have moved the Japanese high seas fleet farther from the Aleutians, affording greater protection for Alaska stocks. In addition, the establishment of 200-mile limit for foreign fishing under the Fishery Conservation and Management Act of 1976 has kept foreigners seeking non-salmon stocks out of Aleutian waters, except in cases where Americans cannot take the available catch. The FCMA has also contributed to a more enthusiastic climate of economic development in commercial fisheries off Alaska, from which the people of the Aleutians could benefit.

With other areas in the state overfished, the industry is at last turning to the rich waters of the Bering Sea, so once again the Aleutian Chain has a strategic place on the map.

Below
Aleut elder Sergie Sovoroff and Father Paul Merculief of Nikolski participated in the discussions and presentations that highlighted the first Aleutian/Pribilof conference held in Unalaska in November 1977.
(Aleutian/Pribilof Islands Association)

Above
Lillie McGarvey was one of the early organizers of the Aleut League, and today is on the Board of Directors of the Aleut Corporation. Her major field of concern has been health care, and she has served on both state and national boards for Native health services.
(Aleutian/Pribilof Islands Association)

Right
A traditional Aleut village on Unalaska Island, Chernofski was decimated by a flu epidemic in 1919-1920 and survivors moved elsewhere except for a few who stayed on to work on a sheep ranching operation established there. The U.S. military built a base here but it, too, was abandoned. Today military docks are used for storage of crab pots, and promoters eye the site as a prospective base for a large bottomfishing operation. The sheep ranch, long run by Milt Holmes, is still active.

Left
Atka had an ambitious paint-up/fix-up housing program in 1978, the first since the village was rebuilt in 1945. It still looks almost the same, however, set amidst its changeless hills and islands, as it did in its heyday during the rich fox trapping years of the 1920s.

Below
World War II veteran Simeon Pletnikoff, who fought the Japanese in the Aleutians in 1943, receives one of eight decorations presented to him in 1978. The fact that Pletnikoff was eligible for all eight awards did not come to light until 35 years after the military service for which he earned the decorations.
(U.S. Army Photo by Victor Johanson)

Above
Many Aleuts who escaped the Japanese invasion of the Chain joined the U.S. Armed Forces during World War II and served with distinction. Here Roxanne Stepetin of Saint Paul proudly tries on a medal awarded to her grandfather, Dan Prokopeuff of Atka.

Left
The Russian Orthodox Church at Attu was destroyed in the battle when Americans retook that island from the Japanese, but recently one of its treasured church bells was located on a distant beach by Fish and Wildlife personnel. Here it is loaded aboard USF&WS boat, Aleutian Tern, *for delivery to Atka, where the Attuans were resettled.*

Below
Former members of the Amchitka Masonic Club would now find their headquarters serving as a comfortable private home.
(Forrest B. Lee)

Left
A gold strike at Unga at the end of the 19th century resulted in construction of a model town, which thrived for a few boom years before the main vein of gold ran out. Mining continued on a limited scale into the 1930s. Virtually a ghost town now, Unga still looks imposing from a distance.

Above
The last holdout at Unga is Maggie Johanson, who still maintains her house in the ghost town. Currently she is renting it to a young couple who appreciate its vintage.

Above
Fishing nets, glass floats and a starfish decorate this Christmas tree, Aleutian style.
(Lorie Kirker)

Left
The most successful Aleutian rancher to date, Milt Holmes hauls wood for kindling at his Chernofski ranch.
(Milt Holmes)

177

Left
At anchor off Agattu Island is Aleutian Tern, *the USF&WS boat.*
Below
The Aleut Provider, *a supply ship serving the Aleutians and Pribilofs, is based in Seattle.*
(Tim Thompson)

A New England-style dory lies aweathering in the fields of Little Koniuji Island in the Shumagins.
(R.H. Day)

Left
Japanese freighters are an increasingly common sight at Unalaska/Dutch Harbor, especially during crab season when foreigners constitute the largest percentage of the buyers. Despite heavy traffic, Unalaska has no harbor master, and harbor pilots are flown in from Anchorage to handle traffic.

Below
A landing craft from the Bureau of Indian Affairs' ship, North Star, *brings annual supplies to Atka village.*
(Paul Eskelin)

Right
North Star *captain passes out candy to eager young people at Atka.*
(Paul Eskelin)

Left
The anniversary of the Unalaska Recreation Center's founding was observed with a party in the fall of 1978. Agnes and Sergie Sovoroff are in line for some of the anniversary cake, served by Irene McGlashan.

Right
Philemon Tutiakoff prepares for his class in baidarka *construction at the Unalaska school. The school district has an active Aleut cultural heritage program, and Tutiakoff is a master carver.*

Below
Anna McGlashan instructs a class in Aleut basketry at the Unalaska School library. There are many non-Aleuts in the class, and although it was not a skill traditionally demonstrated by men, these young men seem to enjoy the challenge.

Flora Tutiakoff of Unalaska and Anesia Kudrin of Akutan discuss the concerns of their communities at the first Aleutian/Pribilof Conference at Unalaska, November 1977.
(Aleutian/Pribilof Islands Association)

Below
Long an important cannery site, Squaw Harbor recently slowed production, the school closed down and the town is virtually deserted.

Above
The orderly community of Nikolski on Umnak Island faces 7,050-foot Mount Vsevidov. Father Veniaminov once reported there were 20 Aleut villages on Umnak; today Nikolski is the sole settlement. One of the Chain's most important anthropological sites is located at Chaluka, Nikolski village. (Douglas W. Veltre)

Right
Because its fleet is almost all locally owned and fishing has been consistently good here over the years, Sand Point can boast the second highest per capita income of any small town in the state. This is the most modern of the Aleut villages, with two canneries currently in operation.

In the introduction to a handbook on Aleut grammar written for government personnel during World War II, Fredericka Martin noted the Natives of the Aleutians had developed a "fanatical devotion to their language as their only cultural heritage, the only bond that holds them together as a distinct people.

"The Czarist Russian conquest of the proud, independent sea hunters was so devastatingly thorough that tribal traditions, even tribal memories were obliterated."

During early occupation, however, Aleuts were compelled to learn Russian to communicate with their overseers. Russian words were (and are) naturally used in Aleut conversations for things the conquerors had introduced—*sobaka* for dog, *koffia* for coffee—and for dealings with the Russian Orthodox Church, the faith Aleut people embraced in place of their own.

And it is not surprising that, after more than 200 years of Russian contact, Russian traditions have become Aleut traditions. Because they are strongly rooted in the Russian Orthodox faith, Aleuts celebrate two sets of holidays, the American (western) Christmas and New Year's and those recognized by the traditional church calendar which fall a couple of weeks after the American versions.

Russian recipes remain favorites: *peruga* or *pirox,* Russian fish pie, which is a splendid way to utilize local salmon; *boska* and *kulich,* Easter cakes; *pirozhkies,* deep-fried pastries stuffed with meat; and *alodiks,* fried bread.

Most Aleut family names are Russian: Prokopeuff, Nevzoroff, Shaishnikoff, Pletnikoff. Russian surnames—Agafangel, Sofia, Dmitri, Vasha—remain popular.

The bright candy colors of the Orthodox churches — rich pastel shades of pink, lavender, yellow, blue and green — brighten many Aleut homes. Russian-style storm porches — collidors — front even modern Aleut homes. The *bonia,* Russian forerunner of the sauna, remains an Aleut delight. And most village-based Aleuts are still inveterate tea drinkers, a definite heritage from their Russian past.

Above
The onion-domed cupolas and unmistakable crosses of the Orthodox Church are outlined against a bright sky at Unalaska. One of the accepted explanations of the slanted bar on the Orthodox cross is rooted in the belief that Christ, suffering and dying on the cross as true Man, twisted the footbar in his agony.
(David W. Shapiro)

Right
Priest and altar boys are surrounded by the sacred icons of their faith during celebration of the Sacred Liturgy at Unalaska's Church of the Holy Ascension of Christ.
(Terry Domico: Earth Images)

Left

Nick Lekanoff works on restoration of the Bishop's house at Unalaska. This house was built by the Alaska Commercial Company for Bishop Nestor (formerly Baron Nicholas Zass) in 1882. It cost $3,634.15, and an additional $2,671.27 was charged for the Russian school which was attached to the house. Restoration work is being done by the Ounalashka Corporation through the Unalaska Development Corporation, with the intention of turning the historic building into a museum.

Below

An elaborately decorated star is carried by Orthodox children as they go caroling from house to house at Atka. The starring ceremony originated in the Ukraine and southern provinces of Russia. It has remained a colorful feature of Christmas observance among the Aleut people.
(Paul Eskelin)

Left

The Orthodox churches of the Aleutians are adorned with colorful and often priceless icons.
(Lorie Kirker)

Below

This gravestone is located at the site of Korovinski, about 10 miles from the present village of Atka. The site was occupied from 2,000 years ago through the Russian period and abandoned by the mid-1870s. The stone commemorates the death on February 5, 1837 of Georgii Netzvetov. He was the father of the first priest on Atka, Jacob Netzvetov. Jacob arrived on Atka, with his father and wife, on June 15, 1829.
(Douglas W. Veltre)

187

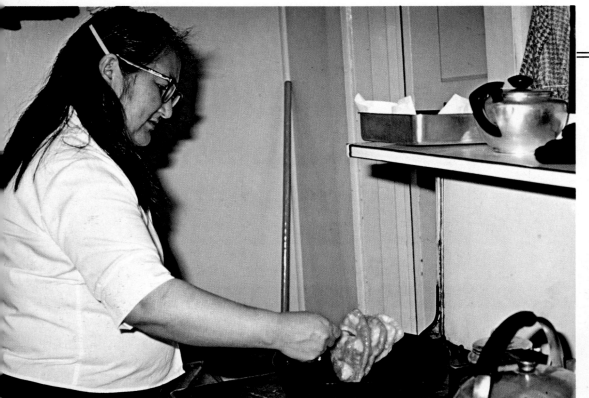

Below
The late Polly Lekanoff of Unalaska helped to prepare the church she loved for its 150th anniversary celebration.

Right
Regularly attended by about 99% of the village population, this small church at Atka is a focal point of village life. It is an exact replica of an earlier building burned by the American military when Japanese invasion was imminent.□

Above
Lydia Dirks of Atka demonstrates the preparation of an Aleut favorite, fried bread or alodiks. A staple originally introduced by the Russians, fried bread takes the place of toast, and also is sometimes served with sugar or jam as a dessert.

Right
Russian treats are featured on a food table, highlighted by a gleaming samovar, at the Unalaska Arts and Crafts Fair.
(Lorie Kirker)

Let the quiet of the eagle high in flight,
Let the grave crashing of magnificent wings,
Let your silence, your history, answer
your children's call.

15
The Future

In 1975 Unalaska wasn't even on the National Marine Fisheries Service list of top U.S. fishing ports in terms of money made and poundage taken, but a year later it was in second place for the nation with $48.3 million in crab landed. By 1978 it had far surpassed Kodiak, Alaska, formerly number two, and had edged out San Pedro, California, for number one spot with a $99.7 million catch.

Sand Point has the second highest per capita income of any small town in Alaska (next to Valdez) and its future looks even brighter because the fleet is locally owned.

Biggest moneymaker at the moment is crab, mainly king but with developing markets for tanner. While some other areas in Alaska have been over-fished, biologists record good escapement for the growing Bering Sea fleet, while a promising bottomfish market has yet to be tapped.

Several multimillion-dollar boats have already been built for the Bering Sea, utilized now for salmon, crab, herring and shrimp, ready to convert for bottomfishing if the price rises, and planners are talking shore-based processing plants that will hire several thousand people.

Seaweed, an important food resource elsewhere in the world, is found in the Aleutians in marketable quantities, but is not being utilized as a resource.

The oil industry is eyeing off-waters of the Chain with considerable interest. Preparations for a lease sale on the north Aleutian shelf are scheduled to begin in 1980 with sale decision to be announced in 1983.

At Unga, resale of the famous Apollo through state auction encountered litigation problems, but, while much mineral potential of the Chain has yet to be explored, the current resurgence of interest in the gold and silver market has reawakened the name of Unga in many minds.

There are numerous sources of geothermal energy in the Aleutians, but as yet they are too remote from population centers for commercial use.

Tourism is being pioneered in areas where hunting and fishing are good. Sports hunting for brown bear and caribou are particularly popular on Unimak, and Adak also offers good caribou hunting. Bird watchers, too, are becoming more interested in the Chain. And should World War II battlefields become na-tional monuments or parks, they will attract more visitors.

Aleuts, who now control most of the land in private hands, are beginning to profit from these various industries, and increased interest in the Aleutians should add to their prosperity, although prospect of future booms is not heartening to most.

"We have lived in these islands for years—without Reeve Airways, processors, war, Bureau of Indian Affairs, disease, growing trees, farms; and just got by on a little trade," muses Phil Tutiakoff, an Unalaska Native who's weathered the worst of it. He has stayed on the Chain for the reason most Aleuts have stayed: because he loves the remote beauty of his land and is proud of his people's great heritage. Preservation of these values will be vitally important to the future if Aleut thought prevails.

A lone fisherman enjoys this peaceful scene at Nazan Bay on Atka Island. Across the waters in center is Uyak, known locally as Cake Island.
(Douglas W. Veltre)

Left
Sand Point historian Andrew Gronholdt has covered almost all of his area and much of the Alaska Peninsula on foot. As a lad he delivered mail to local fox farms. His historical research greatly assisted his Shumagin Corporation with the basis for its land claims.

Below
The Russian Orthodox church at Sand Point was privately built by a local family and seldom used. Unlike the other Aleutian villages the strongest church in this region is Baptist. Neighboring Unga, now a ghost town, once boasted active churches of several denominations.

Upper left
Nina and Mary Dushkin spend a quiet afternoon playing Monopoly at Nikolski. Aleut youngsters are accustomed to providing their own entertainment. Their villages are the last in the state scheduled for TV reception.

Left
Ready, set, go!—a sack race at Nikolski.
(Sherry Spitler)

Right
Colorful laundry dries quickly in Atka's brisk breezes.
(Marian Rohrbeck)

Programs administered by school districts and nonprofit corporations of the Aleutian area are designed to foster and preserve the Aleut cultural heritage. At Atka, the Indian Education program provided the necessary funds to construct a traditional barabara which highlights a recreational area developed just across the bay from the village. Shown during and after the construction project—with the interior of the barabara in lower left photo—are participants Jerry Zaochney, Capt. John Nevzoroff, Raymond Golodoff, Nicky Golodoff, Dan Prokopeuff and Arnold Golodoff.
(Douglas W. Veltre)

Above
Larry Prokopeuff leaves election headquarters at Atka during the 1978 statewide election. The building, originally constructed as housing for the church, also serves as village clinic, housing for the visiting priest and out-of-towners.

Below
Little Eva Nevzoroff hugs her kitten at the home of her aunt Millie Prokopeuff.

Clockwise from right
►*Atkans have to spend a lot of time repairing their worn, wind-battered houses. Greg Golodoff does his share.*
►*With no electricity or refrigeration, Atkans still live by daily subsistence hunting and fishing. Here youngsters return from a successful afternoon of catching salmon.*
►*Stanley Swetzof diligently picks crowberries. Some of the berries even make it home!*
►*This waterfall near Atka is a well-known landmark, though apparently nameless. This is just one of several spectacular falls on the mountainous island. Flattened by the fisheye lens, the horizon at left, on the northeast end of the island, is dominated by Korovin Volcano, 4,852 feet.*

195

Left

Long the headquarters for prominent Aleut chiefs, Akutan has managed to survive as a village against considerable odds. There is a fine harbor, but air connections are far from ideal. After the whaling station closed down here at the start of World War II, employment was hard to come by until the development of the big processing fleet in recent years. The village qualified under the Alaska Native Claims Settlement Act and has claim to valuable land resources.

Below

Luke Shellikoff, Chief of Akutan, shows the old box compass he used for cod fishing when that was a major wage source in his area. Shellikoff also worked with Norwegian whalers.

Top

The late Polly and William McGlashan of Akutan adopted 12 children orphaned when flu devastated their area, and they did a good job raising the clan that now carries their name throughout the Chain. McGlashan was the descendant of a Scot trader who married locally; his wife came to Unalaska from the Pribilofs (on a boat towing eight whales) to be his bride.

Above

Delivering oil at Akutan can be a back-breaking job. Even if the village had a truck it couldn't negotiate the boardwalk.

Top

In country where it rains so much of the time a tight roof is essential. Here Sandra Kudrin and her uncle Sergie Kudrin make repairs at Akutan.

Above

Anna McGlashan brought her new baby home to Akutan in 1975. The village has a modest clinic, but residents have to travel to Anchorage for serious medical help.

Left
Boaters enjoy a calm day on Town Creek near the old boat landing at Unalaska, looking toward Dutch Harbor.
(Martin Butz)

Below
Abi Dickson is a fisherman's wife and a member of the Unalaska City Council. Her hillside home, formerly an Army latrine, has been made comfortable and attractive through her resourcefulness. Here she is examining wools she acquired from Chernofski which she dyed using local lichens, then spun on the wheel shown against the backdrop of her thriving greenhouse.

Clockwise from right
►*Some things are the same everywhere, especially when basketball's the name of the game! Unalaska youngsters enjoy some free-throwing.*
►*Early Russians discovered to their delight that Aleuts generally excelled at chess. It's still a favorite game with them, along with checkers and cribbage. Here Feddie Krukoff Jr. and George Bezezekoff of the Reeve ground crew at Dutch Harbor play a hand of cribbage as they wait for a plane to come in.*
►*Sophie Pletnikoff of Unalaska is skilled in weaving, basketry and needlework arts, and willingly shares her time and talents to teach these artistic skills to young people at the Unalaska school.*
(Raymond Hudson)
►*Night lights illuminate the busy harbor at Unalaska.*
(Tim Thompson)

199

Left
Skipper Magne Nes of the Northern Aurora *looks over the equipment of his modern pilot house.*

Below
The World War II dock at Chernofski is used for commercial crab pot storage. Beside the Northern Aurora, *Skipper Magne Nes and sheep rancher Milt Holmes enjoy a chat.*

Above
A False Pass waterfall blows sideways in high winds. The pass is deceptively shallow and requires skill, knowledge and good luck to navigate.

Right
Young Billy Dushkin stands at the entrance of a sod barabara *at Sandy Beach, a traditional summer settlement near Nikolski.*

Left
From the northeastern end of Adak Island gleaming waters highlight the flanks of Mount Moffett, with Kanaga Volcano beyond.
(Michael Gordon)

Below
Pete Culbertson takes advantage of hot springs that warm tide pools on an Adak beach. Away from the springs, the Aleutian beaches are not generally regarded as a bather's dream.

Left
The Coast Guard LORAN station, on the northern tip of Adak Island, stands out brightly on an exceptionally fine day.
(Michael Gordon)

Opposite
A stormy sea pounds the rocks at Kirilof Point, Amchitka, near the entrance to Constantine Harbor.
(Charles A. Simenstad)

Above
Weather and tides have sculpted many different and strangely beautiful forms in the lava rock. The larger "sea stacks" are often eyries for eagles and falcons; the smaller serve as perches for flocks of gulls and cormorants.
(Michael Gordon)

Left
A waterfall spills in shining ribbons on Kanaga Island.
(Robert Kay)

Overleaf
Sunrise illuminates countless small islands near Atka.
(Paul Eskelin)

. . . Aleutian Islands . . .
belt of emeralds . . .
a bracelet abandoned in the sun . . .

Listing of Aleutian Islands

The authors were unsuccessful in compiling a truly complete list of Aleutian Islands. Even the most detailed maps show unnamed islands, rocks, reefs, and sea stacks (lava rock formations), which are known and named locally. And often one island is known to various agencies and groups by different names.

This list derives from the *Dictionary of Alaska Place Names*, Geological Survey Professional Paper 567; from the lists of refuge managers which often include names not listed in the dictionary; from the unpublished works of linguist John P. Harrington, who worked at Unalaska before World War II and whose island lists are now in the Smithsonian Anthropological Archives; and with old fox farming permits in the National Archives.

We have done our best to eliminate duplicates and to identify the locations as accurately as possible. Occasionally we have included a name despite very little information about size and location, if there are strong indications that it is a bona fide listing.

Corrections offered by readers will be of service to the next researcher who attempts a complete "Listing of Aleutian Islands."

ALEUTIAN CHAIN—A 1,100-mile 279-island archipelago extending from the Alaska Peninsula nearly to the western Russian coast. Once known as Katerina Archipelago in honor of Catherine the Great under whose patronage the Russians discovered it. *Aleoutiennes, Aleotskia,* Fox Islands and Billy Mitchell Islands have also appeared on various maps.

Actually the archipelago comprises eight lesser groups: the Andreanof Islands, Delarofs, Fox Islands, Islands of the Four Mountains, Near Islands, Rat Islands; and the Shumagins and Sanaks, often omitted, but traditionally occupied by Aleuts and an integral part of their government and trading system.

Also included in this coverage are the Komandorskies, generally omitted because they are in Russian territory and were unsettled at the time of Russian exploration. They are, however, a logical extension of the Chain and populated today by descendants of American Aleuts.

The mountains and waters of the Aleutian Chain stretch as far as the eye can see in this view over Sand Point looking toward 8,905-foot Pavlof (Pavlov) Volcano.
(Lorie Kirker)

Bristol Bay

Volcanoes of the Aleutian Chain

Asterisks indicate those believed to have been active since 1760
Compiled from "Volcanic Activity in the Aleutian Arc" by
Robert R. Coats, *Contributions to General Geology, 1950,*
Geological Survey Bulletin 974-B

Bering Sea

U.S.S.R.
U.S.

Pacific Ocean

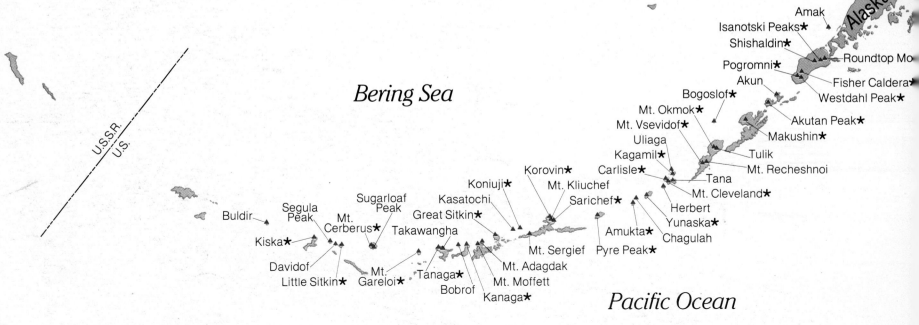

Biologist Olaus J. Murie traveled throughout the Aleutian Chain in the 1930s, cataloging bird and mammal populations for each island. The results of his survey appear in Fauna of the Aleutian Islands and Alaska Peninsula, *a publication of U.S. Fish & Wildlife Service. His field sketches, showing some of the islands in profile, appear in this listing of the Aleutian Islands.*

Sketch elevation of Ananiuliak Island, looking southerly. Umnak Island in background.

Alphabetical Listing and Description
Island groups are in parentheses.

ADAK—Andreanofs, called by Natives *Ayasgh* or *Kayaku* or perhaps coming from the Aleut *adaq* meaning "father." Length: 28 miles, dominated by Mount Moffett Volcano, 3,924 feet. Probably discovered by Alexei Chirikof September 8, 1741; when frightened by the roar of breakers, he anchored there in the fog and met Aleuts in canoes.

ADOKT—Baby Islands in Akutan Pass.

ADUGAK—Fox Islands, near southwest tip of Unimak. Length: 3 miles by 1.5 miles. Name may be Aleut translation of "something long."

AGATTU—Near Islands, 30 miles southeast of Attu. Length: 20 miles. Aleut name, *Agataku.* Russians called it *Ostrov Kruglyy.* Probably discovered by Chirikof September 21, 1741, or perhaps by Vitus Bering October 29, 1741, and mapped as Saint Abraham.

AGLIGADAK—Andreanofs, east of Amlia. Length: 2 miles.

AIKTAK—Fox Islands, Krenitzin group. Length: 1.3 miles. Aleut name first mapped in 1852 may translate "travel" or "going on a voyage."

AKUN—Fox Islands, second largest of Krenitzins. Length: 10 miles with Mount Gilbert, semiactive volcano of 2,685 feet.

AKUTAN—Fox Island, largest of the Krenitzins. Length: 18 miles, topped by active Akutan Volcano, 4,275 feet.

ALAID—Near Islands, westernmost of the Semichis. Length: 3 miles by 1 mile. Joined to Nizki by strand even at high tide. Named by Russians for resemblance to one of Kurile Islands. American whalers called it Alida.

AMAK—Easternmost of the Aleutian Chain near Cold Bay. Length: 3 miles. Also known as Walrus Island, for it was a source of ivory for the Aleuts.

AMAKNAK—Fox Islands, in Unalaska Bay. Length: 4.3 miles, elevation 1,640 feet on west end. Aleut name apparently meant "burial place."

AMATIGNAK—Andreanofs, Delarof group. Length: 5 miles by 5 miles with 1,690-foot elevation.

AMCHITKA—Largest and southernmost of the Rat Islands. Length: 25 miles by 3 miles. May have been named Saint Makarius by Bering October 25, 1741.

AMLIA—Andreanofs. Length: 45 miles by 8 miles. Stark headlands rising to 2,020 feet at highest point. Discovered by party under command of Simeon Polevoi in 1759.

(AMTAGIS ISLANDS)—Andreanofs, off south coast of Atka.

AMUKTA—Westernmost of Islands of Four Mountains. Length: 5 miles. First sighted by Krenitzin in August 1768.

ANAGAKSIK—Andreanofs, south of Great Sitkin. Length: 1 mile.

ANANGULA—See Ananiuliak.

ANANIULIAK—Fox Islands, three miles from Nikolski. Length: 5 miles by ¼ mile. Also known as Anangula.

(ANDREANOF ISLANDS)—A 310-mile chain between Islands of Four Mountains and Rat Islands. First explored in 1716 by merchant Andreian Tolstyk.

ANDRONICA—One of the Shumagins near Unga. Length: 3.5 miles. Also listed as Foggy Island and *Yasni,* meaning "clear."

ASUKSAK—Andreanofs. Length: 1 mile by ⅜ mile. Domelike rock of 700 to 1,800 feet. Once called Isoso.

ATKA—Largest of the Andreanofs. Length: 55 miles with 4,852-foot Korovin Volcano. Apparently discovered by Trapeznikof in 1745.

ATKINS—Shumagins. Northeast headland of Little Koniuji Island, connected by a shoal. Length: 1.5 miles by .6 mile. Named about 1880 by William Dall for the fishing schooner *Minnie G. Atkins.*

ATTU—Westernmost of Near Islands. Length: 37 miles. Dominated by Mount Attu, 3,100 feet. Probably sighted by Bering but officially discovered by Chirikof September 6, 1741, and named Saint Theodore by him.

AVATANAK—Krenitzin Chain, Fox Islands. Length: 9 miles by 2 miles. Mountains to 1,635 feet.

AZIAK—Andreanofs, between Great Sitkin and Umak. Length: 1 mile.

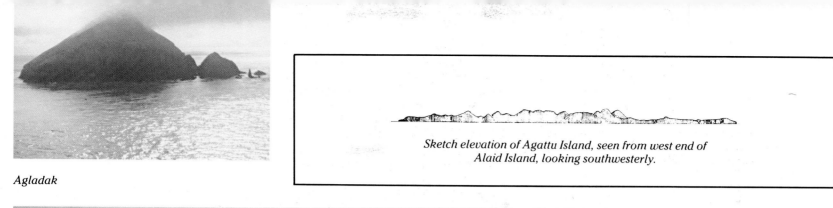

Agladak

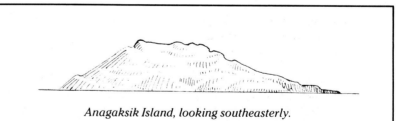

Sketch elevation of Agattu Island, seen from west end of Alaid Island, looking southwesterly.

Amak from Neumann Island
(Palmer C. Sekora, AINWR)

Amlia from Atka

Anagaksik Island, looking southeasterly.

Anagaksik
(Palmer C. Sekora, AINWR)

211

Carlisle
(G. Vernon Byrd, AINWR)

Chagulah
(AINWR)

Buldir

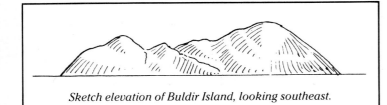

Sketch elevation of Buldir Island, looking southeast.

Chuginadak
(G. Vernon Byrd, AINWR)

Chugul from Umak Bight
(Palmer C. Sekora, AINWR)

212

North side, Castle Rock
(R.H. Day, AINWR)

(BABY ISLANDS)—Fox Chain extending 2 miles into Akutan Pass. Also known as Gull Islands and Seagull Islets.

BAT—Rat Islands, off Amchitka.

BENDEL—Shumagin Islands. Length: 3 miles. Bering's men landed here August 30, 1741. Also known as Turner Island and later Morse.

BERING—Komandorskies. Crew of Vitus Bering shipwrecked here November 4, 1741.

BIG KONIUJI—Shumagins. Length: 15 miles. Aleut name *Kiuniuiu Tanani* translates "big-crested Auk" and original Russian *Bolshoi Koniuzhi* means the same.

BIRD—Shumagins. Length: 5 miles. Name is translation of Russian name *Ostrov Pichnoi*. On September 4, 1741, Bering's ship anchored here but it was too rocky for a safe landing. Two sailors and an interpreter swam in and back.

BOBROF—Andreanof Islands. Length: 2.5 miles topped by 2,419-foot Bobrof Volcano. Earlier known as Beaver Island, the Russian term for sea otter: in Russian *Ostrov Bobrovoy Vilga*.

BOGOSLOF—North of Fox Chain and newest of the Aleutians. Length: 1 mile.

BOLSHOI—Andreanof Islands, Nazan Bay, Atka. Length: 1 mile.

BOX—Andreanofs, in Great Sitkin Pass. Length: 150 feet.

BREADLOAF—Fox Islands, southwest coast of Umnak.

BUCK—Fox Islands, Kashega Bay, Unalaska. Length: .4 mile.

BULDIR—Rat Islands. Length: 4 miles with 2,152-foot elevation. Bering supposedly sighted it October 28, 1741, and named it for a navy cooper who died of scurvy; however, historians challenge this.

CARLISLE—One of the handsomest of the Islands of Four Mountains. Length: 5 miles with almost perfect volcanic cone of 5,283 feet. Sometimes called *Ylyaga, Kigalgin, Ollaga* or *Tanakh-Angunakh,* the island was finally named for John G. Carlisle, Secretary of Treasury, 1894.

CASTLE—Fox Islands, off southwest coast of Kanaga, Unalaska. Length: 3 miles.

CATON—Easternmost of Sanaks. Length: 5 miles by 2 miles. Named by a fish commissioner in 1888, perhaps for a well-traveled local man.

CHAGULAH—Islands of Four Mountains. Length: 2.5 miles with 4,300-foot elevation. Often wrongly on the map as *Chugul* or *Ostrov Chugula.*

CHERNABURA—Most southerly of the Shumagins. Length: 5 miles. Original Aleut name *Tananak*. Russians called it Chernabura from *chyorny* meaning "black" and *burnastyy* meaning "brown." Aleut name was *Nunik* meaning "porcupine."

CHINKOFF—Andreanofs, Bay of Islands, Adak. Length: 1.5 miles by 1.5 miles.

CHISAK—Andreanofs, south of Little Tanaga. Length: .6 mile.

CHUGINADAK—Largest of Islands of Four Mountains. Length: 14 miles by 5 miles, topped by Mount Cleveland, 5,675 feet. Name in Aleut translates "to roast or fry."

CHUGUL—In Andreanofs, just south of Great Sitkin. Length: 5 miles by 2.5 miles with 1,700-foot elevation. Originally on Russian map as *Tshugulla* or *Tcugula*. Both Chagulah and Segula have been called Chugul, causing confusion.

CHUSUGA—Fox Islands, extreme southwest of Unalaska. Length: 1 mile round.

CLIFFORD—In Sanaks. Sometimes confused with Long Island. Length: 2.5 miles by 1.6 miles.

(COMMANDER ISLANDS)—See Komandorskies.

Sketch elevation of Bobrof Island, looking southwesterly.

CONE—Andreanofs, in Nazan Bay, Atka.

COOPER—Near Islands off northeast coast of Attu. Named for U.S. Navy survey schooner *Fenimore Cooper* in 1855.

COPPER—Second largest of the Komandorskies. Also known as *Mednyy*. First explored by Andrei Vsevidof in 1743.

CRONE—Andreanofs, south of Adak. Length: 1.5 miles.

CROSS—Shumagins. In Delarof Harbor, Unga. Length: 300 yards.

DAVIDOF—Rat Islands, west of Kiska. Length: 2.3 miles by .5 mile. Named in honor of Russian naval officer Gavriil Davidoff, who explored Alaska from 1802-1804. Originally name applied to Segula.

DEER—Near King Cove. Length: 11 miles. Also called Animak and *Itkhayak Oleny*. Russian translation also meant "deer" although there is no record of deer being on the island; however, caribou have been reported there.

(DELAROFS)—An island chain just west of the Andreanofs and sometimes included as part of them. Named in honor of Estrate Ivanovich Delarov, director of the Russian-American Company, 1784-1791.

DERBIN—Krenitzins, southeast shore of Tigalda. Length: .5 mile.

DOLGOI—Pavlofs. Length: 10 miles. Called by Aleuts *Ananakeik*, Russian translation "Long Island."

DORA—Andreanofs, west of Adak. Length: 1 mile. Named for trading schooner *Dora*, 1934.

DORA—Sanaks, 3 miles south of Sanak Island. Length: .1 mile.

DUAHASON—Fox Islands in Beaver Inlet, Unalaska. Length: ¾ mile by ¼ mile.

DUSHKOT—Fox Islands in Beaver Inlet, Unalaska. Length: 4 miles.

EGG—Andreanofs, off north coast of Atka. Length: .7 mile.

EGG—Fox Islands, off Sedanka. Length: .7 mile. Also known as Gagalgin, Iachnoi, Jaitschoi, Kigalgin, Hazel, and The Signals.

EGG—Shumagins, in Popoff Strait. Length: 4 miles. Listed as both Egg and Little Egg in early sailing directions.

EGG—Pavlofs, near Wosnesenski.

ELF—Andreanofs, southeast of Adak. Length: 2 miles.

ELMA—Sanak Islands. Length: 2.2 miles.

EMERALD—Fox Islands, off Unalaska. Length: .3 mile; height: 200 feet.

EXCELSIOR—Easternmost of Baby Islands.

EXPEDITION—Fox Islands, just off the coast of Amaknak in Unalaska Bay. Length: .2 mile. No longer an island but joined to Amaknak as cannery site.

FINNEYS—Sanak Islands, adjacent to Wanda. Length: .5 mile. Also known as Fenneys.

FIRE—Appeared off Bogoslof in 1883.

FORTRESS ROCK—Fox Islands near Kashega.

(FOX ISLANDS)—Chain in eastern Aleutians. Known to Russians as *Ostrova Lisyy*, which means Fox Islands.

GARELOI—Delarof group. Length: 6 miles with 5,160-foot peak. Originally not considered a Delarof. Called *Goreli* by Russians, which translates "burnt."

GARGOYLE—Fox Islands, across from Surveyor Bay, Unalaska.

GIBSON ISLANDS—Small rocks in Near Islands off Attu near Chichagof Harbor. Named for U.S. Navy Lt. William Gibson, commander of 1855 survey team.

GOLOI—Pavlofs. Length: 2.5 miles. Russian word meaning "bare."

GREAT SITKIN—Andreanofs. Length: 7.5 miles by 7 miles with 5,740-foot Great Sitkin Volcano. Probably sighted September 8 or 9, 1741 by Chirikof.

GUMBOOT—Sanak Islands near Caton. Length: 1 mile.

HALL—Shumagins, between Big and Little Koniuji. Length: .9 mile by .4 mile. Named by William Dall in 1874 for Captain Hall of USC&GS schooner *Humboldt*.

HALUK—Andreanofs, near Tanaklak.

HERBERT—Islands of Four Mountains. Length: 5.5 miles by 3.5 miles with top elevation 5,291 feet. Although it was called *Ostrov Ulyaga* and *Chigula Tcigula* by Russians, the U.S. Hydrographic office named it for Hilary Abner Herbert, Secretary of Navy in 1894.

HERENDEEN—Shumagins, near Little Koniuji. Length: 1 mile. Named in honor of Capt. Edward Perry Herendeen of U.S. schooner *Yukon* who discovered it.

HOG—Fox Islands, just off Unalaska Village. Length: .9 mile. Aleuts called it *Oknodok*, but Russians raised hogs there and named it accordingly *Ostrov Svinoy*.

IGITKIN—Andreanofs, near Great Sitkin. Length: 6.7 miles by 3 miles. First mapped as *Egilka* but the Aleut name prevailed.

IKIGINAK—Andreanofs, west end of Atka. Rocky cone .4 mile in length with 871-foot elevation. Once called *Nerpitchy Ilot* or Seal Island by Russians.

ILAK—Andreanofs, Delarof group, southwest of Tanaga. Length: 1 mile by .5 mile.

INIKLA—Sanaks, between Caton and Sanak islands. Length: .7 mile.

INNER ILIASIK—Pavlofs, southwest of Dolgoi. Length: 3 miles. Native name published by Captain Tebenkov in 1852.

(ISLANDS OF THE FOUR MOUNTAINS)— Major Aleutian group between Fox Islands and Andreanofs. Aleuts called it *Unigun*, the Russians *Ostrova Chetyre Soposhnye*, meaning islands of four volcanoes. Some maps showed a five island group.

ISOSO—See ASUKSAK.

JOHN—Shumagins. Length: 1 mile. Named in 1880 by William Dall.

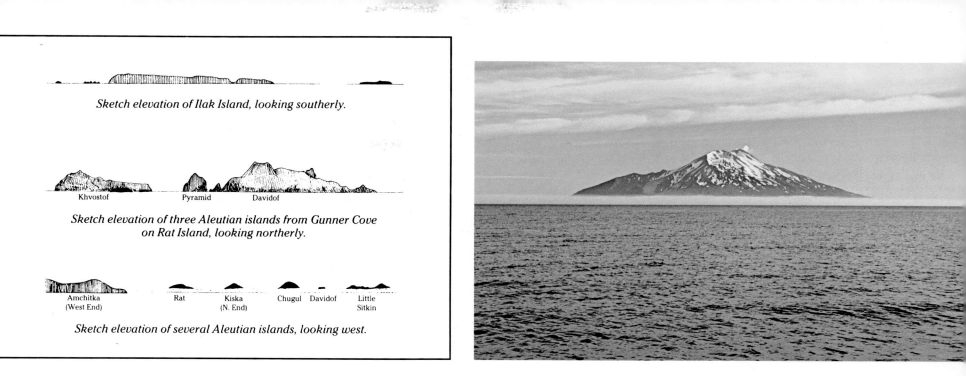

Sketch elevation of Ilak Island, looking southerly.

Khvostof	Pyramid	Davidof

Sketch elevation of three Aleutian islands from Gunner Cove on Rat Island, looking northerly.

Amchitka (West End)	Rat	Kiska (N. End)	Chugul	Davidof	Little Sitkin

Sketch elevation of several Aleutian islands, looking west.

Above
Gareloi from Kavalga
(R.H. Day, AINWR)
Left
Island of Four Mountains
(Craig Harrison)

215

Kanaga
(Floyd Cummings)

Kagamil
(G. Vernon Byrd, AINWR)

Sketch elevations of Kasatochi Island
and Koniuji Island, looking west.

Sketch elevation of Kavalga Island from
West Unalga Island, looking easterly.

Nagai

KAGALASKA—Andreanofs, east of Adak. Length: 10 miles by 5 miles with top elevation in northwest 2,331 feet. Russians took Aleut name.

KAGAMIL—Islands of Four Mountains. Length: 6.2 miles with 2,930-foot volcano. Aleut name.

KALIGAGAN—Fox Islands, Krenitzins. Length: 1 mile by ¼ mile. Also known as Sea Lion Island.

KANAGA—Andreanofs. Length: 30 miles by 18 miles with volcanic cone rising 4,416 feet on north end. Probably first visited by Andreian Tolstyk in 1761 and reported as *Kanaton* by Cook in 1778.

KANU—Andreanofs, south of Great Sitkin. Length: 1.7 miles. Once on books as Unak; name changed by spelling backward to save confusion.

KARPA—Shumagins, near Korovin. Almost circular 1.5 miles. Russian name meaning "carp" replaces Aleut *Inlikak*. Also called *Bouly Bouldyr* meaning "hovel" in Russian.

KASATOCHI—Andreanofs, off Atka. Length: 1.5 miles with extinct volcano of 1,038 feet. Aleuts recall name originally translated "That wasn't there yesterday."

KAVALGA—Delarof Islands in Andreanofs. Length: 5.5 miles by 3 miles.

KEEGAGAN—Fox Islands, 10 miles from Nikolski. Length: 1 mile by ¼ mile.

KEEGALOO—Andreanofs, east of Umnak on Pacific side. Length: .5 mile by ¼ mile.

KENNON—Near Islands, Chichagof Harbor, Attu. Length: 3 miles. Named for Lt. Beverley Kennon of North Pacific Expedition, 1855.

KETNAUGH—Fox Islands, east end of Umnak.

KHVOSTOF—Rat Islands, near Kiska. Length: 1.8 miles by .5 mile with 1,873-foot elevation. Named for Nikolai Khvostov, Russian naval officer who explored Alaska with Davidof in 1802-1805. Name once applied to whole group of islands.

KIGUL—Fox Islands, southeast of Umnak. Length: .5 mile.

KISKA—Rat Islands. Length: 24 miles with Kiska Volcano rising 3,996 feet. May have been sighted by Bering and named Saint Makarius or Saint Stephen. Currently bears Aleut name which translates "gut."

KITHANUSKAN—Fox Islands, east of Umnak.

KOHL—Near Islands, south coast of Agattu. Length: .2 mile. Named for a partner of Hutchinson, Kohl & Co. which bought out the Russian-American Company in 1867.

(KOMANDORSKIES)—Group of two islands and two islets comprising 850 square miles off the Kamchatka Peninsula of Russia. Also known as Commander Islands after Bering who led the Russian discoverers of Alaska here in 1741 and is buried here.

KONIUJI—Andreanofs, northwest of Atka. Length: 1 mile by .5 mile with blunt-topped mountain of 1,000 feet. Named *Kanoozhki* by Russians, their term for crested auks which nest there still in great numbers. Aleuts called it *Kunuliuk*.

KOROVIN—Shumagins, near Popof. Length: 8 miles. Named for Ivan Korovin who explored there in 1762.

KOSCHEKT—Baby Islands, near Unglga, Fox Chain.

(KRENITZIN CHAIN)—Fox Islands. Named by Litke for Peter Krenitzin, who with Levashev explored over 30 islands in the area from 1768-1769.

KUSAGO—Fox Islands, west of Unalaska.

LIDA—Sanak Islands, off Caton. Length: 400 yards by 600 yards.

LITTLE KISKA—Rat Islands, next to big Kiska. Length: 3.5 miles by 1.5 miles.

LITTLE KONIUJI—Shumagins, near Big Koniuji. Length: 8 miles. Aleut name was *Tangimak* and also appeared on Russian maps as *Tounghimik*.

LITTLE SITKIN—Rat Islands. Length: 6.8 miles with 3,897-foot peak. Once called Western Sitkin Island to avoid confusion with Great Sitkin Island.

LITTLE TANAGA—Andreanofs. Length: 10 miles with 1,747-foot summit.

LOAF—Near Islands, off west shore of Massacre Bay, Attu.

LONG—Sanak Islands. Length: 3.5 miles. Sometimes confused with Clifford Island.

MARY—Near Islands, Massacre Bay, Attu.

MARY—One of Sanak Islands. Length: .3 mile.

MEXI—Rat Islands, off Amchitka.

NAGAI—Shumagins. Length: 31 miles. Bering's crew landed here for water August 20, 1741.

NEAR—Shumagins, near Nagai. Bering's ship anchored here September 1, 1741.

(NEAR ISLANDS)—Chain that comprises western Aleutians. Literal translation of Russian *Plishnie Ostrova*.

NIZKI—Semichi Islands of Near Group. Length: 3 miles by 1 mile. Now connected by strand to Alaid. Name probably comes from Russian word meaning "low." Also marked on maps as *Oubeloi*.

NORTH—Andreanofs, at entrance of Bay of Islands, Adak. Length: 7 miles.

NURSERY—One of largest of Baby Islands, Fox Chain.

OGCHUL—Fox Chain, south coast of Umnak. Length: .5 mile.

OGLIUGA—Delarof Islands. Length: 3 miles by .5 mile.

OGLODAK—Andreanofs, near Atka. Length: 1.2 miles by .5 mile. Name may come from Aleut word meaning "albatross."

ORANGEN—Fox Islands, off Unalaska.

OUTER ILIASIK—Pavlofs. Length: 3 miles. Also known as Big Iliazhek and Eliazik.

(PAVLOF ISLANDS)—Seven island group 23 miles in length at southwest end of Aleutian Range. Aleut name *Kadugin* which apparently meant "narrow."

PENINSULA—Mainland Alaska to which the Aleutian Chain was once attached.

PETER—Fox Islands, Makushin Bay, Unalaska. Length: .6 mile.

PETERSON—Sanak Islands. Length: .3 mile.

POA—Krenitzin of Fox Chain. Length: .5 mile round. Named by Fisheries Bureau in 1881 for a genus of grass. On Russian maps it was *Ostrov Tumannoi* meaning "foggy island."

POPERECHNOI—Pavlofs, southwest of Wosnesenski. Length: 4 miles. Translates "crosswise" in Russian. Aleut name *Kuiagdak*.

POPOF—Shumagins, east of Unga. Length: 9 miles.

POSTOI—See Pustoi.

PRIEST ROCK—Fox Islands. Landmark off Unalaska Harbor.

PUFFIN—Krenitzin Chain, off Trident Bay, Akun. Length: 200 yards.

PUSTOI—Fox Islands, in Umnak Pass. Length: .3 mile. Russian name translates to "desert island."

PYRAMID—Rat Islands, in Crater Bay, Rat Island. Length: .4 mile.

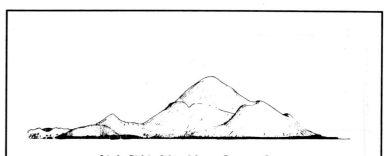

Little Sitkin Island from Gunner Cove on Rat Island, looking northeasterly.

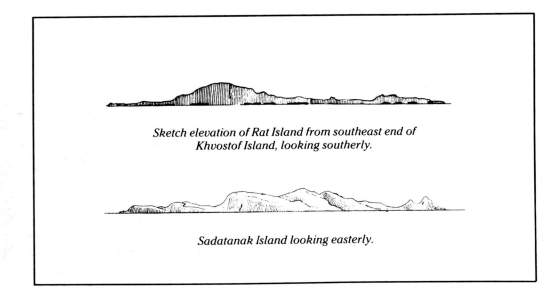

Sketch elevation of Rat Island from southeast end of Khvostof Island, looking southerly.

Sadatanak Island looking easterly.

RABBIT—Sanaks, west of Sanak Island. Length: .3 mile.

RAT ISLAND—Rat Islands. Length: 9 miles. Name translates directly from Russian.

(RAT ISLANDS)—Chain between Near and Andreanofs, extending 180 miles.

RESOF—Fox Islands, Beaver Inlet, Unalaska. Small high rock.

RINGGOLD—Andreanofs, west of Adak. Length: 1.5 miles. Named for Capt. Cadwalader Ringgold, USN, 1855.

ROMAN SENATOR—Baby Islands, Fox Chain.

ROOTOK—Krenitzins, near Avatanak. Length: 3.5 miles by 2 miles with twin peaks 1,545 and 1,532 feet. Called *Aikhak* meaning "travel" by Aleuts. Russian rechristened *Ostrov Goly* meaning "bare."

ROUND—Fox Islands, off Aiktak.

ROUND—Andreanofs, off Amlia.

SADATANAK—Andreanofs, south side of Atka. Length: ¾ mile by .5 mile.

SAGCHUDAK—Andreanofs, off south coast of Atka. Length: 1.3 miles.

SAGIGIK—Andreanofs, south of Amlia. Length: 2 miles. Aleut name meaning "having sharp edge."

SALT—Andreanofs, northwest of Atka. Length: 1.3 miles by .5 mile.

SAMALGA—Fox Chain, west end. Length: 4.2 miles by ¼ mile. Aleut name.

SANAK—Longest of Sanak Islands. Length: 13 miles by 4.5 miles, with Sanak Peak 1,740 feet. Aleut name has survived, but was known as Halibut Island after Captain Cook found good fishing here.

(SANAK ISLANDS)—A 21-mile chain of two large islands and numerous small ones, reported by Russian explorers in 1774 and mapped by Cook in 1785.

SAVAGE—Near Islands, Temnac Bay, Attu. Length: .3 mile.

SEDANKA—Fox Islands, off Unalaska. Length: 11 miles with 2,130-foot peak. Called *Sithanak* by Aleuts meaning "braided" or "curled," but long known as *Biorka*, the name of its main village, which apparently comes from a Scandinavian word meaning "birch."

SEGUAM—Andreanofs. Length: 15 miles with Pyre Peak, 3,458 feet. Variations of Aleut name. Russians called it *Goreli* meaning "burnt" and also *Siguam*.

SEGULA—Rat Islands, west of Little Sitkin. Length: 4 miles with 3,817-foot peak. Because of variations of Aleut spelling—*Chugul, Chigul, Tchougoule*—the island is easily confused with Chugul in the Andreanofs and Chagulah in Islands of the Four Mountains.

(SEMICHI)—Chain 13 miles long in Near Islands. Probably discovered by Bering October 29, 1741. He named it for Saint Abraham. Name comes from Russian *Semik*, which is a religious feast day.

SEMISOPOCHNOI—Northeasternmost of Rat Islands. Length: 12 miles by 9 miles with mountains ranging from 1,200 to Flathead Anvil Mountain, 4,007 feet. Translation of Russian is "seven extinct volcanoes" although there are really nine peaks here.

SHEMYA—Easternmost of the Semichi. Length: 4 miles by 1.8 miles. Originally known as Semichi Island.

SHIP ROCK—Rat Islands, Umnak Pass. Length: 500 yards. Called *Tanghinakh* by Aleuts meaning "islet."

(SHUMAGINS)—A 60-mile chain south of the Alaska Peninsula. Named by Vitus Bering for a sailor who died of scurvy and was buried here when the party anchored offshore in 1741. Aleuts called the chain *Unga* after the largest island of the group.

SILAK—Andreanofs, between Little Tanaga and Kagalaska. Length: .2 mile.

SIMEONOF—Easternmost of Shumagins. Length: 6 miles with 1,436-foot elevation.

SISTERS—Sanak chain, just off Sanak Island.

SKAGUL—Delarof Chain. Length: 1.8 miles.

SPECTACLE—Shumagins, between Big Koniuji and Nagai. Length: 3 miles. Early known as *Kangaiulouk* Island.

STATEN—Andreanofs, west of Adak. Length: 1 mile. Resembles namesake in New York.

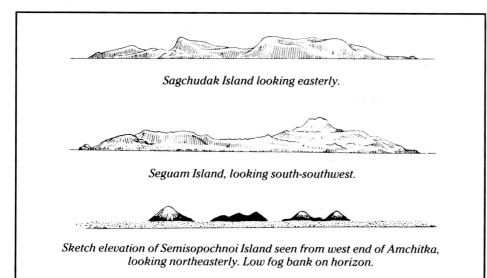

Sagchudak Island looking easterly.

Seguam Island, looking south-southwest.

Sketch elevation of Semisopochnoi Island seen from west end of Amchitka,
looking northeasterly. Low fog bank on horizon.

Segula
(David Spencer, AINWR)

Semisopochnoi from Amchitka
(LeRoy Sowl, AINWR)

219

Tagalak
(Palmer C. Sekora, AINWR)

Tanaga

Ulak
(Palmer C. Sekora, AINWR)

Uliaga
(G. Vernon Byrd, AINWR)

TAG—Delarof Islands, off Skagul. Length: .5 mile. Known to Russians as *Tagachalugis*, which refers to "largest of the group."

TAGADAK—Andreanofs, between Great Sitkin and Umak. Length: 3 miles by 1 mile. Name may come from Aleut meaning "fresh" or "new."

TAGALAK—Andreanofs, between Atka and Adak. Length: 4 miles; height 1,783 feet.

TANADAK—Andreanofs, off Amlia. Length: 1.5 miles.

TANADAK—Delarofs, near Ulak. Length: .5 mile. Aleut name may mean "crab place" or "eternal resting place."

TANADAK—Rat Islands, east of Little Kiska. Length: ¼ mile.

TANAGA—Andreanofs. Length: 25 miles by 22 miles. Tanaga Volcano 5,925 feet. Russian fur hunter Andrei Serebrennikof apparently wrecked here in 1753.

TANAKLAK—Andreanofs, between Great Sitkin and Umak. Length: 1.7 miles by ¾ mile.

TANGAGM—Fox Islands, near Unalga. Length: .5 mile.

TANGIK—Fox Islands, southeast of Akun. Length: .5 mile.

TANGINAK—Fox Islands, east of Akun. Length: .2 mile.

THREE SISTERS—Andreanofs. Three Arm Bay, Adak. Each island .2 mile long.

TIDGITUK—Andreanofs, near entrance to South Bay, Tanaga. Length: .5 mile.

TIGALDA—Krenitzins, east of Akutan. Length: 12 miles by 3 miles with 1,800-foot elevation.

TRINITY—Sanaks, northwest of Long Island.

TURNER—Shumagins. Length: 2.8 miles by .9 mile.

UGAMAK—Krenitzins. Length: 5.2 miles with 1,042-foot peak. Aleut name translates "cemetery island."

UGIDAK—Delarofs, just east of Skagul. Length: 1 mile. Russians called it *Kamen Ugidakh* or Ugidak Rock.

UKOLNOI—Pavlofs. Length 7.5 miles. Four miles northeast of Dolgoi Island. Name reported by Captain Litke in 1836 as *Ostrov Youkolny*, meaning "stone coal." Aleut name is *Kitagutak*, according to Father Veniaminov.

ULAK—Delarofs. Length: 6 miles by 2 miles. Aleut translation, "Everybody's house."

ULAK—Andreanofs, east of Great Sitkin. Length: 1 mile with 688-foot elevation. Early charts show as *Ostrov Ulyadak*.

ULIAGA—Islands of Four Mountains. Length: 2 miles with 3,000-foot elevation. Called *Kigalga* by Russians, which translates "smallest and lowest." Has also been called *Chegulak* and *Ultyaga*.

UMAK—Andreanofs. Length: 6 miles by 3 miles. Also called *Yumakh* or *Oumakh*.

UMLA—Sanaks, between Sanak and Caton. Length: .7 mile.

UMNAK—Third largest of Fox Islands. Length: 70 miles with Tulik Volcano, 4,111 feet; Recheshnoi, 6,510 feet; Okmok Caldera, 3,400 feet; and Vsevidof, 7,050 feet.

UNAK—See Kanu.

UNALASKA—Fox Islands. Length: 20 miles, dominated by Makushin Volcano, 6,680 feet. Probably sighted by Chirikof September 4, 1741.

UNALGA—Andreanofs, westernmost of Delarof group. Length: 1.5 miles. Often referred to as Western Unalga.

UNALGA—Fox Islands, between Akutan and Unalaska. Length: 4.5 miles. Logged by Krenitzin in 1768-69 and by Cook in 1778.

UNGA—Largest and most important of Shumagins. Length: 15 miles.

UNGLGA—Baby Islands, near Koschekt.

UNIMAK—Largest of the Aleutians and of the Fox Island Chain. Length: 67 miles by 22 miles with largest volcanoes in Chain: Shishaldin, 9,372 feet; Westdahl, 5,118 feet; Pogromni, 6,568 feet; Roundtop, 6,140 feet; Isanotski Peaks, 8,025 feet. Probably first recorded by the crew of the *Sv Gavriil* which sailed in 1760.

UYAK—Andreanofs, Nazan Bay, Atka. Length: .15 mile.

VASILIE ISLANDS—Andreanofs, off Atka.

VSEVIDOF ISLETS—Fox Islands, off south coast of Umnak. Length: 1.5 miles. Perhaps named for Andrei Vsevidof who sailed here in 1747.

WANDA—Sanaks, between Sanak and Caton. Length: .2 mile.

WINDY—Rat Islands, off Amchitka.

WISLOW—Fox Islands, near Reese Bay, Unalaska. Length: .1 mile. Known locally as Winslow.

WOSNESENSKI—Pavlofs, northeast of Dolgoi. Length: 4.5 miles. Originally named *Ostrov Peregrebnoy* by Russians, but renamed when Ilia Wosnesenski explored western Alaska in 1842-44.

YUNASKA—Islands of Four Mountains. Length: 14 miles by 5 miles with 2,899-foot elevation. Also recorded as *Junaska* and *Unaska*.

Unga

Umnak from Bering Side

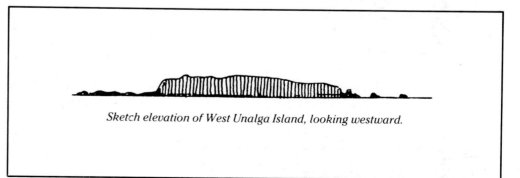

Sketch elevation of West Unalga Island, looking westward.

221

Midway through the battle of Attu in 1943 the pass between Holtz and Massacre valleys became known by the name of Captain Jarmin, the ranking American officer killed there. This was the most bitterly fought-for piece of ground in the Aleutian campaign, as the Japanese, entrenched on the ridges overhead, slaughtered American troops trying to push inland. As seen this day, it is deceptively beautiful, bright with wild flowers and graced with a double rainbow from a passing storm.

SUMMER'S BAY

(For Anfesia Shapsnikoff)
Over a cliff of stone
Above an ocean of silence
Against the silence of walls and burials
Through light that seemed impenetrable
To the trail along the beach
To the city of one street
The gulls drift
   crying crying,
Ivory upon their wings
Wings the color of frost
Flakes of ash on their snowy breasts.

The sun like a halo of clarity rising,
The sea blood-stained, sealion and seal,
Fowl's flesh now rose and salmon: out of nothing
The day is blown towards us.

  Islands
between sea and ocean
  Aleutian Islands
split circle of vanished people
mountainous bow of storms
belt of emeralds
   like the eagle's curved flight above you
carved eyebrow on the death mask
arc of long Winter.

After months of Winter
never the gray fading into black or umber
never igniting into flame
pale stones beneath gray water
ships blue-gray at anchor
an orange buoy blazing once
smoke gray fog locking the harbor:
the dryness of one color shading the spectrum exhausted me.
Along the trail at the bay's end

I found sleeping shoots of rye pale green sunken under
the white yellow slender stems and blades of broken Autumn,
they will sleep until Summer.

In the winding streams on the floor of the valley
fresh-water seaweed darkened, its color withdrawn into the bank.

Then under an overgrowth of Empetrum and blond hairs
its roots stock between stones and beneath stones
heavier roots twisting were ferns thick and stubby
growing into fans as the day broadened into morning:
the ferns green all Winter.
Winter surrendered one green emblem.
Beside the bleached leaves of wild strawberries
the green flames smouldered.
Here in the fist of Winter
I could remember
the shattered history of these islands.
On the side of the rock.
On the volcano.

That fury which from birth is soft,
Never angered into violence,
Shook the sea of these islands,
Sent creation's terrible passion
Confusing the split stock,
Mold, the delicate breeding of spiders,
Centuries of steam and rock,
An age of vegetation.

Against the sea's lisp all the evening was singing.
The islands lay like a bracelet abandoned in the sun.
Do you remember the slow dance of your beginning?
How you came here and prospered?
   at last,
out of deep water
plundering with their eyes the dangerous shore
the fur hunters, Russian,
   sheer sea walls
there the fall of the eagle was straight down,
then at cliff's point
   they coasted, now in the Bay cast anchor
   onto the lips of the valley.
Roof of valleys.
Belly of volcanoes.
Then amid cries and money, a century, you were swept
down the dark aorta into the furious sun.
Sea's end river's end
slaughter and sickness pressed you into silence.

Andrew, Old Man,
you sent your daughter in the close of Winter
after what ferns
   for healing?
Sergie, Old Man, Old Man,
out of the valley and shore,
what ferns
what roots and tendrils
   did you take?

Bring down from your glacial peak, Makushin,
what you had hidden in your heights,
among the scent of orchids,
down rough torrents to the village,
bring what preserved you against slaughter and invasion
to a town of old men with strangers for children.

Let a brilliant redness cover the sky
"like the coming of a new civilization"
with laws, Old Man, it is a new day.
   The door of your room is closing.

A closed door makes the house smaller.
Haul down the door!
Throw open the window!
Let the quiet of the eagle high in flight,
Let the grave crashing of magnificent wings,
Let your silence, your history, answer
your children's call. Call!
All sing or dance in silence but
continue
continue
Pass on
Pass on
to son and daughter
what you shared with the islands
your blood to their blood
yellow eye of the sturgeon
taut sinew of sealion
grass woven baskets as fine as cloth.
Old Man, Old Man,   go silent and
All the fires will be out.
All the fires
   the fight
   the pride
   the calm of your eye as the sea
rages against you.

Eagle.
Aleutian.
Side of the rock.
Moss side of the rock.
Volcano.

Memory moves us
to look; now see
weeds on the surface
in the ocean thin pins of fish.

The water here at valley's end
at Summer's Bay
shallow as the palm of your hand
is filled with light.

Raymond L. Hudson
Hue-Phu Bai, Vietnam
1968

This work and excerpts
which appeared throughout
the book reprinted
by permission:
Raymond L. Hudson,
"Summer's Bay,"
WORLD ORDER, 4, No. 1
(Fall 1969), 27-30.
Copyright© 1969 by the
National Spiritual Assembly
of the Baha'is of the
United States.

Alaska Geographic. Back Issues

The North Slope, Vol. 1, No. 1. Charter issue of *ALASKA GEOGRAPHIC*. Out of print.

One Man's Wilderness, Vol. 1, No. 2. The story of a dream shared by many, fulfilled by few: a man goes into the bush, builds a cabin and shares his incredible wilderness experience. Color photos. 116 pages, $7.95

Admiralty . . . Island in Contention, Vol. 1, No. 3. An intimate and multifaceted view of Admiralty: its geological and historical past, its present-day geography, wildlife and sparse human population. Color photos. 78 pages, $5.00

Fisheries of the North Pacific: History, Species, Gear & Processes, Vol. 1, No. 4. Out of print.

The Alaska-Yukon Wild Flowers Guide, Vol. 2, No. 1. First Northland flower book with both large, color photos and detailed drawings of every species described. Features 160 species, common and scientific names and growing height. 112 pages, $10.95.

Richard Harrington's Yukon, Vol. 2, No. 2. A collection of 277 stunning color photos by Canadian photographer-writer Richard Harrington captures the Yukon in all its seasons and moods, from Watson Lake to Herschel Island. 103 pages, $7.95

Prince William Sound, Vol. 2, No. 3. Out of print.

Yakutat: The Turbulent Crescent, Vol. 2, No. 4. Out of print.

Glacier Bay: Old Ice, New Land, Vol. 3, No. 1. The expansive wilderness of Southeastern Alaska's Glacier Bay National Monument unfolds in crisp text and color photographs. Records the flora and fauna of the area, its natural history, with hike and cruise information, plus a large-scale color map. 132 pages, $9.95

The Land: Eye of the Storm, Vol. 3, No. 2. Out of print.

Richard Harrington's Antarctic, Vol. 3, No. 3. The Canadian photojournalist guides readers through remote and little understood regions of the Antarctic and Subantarctic. More than 200 color photos and a large fold-out map. 104 pages, $8.95

The Silver Years of the Alaska Canned Salmon Industry: An Album of Historical Photos, Vol. 3, No. 4. Temporarily out of print.

Alaska's Volcanoes: Northern Link in the Ring of Fire, Vol. 4, No. 1. Scientific overview supplemented with eyewitness accounts of Alaska's historic volcano eruptions. Includes color and black-and-white photos and a schematic description of the effects of plate movement upon volcanic activity. 88 pages, $7.95

The Brooks Range: Environmental Watershed, Vol. 4, No. 2. Looks at early exploration and at controversy over uses for the region: Native land claims, recreation, proposed national parks and development of resources. Maps, color photos. 112 pages, $9.95

Kodiak: Island of Change, Vol. 4, No. 3. Although half the size of New Jersey, and once the administrative center of Russian Alaska, the 3,588-square-mile island of Kodiak remains well off the beaten path. Past, present and future—everything from Russian exploration to the present-day quest for oil. Maps, color photos. 96 pages, $7.95

Wilderness Proposals: Which Way for Alaska's Lands?, Vol. 4, No. 4. Out of print.

Cook Inlet Country, Vol. 5, No. 1. A visual tour of the region—its communities, big and small, and its countryside. Begins at the southern tip of the Kenai Peninsula, circles Turnagain Arm and Knik Arm for a close-up view of Anchorage, and visits the Matanuska and Susitna valleys and the wild, west side of the inlet. 144 pages; 230 color photos, separate map. $9.95

Southeast: Alaska's Panhandle, Vol. 5, No. 2. Most colorful edition to date, exploring Southeastern Alaska's maze of fjords and islands, mossy forests and glacier-draped mountains—from Dixon Entrance to Icy Bay, including all of the state's fabled Inside Passage. Along the way are profiles of every town, together with a look at the region's history, economy, people, attractions and future. Includes large fold-out map and seven area maps. 192 pages, $9.95.

Bristol Bay Basin, Vol. 5, No. 3. Explores the land and the people of the region known to many as the commercial salmon-fishing capital of Alaska. Illustrated with contemporary color and historic black-and-white photos. Includes a large fold-out map of the region. 96 pages, $9.95.

Alaska Whales and Whaling, Vol. 5, No. 4. The wonders of whales in Alaska—their life cycles, travels and travails—are examined, with an authoritative history of commercial and subsistence whaling in the North. Includes a fold-out poster of 14 major whale species in Alaska in perspective, color photos and illustrations, with historical photos and line drawings. 144 pages, $9.95.

Yukon-Kuskokwim Delta, Vol. 6, No. 1. Temporarily out of print.

The Aurora Borealis, Vol. 6, No. 2. The northern lights — in ancient times seen as a dreadful forecast of doom, in modern days an inspiration to countless poets. Here one of the world's leading experts — Dr. S.-I. Akasofu of the University of Alaska — explains in an easily understood manner, aided by many diagrams and spectacular color and black-and-white photos, what causes the aurora, how it works, how and why scientists are studying it today and its implications for our future. 96 pages, $7.95.

Alaska's Native People, Vol. 6, No. 3. In the largest edition to date—result of several years of research—the editors examine the varied worlds of the Inupiat Eskimo, Yup'ik Eskimo, Athabascan, Aleut, Tlingit, Haida and Tsimshian. Most photos are by Lael Morgan, *ALASKA* magazine's roving editor, who since 1974 has been gathering impressions and images from virtually every Native village in Alaska. Included are sensitive, informative articles by Native writers, plus a large, four-color map detailing the Native villages and defining the language areas. 304 pages, $19.95.

The Stikine, Vol. 6, No 4. River route to three Canadian gold strikes in the 1800s, the Stikine is the largest and most navigable of several rivers that flow from northwestern Canada through Southeastern Alaska on their way to the sea. This edition explores 400 miles of Stikine wilderness, recounts the river's paddlewheel past and looks into the future, wondering if the Stikine will survive as one of the North's great free-flowing rivers. Illustrated with contemporary color photos and historic black-and-white; includes a large fold-out map. 96 pages, $9.95.

Alaska's Great Interior, Vol. 7, No. 1. Alaska's rich Interior country, west from the Alaska-Yukon Territory border and including the huge drainage between the Alaska Range and the Brooks Range, is covered thoroughly. Included are the region's people, communities, history, economy, wilderness areas and wildlife. Illustrated with contemporary color and black-and-white photos. Includes a large fold-out map. 128 pages, $9.95.

A Photographic Geography of Alaska, Vol. 7, No. 2. An overview of the entire state—a visual tour through the six regions of Alaska: Southeast, Southcentral/Gulf Coast, Alaska Peninsula and Aleutians, Bering Sea Coast, Arctic and Interior. Plus a handy appendix of valuable information—"Facts About Alaska." Approximately 160 color and black-and-white photos and 35 maps. 192 pages, $17.95.

COMING ATTRACTION
Klondike Lost: A Decade of Photographs by Kinsey & Kinsey, Vol. 7, No. 4. An album of rare photographs and all-new text about the lost Klondike boom town of Grand Forks, second in size only to Dawson during the gold rush. Introduction by noted historian Pierre Berton: 138 pages, area maps and more than 100 historical photos, most never before published. To be distributed to members in November 1980. $12.95.

Your $20 membership in The Alaska Geographic Society includes 4 subsequent issues of *ALASKA GEOGRAPHIC*, the Society's official quarterly. Please add $4 for non-U.S. membership.

Additional membership information available upon request. Single copies of the *ALASKA GEOGRAPHIC* back issues available, per listing here. When ordering please add $1 postage/handling per copy. To order back issues send your check or money order and volumes desired to:

The Alaska Geographic Society

Box-4EEE, Anchorage, AK 99509